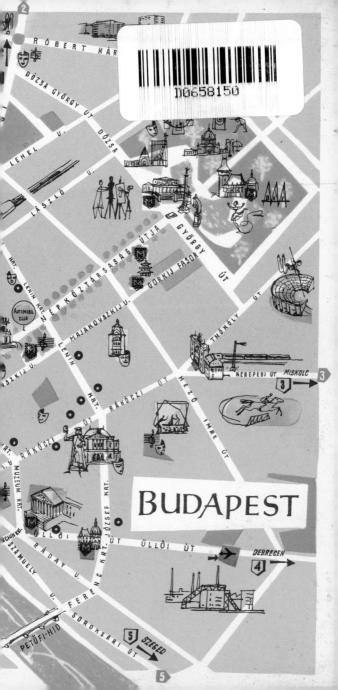

BUDAPEST

BUDAPEST

A GUIDE TO THE CAPITAL OF HUNGARY

CORVINA PRESS

EDITED BY
MIKLÓS PAP
LÁSZLÓ SZÉKELY
ANDRÁS VITÉZ

CONTENTS

III. Practical Information

PREFACE

Budapest—formerly known as Buda and Pest-Buda—has been the centre, the heart of Hungary for seven centuries. Its importance grew especially during the last century, when Budapest assumed undisputed leadership among Hungarian towns. Besides being the political and administrative capital of the country, it steadily gained significance as a centre of economic and cultural life and of communications. The capital of Hungary is similarly the centre of domestic and foreign tourist traffic. The traveller finds here a fascinating and famous panorama, a harmonious unity of a large city and nature, monuments imbued with historical traditions, a wealth of collections, urbanism, culture and entertainment. And beyond these, thanks to the matchless geological endowments of the capital, the best and most popular thermal baths and splendid possibilities for recreation, bathing and sport are here concentrated.

It has been our endeavour to present in this guidebook a many-sided picture of Budapest, with a thoroughness that meets the requirements of tourism, and which corresponds to the dimensions and eminence of this metropolis of close to two million people, and to its past and present. We have given a rather broad interpretation to what a tourist is interested in. We have gone beyond advice on the best way for the traveller to reach his destination, on lodgings, meals, sightseeing, amusements and recreation. We believe that travel in our days cannot be imagined without interest in fundamental information about geology, geography, economics, history and culture, as well as trends of progress with a new content yet rooted in tradition.

This guidebook calls attention not only to the traditionally popular spots of Budapest, frequented for decades by the tourist, but it also wants to extend his sphere of interest. We had to be careful, nevertheless, to select the most important of the wealth of data lest the book became a monograph on Budapest architecture, history, geography, and economics. We were guided in our editorial work by the practical purpose of making the newly arrived tourist feel at home in our town, that he might become familiar with the major points of orientation and be properly assisted in acquainting himself with the points of interests, and the sights of the city.

In compiling this book we have sought to apply scientific thoroughness, as much as possible. The selection of data is recent and reliable. One cannot, of course, present a snapshot-like picture of a metropolis which is constantly growing and changing, this follows from the nature of things.

In the following we inform the reader about the structure of the book and how to use it. *General Information* (p. 9) contains general data on the capital as a whole, arranged according to topics of greatest interest to the reader. This is followed by the "guidebook" proper, *Sightseeing in Budapest*. This, the bulkiest part of the volume (p. 81), takes one on a tour of the city, presenting the sights through systematically planned walks.

The administrative division of the capital, reflected by the numerical order of the districts, does not fully agree with its geographical arrangement. We found it expedient, therefore, not to proceed according to the numerical order of the districts, but rather to deal with them in territorial succession, after starting from a central point. Thus the area has been divided into three major parts. We present the Pest districts first, followed by the Danube and its islands, and lastly the districts of Buda.

Special chapters have also been devoted to the main thoroughfares of the city. Practical considerations have led us to discuss them separately from the districts. The main thoroughfares are also district boundaries in most instances, and were we to discuss them together with the areas, a peculiar situation would arise, namely that one side of a boulevard or a square would be discussed 20 to 30 pages ahead of the other side, which is in another district. The sightseer does not look at the districts, but rather uses the thoroughfares.

Practical Information, the third part of the book (p. 241), calls attention to points of detail which, if we had incorporated them in the walks, would have upset their uniform rhythm. As suggested by its title, it contains, on the one hand, practical information on tourist traffic and lists, on the other hand, detailed catalogue-like data on the most significant art collections, important buildings and institutions.

Orientation in the book is facilitated by an index, which pinpoints all major buildings and important sights.

We trust that the foreign tourist, with the help of this book, will find all the guidance and information about Budapest that he may need.

We wish all our visitors a pleasant time exploring our city.

THE EDITORS

PART I

GENERAL INFORMATION

GEOGRAPHY

Budapest, the Hungarian capital, is situated in Central Europe, approximately half-way between the Equator and the North Pole. It has an administrative area of 525.6 sq. km., of which 173.2 sq. km. lie on the right bank of the Danube and 352.4 sq. km. on the left bank. The total length of its boundaries is 124 km. (right bank 54 km., left bank 70 km.). The area of the capital stretches 25 km. from north to south and 29 km. from west to east.

The major portion of Budapest's area is only 100 to 120 m. above sea level. The deepest point at Budapest (point "0" of the Danube) is 96.5 m. above sea level. Greater elevations can be found only in the Buda hills.

The course of the Danube river in Budapest is 28 km. long. There are no large river tributaries in this area, except a few brooks which practically run dry part of the year. Even the Buda hills are rather poor in surface streams, because they are karstic over large tracts. The city abounds in springs, especially hot springs, which rise to the surface mainly on the eastern fault lines of the Buda hills, on the right bank of the Danube.

Most of the surface of the capital's Buda side consists of varied reliefs of the Buda hills, with only a small part of the Pilis hills on the north stretching into the city area. Lesser units of the Buda hills are the Hill of Three Boundaries (Hármashatár-hegy), János Hill (János-hegy), the Nagykopasz and Nagyszénás groups of hills and the area of the Tétény-Sóskút plateau.

The Pest plain covers the Budapest area on the left bank of the Danube. It is the northwestern expanse of the Great Hungarian Plain. This is where the major part of the capital was built. Its surface is flat or gently rolling and compared to the Buda area, it shows little variation. Its border is difficult to pinpoint. There are a number of terrace-like hills along it, the highest one reaching to the Gödöllő

11

group. Though the Pest plain is bordered by the Danube on the west, morphologically the wide expanse between Szentendre and Óbuda on the right bank of the Danube should be included, as well as the plain of Lágymányos and Kelenföld. The Pest plain is open towards the east and south and joins the Great Hungarian Plain without a sharp definition. The lowland within Budapest's administrative borders, close by the Danube, is only 100 to 110 m. above sea level and 10 to 15 m. above the Danube's level. The area further away from the Danube is of higher elevation, thus the centre of Pestlőrinc is of 142 m., while the hill of 245 metres at Rákoskert is the highest point of the capital's Pest side. The Hungarian capital, like the entire country, is situated in the temperate zone of Europe. Of all the capitals of Europe and the world's big cities Budapest has one of the most pleasant climates. Its most attractive features—relatively high mean temperature, not too humid or foggy atmosphere, together with moderate, though at times brisk winds and abundant sunshine—become evident especially during the spring, summer and early autumn months, which are of major importance from the point of view of tourism.

The annual average sunshine for the past fifty years has been 1,991 hours, 1,300 of which fall into the May to September period (this latter is about equivalent to the annual figure for the British Isles). The sky is sunny during the better part of this period.

Of all the capitals in Europe, Budapest is one of the best sheltered from the wind; it is protected by the Carpathian Mountains, partly by the Alps, as well as by the Hungarian Central Mountains. The direction of the wind is favourable, because the prevailing northwest-westerly wind, blowing especially during the warm months, brings pure air to the capital from the Buda hills. The average annual wind velocity is low, 2 m./sec., and the average velocity during the noon hours for many years has been below 3 m./sec.

The mean temperature over many years has been 11°C, with 22°C in the hottest month (July) and —1.1°C in the coldest month (January). The highest temperature ever measured in Budapest was 39.5°C, while the coldest was —23.4°C. This latter figure is indicative of the protection enjoyed by Budapest, since south of the capital, in the lower stretch of the Great Plain, temperatures lower than —30°C have been recorded.

The cooler heights of the Buda hills are refreshing in high summer. The annual mean temperature on Liberty Hill (Szabadság-hegy) is appr. 9°C, in July the average is 19.5° to 20°C, while in January it is —2° to —2.5°C. The latter figure is quite significant from the standpoint of winter sports, especially if one takes into consideration that the annual precipitation in the Buda hills is about 20 per cent higher than the average.

There are relatively few extremely hot summer days. The temperature is above 25°C for about 80 days a year including some 20 days when it is above 30°C.

For almost 100 days during the winter season the temperature is above the freezing point, and there are only 30 days with a sub-zero temperature.

The trend of the humidity of the air is also quite favourable. The vapour pressure is not too high (7.5 mm. over a long-term annual average). The July average of the relative humidity is 60 per cent and during the noon hours of the same month it is 40 to 45 per cent. The many-years average humidity in December, the dampest winter month, is not more than 82 per cent. High humidity, with summer sultriness bringing on indisposition, is just as rare as are fog formation and raw weather in winter.

The average precipitation fluctuates. Measurements have shown 617 mm. at the Meteorological Institute in Buda, 650 to 680 mm. in the Buda hills, and only 550 mm. on the outskirts of the Pest side. Most of the precipitation occurs during the early summer, mainly in the form of thunderstorms and rain showers. Extremely damp months are very rare (e.g. 263 mm. in August 1955), and devastating cloudbursts over the capital are exceptional. On the other hand, there are frequent thunderstorms in Budapest in the summer months. They are due to the city's geographical location and physical disconformity. The meeting of hills and lowlands and the unnatural surfaces (paved streets, wide expanse of houses) lead to sudden rises of air.

FLORA AND FAUNA

Budapest has a wealth of interesting flora and fauna hardly matched by those of other big cities.

Paleontological fossils—dating back about 600,000 years—have been preserved in the layers of the clay and marl pits of the Óbuda brick works. Scientists have unearthed here prints of the leaves of oceanic Nipa palms, which can be found now only in the tropics, and of laurel and camphor trees. Later, there was a decline in temperature during the several periods of the ice age. This resulted in the destruction of the evergreen tropical plants and the evolution of a flora which thrived under a moderate and cooler temperature.

The forests belong by and large to the oak-tree zone. On the southern, sunny slopes one most often finds turkey and tomentose oaks, while on the cooler northern and eastern slopes the acaulous varieties, mixed with hornbeam trees, are more common. Other species thriving in the oak forests are the wild cherry, mountain and garden ash (sorbus) and maples. Of the latter, the tartar maple trees lend an oriental character to the forests. The parasitic loranthus shrubs, which live on the oaks, are of a southern character. The flora of the oak forests is made up of pulmonaria, lithospermum, stellaria, corydalis and primula, while the fauna consists of a motley array of deers, foxes, squirrels, magpies, jays, butterflies, capricorn beetles, stag beetles, and other long-horned beetles.

In Hungary, beech trees cover the hills upward from 600 metres. In the Buda hills, however, the region of giant trees several centuries old comes down as low as 200 to 250 metres (at Hármaskút, on the crest and the northern slope of János Hill (János-hegy), at Csillagvölgy and Zugliget).

The karstic scrub forests are the most diversified and colourful of all. They are found on the steepest southern, southwestern and southeastern slopes covered with dolomite and limestone or loess. Tomentose oaks, wayfaring trees, hawthorns grow here in thick clumps, the greenish-white flowers of the ash trees being most conspicuous in May. Smoke trees dominate the scene during autumn on the southern and eastern slopes of the Hill of Three Boundaries (Hármashatár-hegy) and Martinovics Hill (Martinovics-hegy), their egg-shaped leaves assuming a flaming red colour. This typically southern bush supplied the tanning material of the famous Turkish morocco leather.

The karstic scrub forests do not grow as densely as the northern oak woods; there are many grassy clearings in them. In the spring these clearings contain patches of colour, made up of large anemones (Pulsatilla grandis) with purple flowers, the stars of pheasant's-eyes almost as big as a palm of the hand, and the dwarf almond. This dwarf shrub has attractive rose-like flowers, and flower vendors sell its flowering branches during the early spring months. This genuine heath plant, only a few inches tall, is gradually becoming extinct.

The karstic scrub forests and the loess heath meadows have a characteristic fauna of their own—pheasants, partridges, gophers, brown hare, nightingales, large golden-green lizards and the much more interesting and hardly discernible Pannonian lizards (Ablepharus kitaibeli). This species, as indicated by its name, was found and identified in the Buda hills by Pál Kitaibel, the famous Hungarian botanist of the early 19th century. It can easily be recognized by its peculiar, snake-like rapid movement. When disturbed, the lizard hardly uses its small, degenerated legs and quickly seeks refuge under the parched grass with a serpentine motion.

The unwooded dolomite slopes, which appear grey and bare from a distance, have a peculiar flora and fauna of their own. The loveliest hillside is the twin-peaked Eagle Hill (Sas-hegy) which has been turned into a nature reserve. On these feathergrass-covered slopes the white-flowered dolomite carnation (Dianthus serotinus) in bluish-grey clusters and the native plant of the Hungarian Central Mountains, the white-flowered seseli (Seseli leucospermum) with its thin, fringy leaves thrive in the hot sunshine. On the northern slopes one finds a characteristic grass of the Carpathian-Alpine region, the Sesleria sadleriana, with its grey-bluish clumps and steel-blue flowers.

A unique representative of ancient flora growing over a

few square metres of the crumbly calcic soil on the northern dolomitic slopes of the Buda hills, is the *Knautia tomentella*, which cannot be found anywhere else, hence it is a matchless specimen of our hills.

There is not enough space to list the many characteristic species of the smaller fauna living on the Buda slopes. We must limit ourselves to mentioning only one, the rare reddish-brown spotted rock thrush *(Monticola saxatilis)*.

The Pest side, the lowland on the left bank of the Danube, has preserved only a few plants from ancient times, on the sand hills of the Academy forest behind the Rákoskeresztúr cemetery and on the dunes of Csepel and Káposztásmegyer. One is the grey, rigid-leaved Hungarian fescuegrass *(Festuca vaginata)*, growing in sandy meadows with feathergrass, and others are rosemary grass shrubs of various sizes which can be found between the sand hills. At one spot, Füredi út in Zugló, there are a few acres of undrained, protected, ancient marshy meadow, which is a home for white-spotted cotton grass, yellow-flowered cowslips and irises, dark-purple great burnet and mauve lousewort during the summer.

More than 400,000 trees decorate the streets, squares and gardens of the capital. Western plane trees of American origin are most common on the Pest side; they are easy to recognise by their grey, spotted trunks. The nettle tree, similarly of western origin, with small leaves and berries, is also quite a favourite. On the Buda hillsides the majority of the trees are the horse-chestnuts and the early and mountain maples. Lately many Hungarian mountain ash trees have been planted. The old fig trees on the southern slopes of Gellért Hill were planted during the years of Turkish occupation in the 17th century.

GEOLOGICAL FORMATIONS

Budapest is located at a juncture of two diverse regions: the Great Hungarian Plain, which developed during the Quaternary period, on the Pest side, and the Buda hills belonging to the Transdanubian Mountains, which consist of sediment deposited by a prehistoric sea during the Mesozoic era. These rocks were subjected to many crustal movements, thus they can be found, even in adjacent areas, at various depths. In Pest the loose sediment of the plain is 200 m. deep in Margaret Island (Margitsziget), and 800 m. at the Millenary Monument in the City Park. The sediment of the prehistoric sea, covering up the crystalline basic mountain, is beneath these layers.

THE HISTORY OF THE REGION

Owing to the gigantic crustal movements of the Mesozoic era and of the Quaternary period, the mountainous area submerged in a zigzag manner and was inundated by sea water coming from the Adriatic. This was not a continuous process: the sea moved forward and then receded four times. The Buda hill area and the Pest lowland were constituted mainly out of the oceanic sediment. The composition of the sediment was different in each geological epoch.

The Danube was formed during the glacial (Pleistocene) period. The gravel and sand deposits of the ancient Danube were 50 to 100 metres higher than those of today. Windstorms in this period formed hillocks out of the sand of the ancient Danube in the area of Megyer, Rákos and Soroksár. On the Buda side yellow loess, forming perpendicular walls, was left by the wind, as can be noted around Gellért Hill (Gellérthegy), Hill of Three Boundaries (Hármashatár-hegy), Cuckoo Hill (Kakukk-hegy) and Csillebérc.

During the Pliocene (about one to twelve million years ago) an inland sea covered the Great Plain, as well as the present flat and low hilly areas of Transdanubia. The Buda hills in the capital's area stood out like islands from the shallow sea inhabited by snails and shellfish. At the end of the Miocene epoch (12 to 26 million years ago) the sea had a rich flora and fauna, shells, echini and myriads of one-celled foraminifera. Under the subtropical climate (an annual mean temperature of 16 to 18°C) a sedimentation of "coarse limestone" took place at Kőbánya, Budafok, Tétény and Kamaraerdő. Limestone is a favourite building material. It was used in building the Parliament, the Opera House, the Western Railway Terminal and a part of the Technical and Economic Universities.

At the end of the Eocene epoch (30 to 40 million years ago) there was a gradual sedimentation of marl, which can be found in certain areas of Castle Hill (Vár-hegy), Gellért Hill and Eagle Hill. In the middle of that epoch (40 to 45 million years ago) limestone was deposited by the sea. Some fossils, like the nummulites (one-celled organisms with lime skeletons) and corals, indicate a tropical climate. The mean annual temperature of the sea and air must have been about 20°C. A seam of good-quality coal was left in the seacoast marshes of the middle Eocene epoch. (When drilling one of the artesian wells in the City Park an 0.8 m. thick seam of coal was found in a depth of 916 m.) During the early Eocene (50 to 58 million years ago) gravel and detritus accumulated in some of the areas of the sea-shore.

There are no Cretaceous and Jurassic formations (60 to 150 million years old) because of the elevation of the area. There is, however, a sediment of Dachstein limestone (about 30 m. thick) with dolomite beneath it, dating from the time of the sea in the upper Triassic period 150 to 160 million years ago. Limestone was deposited by the middle Triassic sea 170 million years ago. It is probable that under this sediment there is a granite-granodiorite crystalline mass of rock, similar to that found in the Velence hills, southwest of Budapest. The thermal springs coming from a great depth have a solvent effect on these granite rocks, adding valuable minerals to the medicinal waters. This is the source of the potassium, lithium, sulphur, fluorine and silicium salt content of these thermal springs.

SPRINGS AND WELLS

Geologically speaking, the springs and wells of Budapest are of a different origin and character. Some are close to the surface, as "layer springs" or ordinary wells. The temperature of the water depends on the composition. It either corresponds to the annual mean temperature ($10°C$ in general, warmest in October and coldest in April), or is 2 to 4 degrees higher, such as in the Epsom salt springs and wells rich in sulphates. Springs with water at the annual mean temperature are Disznófő (in Zugliget) and King Béla's well (Liberty Hill). They give very little water, about one to two litres per minute. The Buda hills are poor in water, because the precipitation easily passes through the limestone and dolomite layers into the lower levels.

The lukewarm and hot springs and artesian wells are well known. They give medicinal waters rich in radioactive mineral salts and spring forth alongside the geological fault line. They include the lake springs of the Roman Baths (Római-fürdő, 18 to $20°C$), with an average capacity of 8,000 litres per minute (at present the spring runs dry during certain periods), the Turkish (Török) spring of the Császár Baths ($27°C$, 5,000 to 6,000 litres of water per minute), the natural springs of the Rudas Baths, the Matthias spring ($42°C$, 50 to 60 litres per minute), and the Juventus artesian well ($45°C$, 255 to 650 litres per minute), the natural springs of the Gellért Baths (46 to $48°C$, 570 to 2,700 litres per minute), the artesian well No. 1 on Margaret Island (Margitsziget) ($42°C$, 4,000 litres per minute), the Béke spring of the Szabadság Baths in Dagály utca ($42°C$), the artesian well No. 1 of the Széchenyi Baths ($72°C$, 400 to 490 litres per minute) and the artesian well No. 2 ($76°C$, 4,200 to 4,500 litres per minute). The medicinal use of these thermal waters will be discussed in a separate chapter (see page 281).

These hot springs also serve industrial purposes. Their waters have been providing heat for the Lukács Baths since 1919 and also for the Széchenyi Baths. The hot artesian wells on Margaret Island (especially No. 2) heat the blocks of houses on the Danube embankment, while the wells of the Lukács and Császár Baths supply hot water to the blocks of dwellings up to Zsigmond Square.

CAVES

There are many caves between the limestone and dolomite layers of the Buda hills, some even with hot-water springs. The formation of the caves was started by crustal movements (huge earthquakes) and completed by the erosive and dissolving effect of water. The latter resulted in the formation of stalactites and stalagmites of striking beauty, including golden-yellow pyrite crystals on snow-white gypsum.

The Molnár János spring cave lies in the hillside behind the Mill Pond (Malomtó) of the Lukács Baths. Of particular interest is the presence of crystal-clear water of 25°C on its bottom, while the side walls display snow-white stalactites and stalagmites and traces of an ancient rivulet. The springs of the Imre Baths come to the surface in the Matthias thermal spring cave; 3 to 4 cm. large lumps of pyrite in the decomposed marl indicate the sulphur content of its medicinal water.

The Matthias, Árpád and Rákóczi wells gush forth of dolomite crevices at the eastern foot of Gellért Hill. The Iván cave is located on the southeastern side of Gellért Hill. The Observation Hill (Szemlő-hegy) cave, which is one kilometre long, has fine snow-white gypsum crystals. The Pálvölgy cave in the area of the Hill of Three Boundaries contains many crevices formed in Eocene limestone. They show a large variety of fine stalactite and stalagmite formations. The passage-ways of the cave are one kilometre long. To the northeast, and opposite this cave, lies the Matthias Hill (Mátyás-hegy) cave, also formed in Eocene limestone. Its labyrinthine passages are two kilometres long, where many people had lost their way before it was closed. On the bottom of the cave there is a lake fed by karstic water. Many such caves and crevices, though small, may be found in the quarries on the side of Matthias Hill. The largest set of crevices in this area, the Solymár cave, with passages two kilometres long, cannot be traversed without an experienced guide.

The Ferenc Hill (Ferenc-hegy) cave was discovered during the construction of a road at 65 Törökvészi út. It is one kilometre long, with a most interesting group of stalactites and stalagmites, and numerous crystals. There are several caves in the Cool Valley (Hűvösvölgy) area, such as the Báthori cave in the slope of Linden Hill (Hárs-hegy), and the Seven Holes (Hétlyuk) cave at Nagykovácsi, which

can be reached by a 30-minute bus ride from Hűvösvölgy.
In the latter daring and skilful explorers may descend
through a 20-metre-long perpendicular sump into a large
cave at the bottom.

The system of caves in Castle Hill is partly man-made,
and was dug into tufa originally for the protection of the
population. There are scores of interesting cellar caves
in this area, containing the muddy sediments of the prehistoric Danube. These caves and cellars, products of both
erosion and human labour, contain many historic relics;
some of them are real museums.

The breweries at Kőbánya and other industrial works on
the Pest side had artificial caves cut into the pliable Miocene limestone. Today they are still utilised for storing,
mainly by breweries. The limestone of more recent
origin at Budafok is used for similar purposes, especially
for wine cellars and for the growing of fungi.

The large networks of cellars and the caves in Castle
Hill, Matthias Hill and Pálvölgy were used as air-raid
shelters during the Second World War.

HISTORICAL BACKGROUND

The geographical location of the Hungarian capital was favourable for founding of early human settlements. The meeting point of the hills and lowland by the Danube attracted people from the dawn of history up to the Roman conquest, as proven by findings from various epochs. The area, though sparsely, was inhabited continuously. The last settlers preceding the Romans were the Celts who had a comparatively primitive civilisation, as shown by the relics unearthed. The settlement of the Eraviscus tribe was called Ak-Ink, i.e. Abundant Water.

It was on the site of this small settlement, on the right bank of the Danube, in the northwestern part of the city, that the Roman conquerors set up their military camp, which was named Aquincum, the latinised form of the Celtic name. During 9-11 A.D. the Roman legions occupied the western part of present-day Hungary, which they organised into a province named Pannonia. The Limes, the fortified frontier of the empire, was along the Danube. The Limes remained for a while the starting point of subsequent conquests, consequently Aquincum was a military settlement, with a thriving civilian town to the north. This town was inhabited by artisans who worked for the military, and tradesmen who maintained contact not only with the rest of the province but with the whole empire. They kept slaves of various ethnic origins, brought from everywhere and put to work in the many workshops.

Aquincum became a major centre of the Limes by the Danube. The one-time Eraviscus settlement grew into a flourishing town. One military barrack after another was built, together with public buildings, a theatre, a market place, temples, an aqueduct, and two amphitheatres—one for the military settlement and the other for the civilian town. Their ruins are today points of major interest of Budapest. This flourishing town was not only a thriving economic centre with a population of soldiers and artisans, tradesmen and slaves, but a cultural centre as well. The walls of the proconsul's palace and of the villas of wealthy citizens were decorated by local artists, who also carved the statues of the gods in the temples. Aquincum, as the capital of the province of Pannonia, became a significant representative of Roman urban life. The relics of its art and economic advancement, unearthed in large numbers recently, are remarkable.

This rich and multi-coloured urban life, however, was rather short-lived. The flowering of the first two centuries of imperial Rome was followed shortly by a decline, and the disintegration of the slave society became evident here too. The legions of Pannonia played a prominent part in the life of the 3rd-century Roman empire, which, however, had to brace itself up against enemy attacks coming from all directions at that time. As has already been mentioned, Aquincum was at first a starting point of economic and political conquest, beyond the Limes. In fact, Contra-Aquincum, a settlement built on the left bank of the Danube, in the present centre of Pest, was founded with this aim in mind. The new settlement, however, remained far behind the town of the right bank in wealth and size. And before long both were faced with the multiplying tasks of defence. The soldiers of the Roman legions looked, with growing anxiety, beyond the constantly reinforced walls of the two towns. They had to meet the continuous incursions of barbarian peoples, attacking from the other side of the Limes, threatening the thriving, vigorous life of the province with destruction and ruin.

Their fear was fully justified. The world empire based on conquest was shaken to its foundation and later it collapsed under the blows of the barbarian tribes. The Roman legions withdrew from the province, having evacuated Aquincum. They were soon followed by the civilian population of wealth and eminence. The town was left without protection. The poor population could not join those in flight. They sought refuge amidst the walls of the old Roman settlement, but were soon engulfed by the successive waves of migrating peoples. The centuries of the great invasions ruined the town, its richly decorated public buildings fell into decay, and the settlement was reduced to the low standard of the period preceding the Roman conquest.

The great migrations from the East brought in the Huns, followed by the Ostrogoths, then the Lombards, and finally the Avars, who occupied the town and its surroundings, but they could only keep it for a short period of time; they were unable to strike roots here. Their primitive social conditions did not allow them to carry on or renew the former urban life. The population of the settlement engaged only in certain agricultural pursuits. Surviving documents make no references to industrial activities in these periods. Following the collapse of Avar rule, the area was conquered by Charlemagne, the King of the Franks, but it remained only a distant border outpost of the Frankish empire, without new settlers, and the Franks later relinquished it to the Slavic peoples who came in from the north. (The area of Budapest proper was little affected by the slow Slavic infiltration; there are no relics showing that Slavs lived there.)

The nomadic Magyar tribes coming from the region of the Black Sea settled on the plains of the Carpathian basin about 900. When crossing the Danube, they only found ruins in place of the previous town. Yet the site was very important to them because of its central geographical location in the recently conquered country. For this reason one of the major tribes making up the alliance of Magyar tribes settled in the area south of present-day Budapest, and their leading chief, Kurszán, most probably built his fort out of the ruins of the former Roman amphitheatre.

Following the conquest of the Carpathian basin, the Magyar tribes continued their nomadic existence for a while. The territory was temporarily suitable for the migratory life of animal breeding. The settling down of the Magyars, therefore, was a long drawn-out process, which must have taken a few centuries. But the establishment of a state—about 1000 A.D.—speeded it up, at any rate, and within a short time, completed it. The area of present-day Budapest again became important. Although the seat of the sovereign was in various other parts of the country, and Budapest became the capital only much later, the town's central location always gave it a great advantage. This was further enhanced with the final settlement of the population and the development of agriculture followed by the growth of handicraft trades.

Commerce played a major role in the development of the town, since the settlement was the centre of the network of trade routes covering the entire country and of trade developing along them. It did not take long for the two towns to emerge: Buda, on the site of the former Roman settlement, which later assumed the name of Óbuda (Old Buda), and Pest on the other side of the Danube. According to recent research, Buda was named after a Hungarian nobleman, while the name of Pest, referred to in written sources for the first time in 1171, is of Slavic derivation, meaning oven.

The development of the town gained fresh vigour in the 12th century, with the coming of new settlers. The many merchants and handicraftsmen of German, Walloon, French and Italian descent, and from other western nations, soon outnumbered the original Hungarian population. The influx of these settlers made Buda and Pest major centres of trade and handicrafts before long. An indication of their importance was the fact that Buda became a provostship, the seat of a high-ranking office of the Roman Catholic Church.

This initial rapid growth was temporarily halted by invaders from the East. In 1241 Hungary was overrun by the conquering armies of Genghis Khan, the Mongolian ruler, who looted and burned Pest. For a while it appeared as if everything was finished and the destruction would reduce the settlement to its earlier primitive level. But the Mongolian armies withdrew the next year. To forestall the threat of any further invasions, King Béla IV (1235-1270) planned the construction of a network of stone fortresses throughout the entire country.

The building of one such stone fortress in Buda began in 1247. The major part of the stronghold was completed in 1255, when the king granted Buda the right to hold fairs and to levy duties, raising the settlement, in a legal sense as well, to the status of a town. From that time on the settlement around and below Castle Hill was known as Buda, while the town built on the site of the old Roman settlement was called Óbuda, i.e. Old Buda; the one on the left bank of the Danube kept the name of Pest. Óbuda gradually lost its significance in comparison to the two other towns.

The Buda fortress was at times also the royal residence. King Béla IV spent much of his time there in order to be close to his daughter Margit, who lived in the Dominican convent on the island between the two towns. [This island was then called Island of Rabbits (Nyulak szigete), but was later named Margaret Island (Margitsziget) after the princess.]

The successors of Béla IV also resided in Buda at times and the Diet, the assembly of the Hungarian nobility, was held for the first time in 1286 near the fortress, on the field of Rákos, on the other side of the Danube. Buda, being the king's part-time residence, increased in size with new settlers arriving from various parts of the country and from abroad. During this period many farming communities were established around the three towns.

The fourteenth century was an important period of urbanisation, of commercial and industrial development in Hungary. The sovereigns from the House of Anjou greatly contributed to this growth with their ambitious economic policies. The three towns became important centres of trade within the country and with foreign lands, and the Danube facilitated communication with the western countries. Handicrafts also thrived, articles of many kinds were produced in the three towns, and the craft of silversmiths became especially famous. Large-scale construction started again on Castle Hill and in its vicinity, several-storey dwellings of wealthy citizens, together with churches of the various orders, were built. The importance of Buda as a trading centre was emphasised by the 1347 decree of King Louis I (1342-1382) which granted the town staple right. This meant that merchants had to stop in Buda, no matter where they came from, and display and sell their fabrics or other goods before proceeding further.

The result of the urbanisation fostered by the sovereigns in Buda, the now wealthy and well-fortified town situated in the heart of the country, was that the town became the capital. King Sigismund of Luxembourg (1387-1437), who later became the ruler of the Holy Roman Empire and, like the Anjou kings, was a great patron of urban development, spent most of his time in Buda during his stay in Hungary. He rebuilt the fortress, which was used originally, like the other forts of Hungary, only for purposes of defence. It is quite probable that he built the famous "Friss" (new) palace in the southern part of Castle Hill. This sumptuous palace won the admiration and envy of foreign visitors. The wealthy burghers did not want to be outdone by the haughty pomp of the royal residence. Alongside the palaces of the nobility near the castle, stately burghers' houses were erected numerous remnants of which have survived to our days.

26

This epoch, the epoch of growth and prosperity, was also significant from another point of view in the history of the three towns. While their earlier population consisted of the many different nationalities, drawn in by royal favour, at this time it was made up of two major groups. The wealthiest burghers, merchants, councilmen and many of the artisans organised into guilds were of German origin. But the number of Hungarian guild members, masters and journeymen, kept increasing, and so did the role they played in economic life. Consequently, these two major groups—Hungarian artisans and German burghers —shared the seats in the town council and participated in the direction of urban life.

The internal and external political difficulties of the country, the strengthening of the aristocracy's power at the expense of central royal authority, and the menace of the Ottoman Turkish Empire hardly cast their shadows at that time upon the development of the three towns. Under the reign of King Matthias (Corvinus) Hunyadi (1458-1490), Buda, the royal residence and the capital of the country, enjoyed its golden age. The king enlarged the castle, enriching the sombre Gothic palace of Sigismund with the livelier and more colourful art of the Renaissance. The few relics of this period show that the reconstructed castle did not lag behind the standard of European Renaissance architecture of this epoch.

Matthias's library, the Corviniana, renowned throughout the world, was in the castle. The library contained the most important works known during that period, in richly ornamented, finely bound volumes. Side by side with these hand-written works decorated with fine drawings, there also appeared the first books coming out of the print-shop established in 1472, also in Buda. Scholars from many lands carried on their discussions in the royal castle, it was in this building that Matthias received the ambassadors and foreign delegations in audience. Furniture and other objects imported from many lands decorated the castle; porcelain from China was just as common here as glassware from Italy or pottery from Cologne. The stone-carving shop established for the decoration of the castle also helped decorate the town and affected the architecture of the entire country.

The urban bourgeoisie did not lag behind the brilliant development of the royal court. At this time the Hungarians were predominant, Hungarian merchants and guild masters said the last word in the town council, the Germans and the less numerous other foreigners played a secondary role. Hungary's capital, admired in distant lands, became the largest Hungarian town. Pest's position was less prominent than that of Buda, the royal seat, but the advance of its commerce and industry ensured it a rank almost equal to the latter. Only Óbuda, which was in the possession of the queens, developed more slowly and on a lesser scale.

The outlook was very promising for the further enrichment and growth of the three towns. Yet, following Matthias's death, ominous signs appeared, making the possibilities of further progress doubtful. The oligarchs again grew strong at the expense of royal power, and the spread of feudal anarchy greatly jeopardised the future of the entire country, hampering urban progress. The luxurious palace of Matthias gradually became the centre of a penurious royal court and desintegrated.

The advance of feudal anarchy worsened the lot of the peasants. Driven to desperation, they attempted to improve their lot themselves. An army of crusaders recruited primarily from among the serfs, gathered in 1514 to resist the Turkish onslaught. The nobles, fearing the armed peasant masses, wanted them to disband. This led to the peasants' uprising under the leadership of György Dózsa against their unbearable oppression. It took all the effort that the nobles could muster to defeat this peasant uprising, which was similar in importance to the Jacquerie in France, the Wat Tyler peasant movement in England, or the 1525 peasants' revolt in Germany. With their military superiority the nobles drowned the peasants' revolt in a sea of blood, and the Diet held in the field of Rákos codified their ruthless victory in a decree binding the serf to his master's land eternally.

These peasants, however, were badly needed in the face of the growing Turkish threat. The forts along the southern borders fell one after another under the powerful onslaught of the Turks. The Hungarian army of nobles was compelled to take a stand during the summer of 1526 against the foreign conquerors. They lost the battle on the lowland around Mohács by the Danube, and the Turks administered a crushing defeat to the Hungarian army deprived of the assistance of peasant troops. Hungarian chronicles have called this defeat the Mohács Disaster, and a historical turning point.

The road ahead was thus opened before the conquerors. Buda was held alternately by the two claimants to the throne who were engaged in struggle for power: Ferdinand Hapsburg (1526-1564), who controlled the western part of the country, and János Zápolya (1526-1540), who had defeated the peasants in 1514 and ruled over the eastern parts of Hungary. The Turks exploited this rivalry; they seized Buda by ruse on September 2, 1541, and the royal seat remained under Turkish occupation, together with the richest central areas of Hungary, for close to a century and a half.

The Turks made Buda the capital of the new province of their empire. The looted royal castle was turned into a storage place, and the town, headed by the pasha of Buda, was opened up to an influx of Turks and other nationalities coming from the Ottoman Empire. The once thriving urban life of a largely Hungarian population was restricted considerably. Turkish rule was unable to ensure the town the former possibilities of development. It is true, the decline came gradually. The guilds carried on their work; new construction, the erection of mosques and minarets, kept people busy. The Turks made use first of the thermal springs of Buda, they built baths, some of which are still functioning today in their original buildings. But while the three towns were previously the centre of a thriving, rich country, enjoying the benefits of a prospering nation, they became a modest and distant outpost of a far-flung empire, often in a precarious military position, cut off from European trade and thereby deprived of the possibilities of the industrial development enjoyed by the western countries.

The Hapsburg emperors who controlled the western areas of the country and retained the title of king of Hungary, made a number of attempts to retake the former capital. They attacked the Buda fortress for the first time in 1542, one year after the Turkish seizure, but the considerably strengthened defences withstood the siege. The same thing happened in 1598 and in 1602. The Hapsburg armies fared somewhat better in the case of less fortified Pest. They recaptured it in 1602 and kept it until 1604, when it was retaken by the Turks. All these sieges, of course, led to serious damage and destructions over many decades, up to the last unsuccessful assault in 1684.

But by this time liberation was not far off. The Turks, gathering all their strength, launched in 1683 a last desperate attack against Vienna, but were badly defeated by the Hapsburg armies, making preparations to reconquer Hungary. The siege of Buda, carried out with a large deployment of forces, began on June 17, 1686. On July 22, the gunpowder stored in the royal castle exploded, destroying the building and playing havoc with the already severely damaged town. On September 2, the final assault of the liberating armies with Hungarian troops fighting in the front lines shattered Turkish resistance, but found only ruins with dead bodies of the enemy, including that of the last pasha of Buda. The once proud seat of the sovereign was liberated, but an enormous price had to be paid for it. Most of Buda's population perished under the Turkish rule, only a few hundred people lived to see liberation. The town's progress was halted and even fell behind the standard achieved in the 15th century.

It was not before the 18th century that urban life began to gain new impetus. It is true, the population of the three towns was engaged mainly in agriculture, only a minority carried on guild handicrafts and trade. The baroque palaces and churches built gradually were, for a long time, of a provincial standard. Buda did not regain its former rank of capital. This was also a factor retarding rapid development, although the highest judicial authorities of the country were transferred to Buda in 1723, and the sole university of Hungary moved to Buda in 1777 and then to Pest in 1784. The regency council, the governmental body directing the country in the name of the Hapsburg king, also functioned in Buda. The political life of the country, however, was not centralised there and, except for one occasion, the Diet did not meet there either: the representatives of the clergy, the nobility and the towns met in Buda between 1790 and 1792.

After this session of the Diet the political significance of Buda and Pest continued to increase. The movement of the Hungarian Jacobins, following the example of the French Revolution, developed here. This movement, which won only a few hundred supporters, set as its goal the overthrow of the feudal system and the realisation of reforms in Hungary which would open the way to unhampered bourgeois development. Other parts of the country were also involved, but the leaders of the movement, Ignác Martinovics, József Hajnóczy and others lived here. This was where they were arrested by the gendarmes of the Hapsburgs, who were frightened by the spectre of a revolution. The five leaders of the movement, the first martyrs of the "Martinovics conspiracy" were executed in Buda. The development of the three towns advanced with somewhat greater vigour at the beginning of the 19th century. Feudalism still reigned, but capitalism in Hungary was developing at an accelerated pace. Buda, and especially Pest, again became the centre of national trade. The tow-barges on the Danube delivered grain and other agricultural produce here from the entire country. Manufactories and even factories were set up, following the initiatives during the last century, alongside the handicraft shops. The population grew rapidly and the bulk of the people were engaged in industry and trade. Street lighting, the unmistakable indicator of urban development, was introduced at the end of the 18th century. The "Embellishment Commission" established in 1803 undertook the task of ensuring proper urban surroundings for the advancing economy. The growth in the number of the population led to increased building. A row of palaces was built on the Pest side of the Danube, opposite the royal castle; they were dwellings of the prosperous urban bourgeoisie, built in the neoclassic style.

Buda and Pest also became the centres of a Hungarian national revival, the focal point of literary life, where the first important periodicals and political journals were published. The Hungarian Academy of Sciences, founded in 1825, began its activities here. The Hungarian National Museum and its Library, established in 1802 and moved into their present building in 1847, became a stronghold of intellectual life, alongside the university and its library. In 1837 this was where the first permanent Hungarian theatre, the National Theatre, was organised. One year later a disastrous Danube flood threatened almost everything with destruction—most of the houses were ruined or badly damaged. After the flood new dwelling houses were built, and both towns took on the appearance of a modern capitalist city. The erection of the first permanent bridge linking Pest with Buda was of great significance; the Suspension Bridge (Lánchíd) built by Adam Clark upon the initiative and with the support of Count István Széchenyi, the outstanding public figure of the Hungarian bourgeois "reform period", was opened in 1849.

The feudal system, however, still had a paralysing effect on urban development. Feudal conditions prevented the development of capitalism and social progress, thus the

31

unhampered prosperity of all the three towns. Feudalism had to be destroyed sooner or later, and the road thrown open through bourgeois revolution for the development of capitalism. This bourgeois revolution also started out from here, and university students and young intellectuals known as the "youth of March" played a decisive part in its preparation. The leaders of the youth included Sándor Petőfi, the greatest Hungarian poet, and Mór Jókai, who later became a novelist of world renown. On March 15, 1848, inspired by the news of the Paris and Vienna revolutions, the people of Pest acted and achieved the freedom of the press, liberated political prisoners gaoled by the bankrupt regime and launched the revolution and the War of Independence which constitute one of the most glorious chapters of Hungarian history. Hapsburg absolutism was compelled to beat a temporary retreat and the first parliamentary government of Hungary, with the active participation of Lajos Kossuth, the political and spiritual leader of the struggle for freedom, later governor of Hungary, was formed here and began its activities of rousing and reshaping the entire country.

The forces of absolutism and counter-revolution, however, did not give up the struggle and opened an offensive against the bourgeois revolution in Hungary. The Hungarian government was compelled to leave Buda and Pest during the early days of 1849, and the towns were taken over by Hapsburg troops. The Hungarian armies, fighting for national independence and to protect the achievements of the bourgeois transformation, went into a counter-offensive in the spring of 1849. They liberated Pest, then Buda, following a siege on May 21, but the success was short-lived; the counter-revolution gained the upper hand, and with the intervention of czarist troops the Hungarian War of Independence was defeated.

The large-scale economic and social transformation initiated by the 1848 revolution, however, could not be stopped, the wheels of progress could not be turned backward. The new capitalist system triumphed and grew by leaps and bounds with Buda and Pest as its centre. New factories were built in rapid succession, metal-processing and engineering works were established alongside light industrial works. This considerably changed the outward appearance of the two towns. The rapidly developing suburbs became grimy with the smoke and soot of the factories, the working class came into existence.

The Austro-Hungarian compromise of 1867 removed additional obstacles barring the road to economic progress. This development called for the unification of the three towns. They were considered one city even in the decade preceding the revolution, and they were officially amalgamated in 1872; Budapest became the largest and most rapidly growing city of Hungary.

The last three decades of the 19th century and the first years of the 20th brought profound changes in the life of the capital. The wealthy capitalists built new factories and blocks of flats at a feverish rate, Budapest was soon the biggest industrial city of the country. By 1910 forty-four per cent of the industrial workers of Hungary were employed here.

The capital's leading role was not limited to the economic field. Here was the centre of political life, the meeting place of parliament and the seat of the government and the various leading national institutions and offices. The Academy and the University continued to dominate scientific activities and the Technical University became shortly famous throughout Europe. Budapest attracted writers, artists and actors. The city drew money and talents like a magnet and practically became synonymous with Hungary. In the shadows of the factories there emerged a large working class, whose greatest struggles are interwoven with Budapest's history. The labour movement was spontaneous at first, strikes and demonstrations took place without serious organisational support. The Paris Commune had a profound influence on the Budapest working class. Street demonstrations took place in Pest on May 8 and 10, 1871, expressing the solidarity of the Hungarian workers with their Paris brothers and their determination to wage a relentless struggle against exploitation. The march of the Budapest workers on July 11, in protest against the imprisonment and mass execution of the Paris Commune's heroes, was the most outstanding action of this period.

By 1890 the Budapest working-class movement had become so strong that it was among the first to answer the appeal of the Second International. May 1, 1890, was the first of the traditional working-class demonstrations in the streets of Budapest, an expression of international solidarity and support of the principles advocated by the Socialist International.

The greatest action took place in the years preceding the

First World War, on May 23, 1912. Barricades were set up in the Budapest streets, and the workers, taking up positions behind overturned tramcars, battled the armed force of the oppressive state machinery.

The capital had its full share of the sufferings and want of the First World War. When it became obvious to the people that the country had lost the war, the workers and soldiers who rallied to support them seized the railway stations and public buildings of the city on the night of October 31, 1918. The people took power, the bourgeois democratic revolution triumphed. The Communist Party of Hungary was formed not long afterward in Budapest. The coalition government of bourgeois parties and the Social Democratic Party, which was put into power by the revolution, tried in vain to stop the growth of the communist movement. On March 21 it was compelled to turn over power to the "proletariat of the peoples of Hungary"; the Republic of Councils, the second Soviet state of the world, was established. This government lasted only 133 days and was defeated after desperate battles by the overwhelming forces of the counter-revolutionary armies attacking from all directions.

Between the two world wars Budapest's development as an industrial centre and the sole big city of Hungary continued. In 1938, 61.9 per cent of the country's factory workers were employed in Budapest, and in line with this, the capital remained the centre of the labour movement. With the ominous approach of the Second World War the Budapest workers' struggle against fascism and for peace intensified.

On March 19, 1944 the capital was occupied by German armies which later, in the middle of October, thwarted the attempt of the Horthy government to switch over to the side of the victorious allies. Soviet army units, however, were already approaching Budapest, and by the end of December the German troops were encircled and the liquidation of their resistance began. Budapest was liberated on February 13, 1945. The senseless resistance put up by the Germans led to enormous losses: they blew up all the bridges, caused 27 per cent of the houses to be ruined or badly damaged (79 per cent in the Castle Hill area), and subjected the population to starvation.

The situation was desperate, but the people of the capital again rose to the occasion. With heroic effort they began the hard work of clearing the ruins away and restoring communications. Tramway service was resumed in the summer of 1945, two pontoon bridges set up by the Soviet armies linked the two banks of the Danube, and the construction of the first permanent bridge was started. The wheels in the factories began to turn again, production and life, which at the time of liberation seemed to be completely destroyed in the city, started all over again. The First Three-Year Plan drafted upon the proposal of the Communist Party was launched on August 1, 1947. Its objective was to eliminate once and for all the damage caused by the war, and to surpass pre-war production levels. As an essential prerequisite, the nationalisation of factories employing over 100 workers was started in March 1948. Thus the large works of Budapest became the property of the people. Four bridges were rebuilt during the three-year plan period and the construction of two more was started. The factories were producing with great vigour by then.

An important change took place in 1950. The suburban and neighbouring communities were incorporated in the city, and Greater Budapest thus came into existence. The reorganisation of the municipal administration and the establishment of councils resulted in the direct participation of the population in the management of the capital's affairs.

The task of the First Five-Year Plan which followed was the large-scale industrialisation of the country. Although the most important industrial investments were made in the provinces, the Budapest factories were not neglected either; new shops were built and the manufacture of new products was introduced. The enlargement of the Technical University made possible the training of more and better technicians, necessary for economic development. The People's Stadium, one of the prides of the capital, was built in this period, theatres were rebuilt and modernised, and the cultural centres established in the factories enabled the working class, which became the leader in the country's economic and political life, to master the cultural field, too.

The counter-revolution of October 1956, aimed at destroying the people's power, also broke out in the capital, owing to the leading part played by Budapest in the life of the country. After overcoming so many hardships Budapest suffered new losses. The working people of the capital, under the leadership of the Hungarian Socialist Workers' Party, restored order and repaired the damage in an amazingly short time. Budapest soon became brighter than ever. Side by side with the building of new housing and the creation of many housing estates in the suburbs, the restoration of monuments, many of them venerable relics of so many centuries, also proceeded at a rapid pace. Modern, well-stocked shops were opened in the remote sections of the city as well.

It is impossible even to outline here the progress of Budapest during recent years. Nor is this necessary, because in subsequent chapters, in the course of the detailed information on Budapest, a thorough description will be given of all points of interest to the visitor from abroad. Let us conclude this brief historical outline by stating that Budapest is advancing at a rate almost inconceivable in the past and everything possible is being done to keep pace with the development of other big cities of the world.

ECONOMIC SIGNIFICANCE

Budapest, unlike the majority of European capitals, is not merely the centre of the bodies directing Hungarian social and economic affairs, but also a leading economic factor itself.

On January 1, 1960, at the time of the last census, 1,804,606 out of the 9,961,044 inhabitants of Hungary lived in the capital. In other words, 18 per cent of the country's population lived on a 526 sq. km. area in Budapest. In this connection it should be pointed out that there are in Europe only two countries with a population of over 4 million (Denmark and Austria) where a still higher percentage of the population lives in the capital city.

Budapest is the largest industrial centre of the country, a junction of land, water and air routes. It is the headquarters of all the foreign trade enterprises of Hungary and the majority of the wholesale trade enterprises. Thirty-three per cent of the retail trade of the country is transacted in the shops, department stores and catering units of the town.

The annual International Fair of Budapest, the Agricultural Exhibition and several special shows attract many Hungarian and foreign visitors to the capital. If one adds to these the natural beauty, historical monuments, excellent medicinal baths and the outstanding institutions of culture and entertainment of Budapest, it is quite natural that the capital has also become a tourist centre.

INDUSTRY

Of Hungary's 1,268 state-owned industrial enterprises, 513 operated in Budapest on December 31, 1961, employing 420,000 of the 900,000 workers of the nationalised industry. This means that 40 per cent of the country's industrial enterprises and 47 per cent of their employees are concentrated in Budapest.

This leading role played by Budapest in Hungarian industry is not a recent phenomenon. Its favourable geographical location and lively trade developed thereby acted as an attracting force right at the beginning of industrialisation. This advantage increased further in the course of industrial development. General economic progress, the development of steamship navigation and railway communication, which directed the entire economic blood stream of the country through Budapest, brought about such excellent conditions for industrial settlement in Budapest's present area that they could not be matched by the provinces. In 1938 Budapest's share in the manufacturing industry of the country, considering the number of workers employed here, exceeded 53 per cent.

The transformation of the territorial distribution of Hungarian industry has been a matter of constant discussion since 1945. The industrialisation of the provinces has undoubtedly made considerable progress during the last decade, nevertheless many products of great importance— both from the point of view of the population and of the national economy—are exclusively or mainly manufactured in Budapest. Motorcycles, bicycles, film cameras, sewing machines, tape recorders, major pharmaceutical goods, are manufactured overwhelmingly in Budapest, together with tramcars, autobuses, tractors, threshing machines, etc.

Districts 4 (Újpest) and 21 (Csepel) of Budapest are still among the biggest industrial areas of Hungary, with the factories of Districts 8, 9, 10 and 13 also playing a major role.

There are many enterprises in Budapest whose products enjoy an international reputation. The machine-tools, motorcycles and bicycles of the Csepel Iron and Steel Works, the maritime passenger boats and freighters of the Óbuda and other shipyards, the Orion television sets, the silk and cotton fabrics of the 180-year-old Goldberger textile mill, the Ikarus buses, the Red Star (Vörös Csillag) tractors, the Ganz-Mávag motor trains, the highly potent medicinal preparations of the Budapest pharmaceutical works—to cite a few examples taken at random—are well known and appreciated throughout the world.

The period since 1950 has been of greater significance from the point of view of industrialisation than many decades preceding liberation in 1945. The production level of the

Budapest state-owned industry, representing at present 47 per cent of the nation's industrial output, rose between 1950 and 1961 by an average of 12 per cent annually. The industrial enterprises of the capital produced almost four times as much in 1961 as in 1949, and considerably more than five times the 1938 output. The heavy industrial enterprises, representing over 60 per cent of the state industries' production in Budapest, increased their output almost fivefold in 12 years, and the light industrial and food-processing works also raised their output approximately three times in 1961 as compared to 1949.

The volume of production of the handicraft cooperatives and private artisans is dwarfed by that of the nationalised industry, yet they play an extremely important role in meeting the many-sided needs of the population, both in making individual items calling for great skill, and in the production of a large variety of small consumer goods. On December 31, 1961 there were 329 handicraft cooperatives employing 60,000 people, and 19,000 private artisans in the capital.

Budapest is also a leading factor in the building industry. In 1961 there were 66 state-owned building enterprises, employing a monthly average of 80,000 workers, and 48 building cooperatives with a total of 5,000 members; this represented fifty per cent of the building workers of Hungary. Many industrial buildings, dwellings, roads and railway lines, health, social welfare and cultural institutions are built every year, thus adding to the economic growth of Hungary, to the better satisfaction of the population's needs.

COMMERCE

The outward appearance of a town is greatly affected by the standard of its shopping network. The modernly equipped, attractively decorated shops, department stores, the hosts of coffee shops, restaurants and confectioneries greatly enhance Budapest's attraction.

In the middle of 1961 there were 7,114 state-owned and cooperative shops and 1,754 catering establishments in Budapest with close to 55,000 employees.

The network of state-owned and cooperative shops is supplemented by 4,300 privately owned retail shops. Their turnover, however, is insignificant compared to the socialist sector.

For over a century the business centre of Budapest has been the inner town, at present District 5. Its rows of retail shops in Váci utca, Petőfi Sándor utca and Kossuth Lajos utca, together with the Luxus Department Store, and the Úttörő (Pioneer) Department Store, continue to enjoy great popularity among the shoppers.

The development of the socialist retail trade organisation has also resulted in the expansion and modernisation of the shop network in the outlying districts. The Újpest Department Store, built in 1950, is one of the finest, most up-to-date shops in the country.

During the second three-year plan period, between 1958 and 1960, the number of food shops increased by 270, and of shops selling durable consumer goods by about 90. This alone is indicative of the efforts being made in the development of retail trade. Beside numerical growth a great deal of attention is being paid to the modernisation of the older shops, to making them more attractive, while introducing up-to-date sales methods, like self-service, rapid service, mail order and delivery systems.

Commerce is faced with a major job in supplying close to two million inhabitants of the capital with food, and the amount of flour and sugar sold yearly is around 4,500 railway carloads, while the figure for bread and meat or meat products is over 17,000 and 8,000 carloads respectively.

The Budapest shops, especially the nationally known department stores, like the Corvin and the Úttörő Áruház (Pioneer Department Store), attract a large number of shoppers from the countryside, although the network of commercial establishments out of town and the variety of their merchandise can meet all requirements.

TOURIST TRAFFIC

The touristic endowments of the Hungarian capital are so favourable that they alone ensure it a privileged position. Budapest is not only a metropolis, but also one of the outstanding cities of the world in natural beauties, while its hot springs, medicinal waters and open-air baths make it a spa as well. Budapest is therefore attractive to the seekers of recreation and cures and also to tourists interested in becoming acquainted with the sights of a big city. Budapest is visited by a growing number of foreign and domestic tourists. As many as 375,311 guests were accommodated by hotels in 1963. The number of tourists is, of course, much higher because only some of them go to hotels. There are no reliable data on those who stay with relatives and friends or come for a one-day visit.

In 1963, out of the 375,311 hotel guests over 194,000 came from abroad. This represented an increase of 64,000 compared to 1960. The following table shows the changes in the number of Budapest hotel guests over a period of 33 years. It shows the great setback in tourism due to the Second World War, but also a rising tendency in visitors from abroad, whose number will soon surpass the pre-war figures.

| Year | Number of hotel guests | | |
	From Hungary	From abroad	Total
1930	125,207	116,249	241,456
1931	103,720	99,171	202,891
1932	96,830	93,763	190,593
1933	90,752	101,936	192,688
1934	91,656	110,457	202,113
1935	87,176	133,089	220,265
1936	91,685	167,195	258,880
1937	95,347	182,747	278,094
1938	111,427	138,314	249,741
1939	160,875	107,887	268,762
1940	214,472	57,598	272,070
1948	109,053	17,998	127,051
1957	311,208	34,756	345,964
1958	300,530	59,275	359,805
1959	286,470	86,683	373,153
1960	285,823	130,173	415,996
1963	181,186	194,125	375,311

Of the guests from abroad who stayed in Budapest hotels in 1963, 33 thousand came from Czechoslovakia, 27 thousand from the German Democratic Republic, 22 thousand from Austria, 19 thousand from Poland, 17 thousand from the Soviet Union, and 15,000 from the German Federal Republic. The number of guests from other countries is also rising.

Country	Guests		
	1957	1960	1963
Austria	1,856	9,203	21,663
Chinese People's Republic	137	1,165	134
Czechoslovakia	11,489	35,913	32,552
Finland	121	566	927
France	1,663	4,055	5,021
German Democratic Republic	2,529	20,867	27,343
German Federal Republic	2,440	6,962	15,489
India	147	268	272
Israel	111	110	521
Poland	2,306	14,055	19,099
Italy	303	1,986	5,098
Rumania	1,329	4,616	7,999
Soviet Union	2,594	11,152	17,076
Sweden	228	843	1,813
Switzerland	524	849	1,733
Turkey	90	129	323
United Kingdom	390	2,445	5,470
Yugoslavia	2,188	2,111	3,700
Other countries	4,311	12,878	25,714
Total	34,756	130,173	194,125

CULTURE AND SCIENCE

Budapest is the centre of Hungary's scientific and cultural life.

The Hungarian Academy of Sciences and thirty-one of its research institutes and groups reside in Budapest, which is also the home of 50 other scientific institutions.

The capital has seven universities, a number of colleges, about 150 secondary schools of all kinds and more than 300 eight-form primary schools.

Budapest is also the most important scene of Hungary's literary life, the creative centre of most of the writers and poets, the headquarters of the Hungarian Writers' Association and the Literary Fund, established to assist the men of letters who are members of the Association.

There are eighteen publishing firms in the capital, and also the largest and most up-to-date printing shops. They produce 30 million volumes of books, 50 million copies of periodicals and weeklies, and daily newspapers with a circulation of 150 million.

Budapest is also the centre of Hungarian arts. Our theatres have a past of 200 years. The first permanent theatre was opened in 1774 in Pest. Since the country was a part of the Hapsburg monarchy, its performances were given in the German language. The first permanent Hungarian-language theatre was opened in 1837. It was first named "Pest Hungarian Theatre", then the "National Theatre" (Nemzeti Színház). (The opening performance, the presentation of a play by the great poet Mihály Vörösmarty, took place on August 22, 1837.) Many Hungarian plays had their premieres here, together with well-known masterpieces of the world's dramatic literature. One of the first Hungarian operas, "Báthori Mária" by Ferenc Erkel, was also presented in this theatre, in 1840.

The first Hungarian stage was followed, during the latter decades of the past century, by other theatres. The Budapest Opera House was founded, then the Comedy Theatre (Vígszínház) and the Magyar Színház, followed by dramatic and operetta theatres, repertory theatres, cabarets and others.

At present there are twenty-odd permanent theatres, two opera houses, several open-air stages in Budapest. There are also many cultural centres in the factories and outlying districts, where professional and amateur stage performances and concerts are given, in addition to cinema showings. Mention should be made here of the up-to-date theatre of the Hungarian Optical Works and the Ironworkers' Cultural Centre of Pesterzsébet, a major working-class district of the capital.

The open-air stages give complete programmes during the summer. This goes also for the Circular Theatre (Körszínház), initiated by young artists, which is specialising in Greek classic dramas.

Music has always played a prominent role in Budapest's artistic life. The Academy of Music (Zeneművészeti Főiskola) can be proud of its distinguished professors like Ferenc Liszt, Béla Bartók, Leó Weiner, Ede Zathureczky, and at present Zoltán Kodály and Bence Szabolcsi. The concert hall of the Academy of Music is the scene of outstanding musical events almost every evening. There are other well-known concert halls, like the Bartók Hall (Bartók Terem) in Váci utca—where stage plays, children's operas and operettas are also presented—and the chamber music hall of Filmharmónia in Semmelweis utca. The Erkel Theatre is often used for concerts by Hungarian and foreign orchestras and artists. Of the summer concerts held at outdoor stages those given in the Károlyi Garden (Károlyi-kert) are the most outstanding. The "Budapest Musical Weeks", a series of concerts organised every autumn, is the highlight of the musical events. Foreign artists, including the best in the world, and music lovers come in large numbers from abroad for this occasion. Musical competitions, arranged to commemorate some renowned composer, attract young musicians from all parts of the world. The International Liszt-Bartók Piano Competition, held in 1962 with the participation of the best young pianists from some twenty countries, was a great success.

Budapest is also the centre of cinema art. The majority of the feature films in Hungary are produced by Hunnia, while the Budapest Film Studio specialises in newsreels and shorts, besides making feature films. The studio of the

Hungarian Television and the two main transmitters of the Hungarian Radio are located in Budapest.

The fine arts have a great tradition in Hungary. The centre of the bustling artistic life is Budapest. Most of the exhibitions are held here. The major galleries include the Art Gallery (Műcsarnok) which is the scene of the biennial national art exhibitions. The expenses of the exhibitions and shows are covered entirely by the state. Public organisations (Councils, the Patriotic People's Front, youth organisations) in the various districts arrange many art shows, mainly in the cultural centres.

Architecture has also made great progress recently. The up-to-date housing estates built in Budapest reflect modern methods in artistic expression and in forms. Many of these new buildings are decorated with works of art, which use the media of metal work and ceramics to the best advantage.

MONUMENTS

Although Budapest is not as rich in architectural monuments as Rome or Paris, remains of Roman and Turkish
buildings as well as art memorials from other bygone ages
lend it a peculiar charm. In some respects these monuments are more varied and unique than those of many
other capitals.

The region of present-day Budapest has shown traces of
man of the neolithic and the copper age, and Celtic and
Eraviscus settlements have been unearthed on Gellért Hill,
but the few relics found are primarily of archaeological
interest.

The situation is entirely different when it comes to Roman
ruins. From the northern tip of Budapest's 526 sq. km.
area to the south there are scattered Roman monuments
everywhere. The most important are the remnants of
Aquincum, the erstwhile capital of Pannonia Inferior, which
flourished from the first century up to the Hun invasion
at the end of the 4th century. The ruins disclosed during
the systematic excavations of Aquincum give a clear picture of everyday life in the capital of a Roman province.
The civilian town had an amphitheatre, which lies north
of the town's ruins. The remains of the Roman proconsuls'
palace were found on the island now occupied by the
Óbuda shipyard, while south of the civilian town there are
vestiges of the one-time military town. A stairway leads
from the basement of the house at 3 Flórián tér to the
remains of a Roman bath, now right under the roadway.
During the building of the house at 63 Korvin Ottó utca,
in 1950, relics from Roman days, including a bathroom and
a fresco depicting a hunting scene, were unearthed. These
are exhibited in the basement of the dwelling built above
them, and partly in the adjoining collection of ruins, called
the Roman Camp Lapidary. The ruins of the military town's
amphitheatre are nearby, alongside Korvin Ottó utca.

The foundation walls of a Roman watch tower can be seen in the Tabán park, between Castle Hill and Gellért Hill, while on the other side of the Danube, on Március 15. tér, the tower and wall of the Contra-Aquincum *castrum* built in 294 A.D. form part of the underground museum. Additional relics may be seen in District 11, the Albertfalva ruins of a Roman military camp, and at Nagytétény, District 22, where the ruins of Campona, a fortified camp of the Danube Limes, have been excavated.

There are no relics of buildings for a period of several centuries following the collapse of Roman rule in Pannonia, because the peoples and tribes who lived here during the Great Migrations did not build. In the 11th and 12th centuries the Hungarians founded in the area of present-day Budapest several settlements which in time became known as the communities of Buda, Pest and Óbuda.

The first proof that there existed a Christian church of Romanesque style in the region which is known today as Budapest can be found in the Inner City Parish Church built over the walls of the Roman *castrum*, at Március 15. tér. Inside the southern tower (to the right when facing the church) there is a semicircular Romanesque cornice built in a style characteristic of the twelfth century. According to ancient chronicles the engagement of St. Elizabeth of Hungary and Margrave Ludwig of Thuringia took place in this church in 1211.

This church was reconstructed, remodelled with additional structures in practically every period. This is a mute testimony of historian Ferenc Salamon's statement that "there is hardly a town in Europe which was destroyed so many times and to such an extent, and consequently had to be rebuilt from the very foundations so many times as Budapest".

The church built originally in Romanesque style was fully destroyed by the invading Mongols in 1241. In the fifteenth century a new Gothic church was built on the same place, as shown by the ambulatory sanctuary, the sediles around the sanctuary and the gates to the right. Its side chapels contain two richly ornamented ciboria in Renaissance style from 1507. The period of the Turkish conquest (1541-1686) also left its mark on the church. Turkish mihrabs (niches) can be seen at the right end of the row of Gothic sediles, as mementoes of the period when it was transformed into a Mohammedan mosque. The church was again destroyed during the siege of Buda, and its roof was restored only

47

during the year of Buda's recapture. The façade and the nave were reconstructed in baroque style between 1725 and 1739, while the sanctuary remained Gothic. Yet the Gothic outer wall of the sanctuary contains a baroque statue of St. Florian from 1725. Classicism is represented by the sepulchre of István Kultsár, a pioneer Hungarian journalist, modelled by István Ferenczy. It is located in the first side-chapel on the left of the main entrance. The organ loft was enlarged, also in neoclassic style, in 1835. The church again suffered heavy damage in 1944-45. A new, modern main altar replaced the old one destroyed during the war, and the venerable ancient church was again restored in 1958.

The Mongol invasion (1241) left only ruins in place of the scanty building monuments of Buda and Pest. The reconstruction of the town is credited to King Béla IV (1235-1270). He built a fortress and a royal castle on the steep Castle Hill (Vár-hegy) of Buda, and the construction of the church of the Blessed Virgin, later renamed the Matthias or Coronation Church, also began during his rule. Béla IV had the convent of the Dominican order built on today's Margaret Island (Margitsziget), named after his daughter Margit who was later beatified. The ruins of this building are still standing today, near the Grand Hotel. The ground-plan of the former church and convent is revealed by the walls of the ruins. The sepulchral chapel of the pious princess who died in the convent in 1270 was to the west next to the church. Close to the Dominican convent the king also built a cloister for the Premonstratensian order. The chapel, which is still used, was built in the original style on the scanty ruins about 30 years ago. In 1272 a church was constructed on the island for the Franciscans. Its ruins or rather well-preserved walls can be seen alongside the motor-road leading across the island. The tower of the Dominican St. Nicholas Church at 1 Hess András tér also dates from the Middle Ages, similarly to the tower of the Mary Magdalene Church (formerly Garrison Church) in the Castle District. In its original form it was built by Béla IV for the order of the Observant Franciscans.

The medieval remains of the former royal castle, recently uncovered, are important Gothic relics. One of them is the Stephen tower, built by Stephen, the younger brother of King Louis I (the Great, 1342-82), then the three annular-vaulted halls from the luxurious palace of Sigismund of Luxembourg, later Holy Roman emperor (as Hungarian king he reigned from 1387 to 1437)—these halls adjoin the Stephen tower—and thirdly the excavated crypt of the Sigismund Chapel.

These modest remains, which are being restored at present, give only a scanty picture of King Sigismund's luxurious palace.

Mention should be made of the secular buildings from the Middle Ages, also in the Castle District, some of which have been relatively well preserved. Their disclosure can be attributed to the bombing and artillery bombardment during the 1944-45 siege of Budapest when layers of mortar of fairly recent origin were removed by the shock waves of the explosions, and Gothic sections of exquisite beauty were revealed.

The house at 18 Országház utca has a closed balcony set on Gothic consoles, dating from the 15th century. The portal is also Gothic. The carved trefoil stone cornice of the house at 20 Országház utca, placed on double consoles above the ground floor, dates from the end of the 14th century. There are four Gothic trefoil sediles in the portico, which are quite common in the Castle District. The house at 31 Úri utca, with an interesting Gothic façade, built around 1440, reflects the influence of the trecento palaces of Italy. Three vaulted windows to the left on the first floor are held together by struts of segmental arches, the other windows have a beaded Gothic frame. There are also Gothic sediles in the portico. The nucleus of the house at 14 Tárnok utca was built during the 14th century, but a protruding storey was added during the 15th century. The exterior wall painting dating from the 16th century was restored authentically. Scores of buildings in this district contain Gothic elements which are not revealed from the outside. The house at 4 Hess András tér, where the Fortuna restaurant, coffee shop and bar is located, is one of these buildings.

Buda has not a single Renaissance building of any significance in spite of the fact that many Italian architects, who came to Hungary upon the invitation of King Matthias Corvinus (1458-1490), worked in the Renaissance style. Their activities centered primarily on giving a Renaissance exterior to the existing Gothic buildings. Moreover, Gothic architecture was perpetuated in Buda because the conservative burghers stuck to the old style instead of following in the footsteps of the Renaissance king.

Basically the lack of Renaissance relics in Budapest, however, is due to historical events. The Turks gradually moved northward and occupied Buda in 1541. The century and a half of Turkish rule prevented the onward march of the Renaissance in Hungary.

Except for fortifications the Turks limited their building activities to baths and sepulchral chapels. They cared little for the maintenance of the existing buildings and made their mosques and djamis out of Christian churches. However, not a single tall minaret adjoining the old mosques has survived. Turkish architectural remains are limited to the halls of three baths, the Király, Rudas and Imre Baths, one of the basins of the Császár Baths and the sepulchre of Gül Baba, a dervish, on the Hill of Roses (Rózsadomb). They are all in Buda.

As to Pest, let us limit ourselves to one quotation from János Bocatius, mayor of Kassa (now Košice, Czechoslovakia), who wrote the following on what he saw in Pest in 1602: "Alas, poor Pest (it should rather be called pestilence, the plague)! Not a single building has remained intact, they are all demolished, and its few inhabitants are all scums of the earth."

Buda was retaken from the Turks in 1686, following a bitter, prolonged struggle by Christian armies, consisting of Germans, Hungarians and other nationalities. In the reconstruction of the houses use was made of the ruins, this is the reason why so many buildings have oddly arranged windows and lack of symmetry. The poverty of the population was another factor. Luxurious palaces were built by the aristocrats and the high clergy, ordinary burghers were satisfied with modest dwellings.

Many of the civic buildings in Buda, and far more on the Pest side, suffered from fire, sieges and frequent reconstruction. While the building boom towards the end of the 19th century caused relatively few changes in the houses on the Buda Castle Hill, the ruthless business drive wrought great havoc on the Pest side, and ugly, unshapely tenement houses replaced the ancient buildings.

The old town hall (2 Szentháromság tér) of Buda of medieval origin in the Castle District was rebuilt in 1692, six years after the recapture of the town. At present it is the seat of the Castle Museum. Venerio Ceresola, imperial architect, still used late Renaissance forms on the balconies and window heads in the course of the baroque reconstruction.

Another sprawling building, almost fully retaining its old

orm, the present headquarters of the City Council (9 Vá-
osház utca), was erected on the Pest side. Built to the
lesigns of Anton Erhardt Martinelli, it was intended origi-
ally as a home for soldiers disabled during the Turkish
wars.

The large-scale reconstruction of the palace on Castle Hill
egan in 1749, according to the plans of the French-born
rchitect, Jean Nicolas Jadot de Ville Issey. Owing to sev-
ral fires, reconstruction and restoration, only the walls
emained. The southern wing of the present castle con-
eals the block of former baroque buildings.

The construction of the only remaining private baroque
dwelling, the present Százéves (Hundred-Year-Old) Res-
aurant with its exquisite gate (2 Pesti Barnabás utca), was
tarted in 1756. The Erdődy palace in the Castle District
7 Táncsics Mihály utca), which has been preserved in
airly good condition, dates also from the latter part of
he 18th century. Another aristocratic house, at 3 Dísz
ér, was built for Palatine Lajos Batthyány, the highest
Hungarian dignitary next to the king.

The Castle District was otherwise rebuilt in the 17th and
18th centuries with unpretentious burgher dwellings,
which, though not outstanding architectural creations in
themselves, lend an atmosphere of quaintness to the
area.

The many church towers and cloisters built in baroque
style are outstanding elements of the cityscape. The recapture of Buda took place during the period of the counter-reformation. The liberating armies were followed by
armies of the religious orders, which came with the double
purpose of restoring religious discipline among the Catho-
ic population, and of winning back to the Roman Church
the flock that had gone astray in the meadows of John
Calvin, Martin Luther or even Mohammed. The various
orders of monks and nuns (Jesuits, Franciscans, Paulites,
Dominicans, Carmelites, Misericordians, Trinitarians, Cla-
rists, etc.) arriving in the wake of the soldiers went ahead
busily to convert—and construct.

Many baroque church buildings are worthy of mention.
There is the original Pauline church in Pest, at present
known as the University Church, at Egyetem tér, with its
recently restored twin-towered building. Another imposing monument of Pest is the Franciscan Church nearby, at
2 Károlyi utca. The St. Anne Church on the Buda side
(Batthyány tér) with two spires, an ellipsoidal dome

and a central nave, was built in the late baroque style and shows Italian influence.

The St. Michael Church, formerly Mary Ward Nuns' Church (47 Váci utca), the former Servite Church (4 Martinelli tér), and the former church of the Elizabeth Nuns (41-43 Fő utca) are also noteworthy.

The influence of the baroque style declined at the end of the 18th century and was followed by a transitional style, generally known as Louis XVI, and called "zopf" style in the Hapsburg monarchy. The most beautiful examples of this transitional style can be found in the Castle District (e.g. the houses at 5, 8, and 24 Országház utca). A baroque Carmelite church was rebuilt in the Louis XVI style, following a decree by Joseph II (1780-1790) dissolving the religious orders, and turned into a theatre (Castle Theatre, 24 Színház utca). The building which was destroyed during the Second World War is being restored. The same decree of Joseph II also resulted in the transformation of the building at 28 Országház utca into the Louis XVI style where the order of the Poor Clares wanted to erect a huge block of houses for its nuns in 1781-82. Joseph II intervened, however, before construction was finished, and made Franz Anton Hildebrandt turn the almost completed convent into the seat of the Diet transferred from Pozsony (now Bratislava, Czechoslovakia) to Buda.

It is worth while taking a good look at the houses at 35 and 62 Úri utca, 3 Táncsics Mihály utca, 8 and 10 Fortuna utca and at the row between 5 and 8 Bécsikapu tér (Vienna Gate Square), because they are fine examples of the Louis XVI style as applied in Buda. The house at 7 Bécsikapu tér is interesting not only because the fine engravings on its façade, depicting classic authors, but also because this is where Thomas Mann was a guest on three occasions in 1935 and 1936.

The remains of the various style periods were concentrated in Buda's Castle District, but with the turn of the 18th to the 19th century the emphasis shifted to the Pest side. The new city district of Pest was built on the basis of the over-all architectural directives and town planning of the city Embellishment Commission established in 1803. This led to the construction of a row of neoclassic buildings during the first half of the 19th century on the Pest bank of the Danube and the former inner Lipótváros, at present District 5, from Vörösmarty tér to the Margaret Bridge (Margit-híd). Many of these buildings became

the victims of demolition, reconstruction—and of bomb-
ings during the Second World War.

Several imposing buildings, however, have been preserved
from this period, like the National Museum (14-16 Múzeum
körút), the work of Mihály Pollack, constructed in 1837 to
1847. The former County Hall built in 1838 to 1841 at 7
Városház utca (at present the seat of the Pest County
Council) is worth noting because of its imposing façade
and fine court with arcades and columns.

We shall mention only a few of the many neoclassic private buildings, those which are located in the busiest
thoroughfares.

There are two outstanding buildings in Akadémia utca,
Nos. 1 and 3, at present the seat of the Ministry of Food.
Facing the Duna Hotel, the houses at 3, 5 and 7 Apáczai
Cseri János utca were built beetwen 1811 and 1813. In the
area around Engels tér attention should be called to houses
1 Engels tér (corner of József Attila utca), 16 József Attila
utca (corner of Október 6. utca) and to 1 József nádor tér
(corner of József Attila utca). In earlier years the entire
street and, in fact, the whole section consisted of such
houses, built in the same style and of the same height.

It is not by accident that the two neoclassic Protestant
churches on the Pest side were built outside the former
city walls. The rapidly growing Protestant population of
Pest was permitted to build churches only as late as the
19th century, and only beyond the walls. The Lutheran
church without a spire at Deák tér and the somewhat
provincial looking Calvinist church at Calvin tér also belong to this category.

One cannot close the listing of neoclassic monuments
without mentioning the first permanent bridge of Budapest, the Suspension Bridge (Lánchíd), monumental yet
simple in its lines (constructed in 1839 to 1849).

The Hungarian bourgeois revolution of 1848 marked the
end of the neoclassic period. The pace of the city development and the number of constructions decreased considerably during the oppression following the defeat of the
War of Independence. The only outstanding building of the
period, the Concert Hall (Vigadó) at 2 Vigadó tér, built
between 1859 and 1869, and destroyed by fire in 1945, is
under reconstruction at present. Its style compounded out
of Byzantine, Moorish, Romanesque and other elements
was the forerunner of the historicising style which assumed
practical hegemony in the subsequent decades. The erec-

tion of this decorative building, with an almost exotic atmosphere was undoubtedly a daring undertaking.

A host of state, municipal and religious buildings, tenement houses and private dwellings were designed in an eclectic style in the ensuing period. It is regrettable that the most productive construction period of the capital coincided with this sterile period in international architecture. Fortunately most of the buildings from this time are more moderate creations of an artistic inspiration, like the building of the Hungarian Academy of Sciences (9 Roosevelt tér, built between 1862 and 1864), the Opera House (22 Népköztársaság útja, 1875 to 1884), the Parliament (1-3 Kossuth Lajos tér, 1884 to 1904), the Hungarian National Gallery (12 Kossuth Lajos tér, 1892 to 1896), the Fishermen's Bastion (1895 to 1902), and the Museum of Fine Arts (Hősök tere, 1900 to 1906).

Most of Budapest's monuments were erected in this period. Most outstanding of the many statues are that of the Palatine Joseph (József nádor tér), of János Arany (in front of the National Museum), and the Millenary Monument (Hősök tere).

Ödön Lechner was the first Hungarian architect to take up the fight against eclecticism. Instead of aping old historical styles, Lechner was blazing a new trail with novel architectural rhythm and decorations and with new building material. His major creations are the Museum of Industrial Arts (33-37 Üllői út, built from 1893 to 1895) the Geological Institute (14 Népstadion út, 1898-99), the Hungarian Foreign Trade Bank Ltd. (4 Rosenberg házaspár utca, 1900).

Béla Lajta was a pioneer of modern architecture as shown by some of his buildings, like the business house at 5 Martinelli tér (1910 to 12), the Gas Works building at 18 Rákóczi út (1911) and the Commercial Secondary School at 9-11 Vas utca (1910-11).

Lajta had no immediate followers in his time and in his own country. Only years later did the modern principles he applied gain the upper hand in Budapest's architecture. At present modern buildings are rising in ever greater numbers all over the city, new housing estates, cultural centres, health institutions, factory and office buildings and sport establishments testify to the rapid development of socialist society. A new housing estate for 40,000 to 50,000 inhabitants is taking shape in Üllői út, the thoroughfare leading to the Ferihegy Airport. This housing estate, being laid out according to the most modern principles of town planning and architecture, is one of several built in Budapest since liberation (1945). These housing estates along main thoroughfares like Üllői út are located in the city's suburbs, showing the path of Budapest's development.

PROTECTION OF MONUMENTS

During the Second World War, Budapest lost more monuments than all the other part of the country combined. Following the liberation in 1945 the protection of monuments was put on an entirely new footing. The objective was twofold. While repairing the damage caused by the war, efforts were made to correct the shortcomings resulting from the feverish building boom which had started at the turn of the present century. The planners of the new buildings disregarded the style and the height of the surrounding structures, and went to the extreme of upsetting the harmony of old architectural styles with modernistic shop fronts and other incongruous features.

The decree of 1949 laid down new principles for the protection of old buildings and monuments. It also called for the protection of the environment of the monuments.

Excavations around the former royal castle revealed the external system of fortifications of the Buda fortress, and this was restored. During the repair of the damage caused by the 1944-45 fightings, valuable remains of fortification walls, towers, turrets, round bastions and other defensive structures were found.

Each protected building bears a plaque on its wall, indicating the name of the architect, the year when it was built, and also the date of the restoration.

NATIONAL ART COLLECTIONS

The valuable national art collections of Budapest are great attractions for tourists.

MUSEUMS

The most important museum of the country is the Hungarian National Museum. Its founding dates back to 1802, when Count Ferenc Széchényi donated his valuable collection of books and antiquities to the Hungarian people. A splendid building was erected for the museum between 1837 and 1847.

This building of the Museum (14-16 Múzeum körút) houses also the Historical Museum, which contains cultural, artistic and historical relics from the time of the conquest of Hungary in the 9th century up to 1848. Several departments of the Museum of Natural History are also located in this old building. The museum suffered serious damage during the 1956 counter-revolution and was not reopened until 1962.

The Museum of Industrial Arts (33-37 Üllői út) houses artistic products made of bronze and copper, of the European silversmith's arts, glassblowing, etc. The museum's collections of ceramics, glassware, textiles, furniture, silver, clocks and bookbindings are very rich both in domestic and European items. The major part of the furniture collection is exhibited in the Castle Museum at Nagytétény (9 Kastélymúzeum utca).

The Museum of Eastern Asiatic Art, founded in 1919 by Ferenc Hopp (103 Népköztársaság útja), with its fine collections from Japan, India, Korea, Vietnam, the Near East, etc., belongs to the Museum of Industrial Arts. Since 1955 its Chinese collection has been exhibited in a separate Chinese Museum at 12 Gorkij fasor.

The Ethnographic Museum (40 Könyves Kálmán körút) consists of two major collections, Hungarian and international, but only a small fraction of the material can be exhibited, for lack of space. The nearly 40,000 items of the international collection are shown at special exhibitions. The folk-music collection is very valuable and bears the imprint of such outstanding collectors as Béla Vikár, Béla Bartók, Zoltán Kodály and László Lajtha.

The Museum of Fine Arts (Hősök tere) has an outstanding collection of old masters. The Old Gallery (Régi Képtár) has fine paintings by Italian masters (Raffaello, Boltraffio, Correggio, Giorgione, etc.) and Spaniards (Velásquez, Goya, El Greco). The collection of old statues also has many items of great value.

Other museums contain historical, archaeological, artistic and other local relics of Budapest. They are under the jurisdiction and supervision of the Budapest City Council. The relics of the Roman era are exhibited in the Aquincum Museum (193 Szentendrei út) and several small local museums. The Budapest relics from antiquity, the Middle Ages, the Renaissance period and the Turkish occupation of Hungary are gathered in the Castle Museum (2 Szentháromság utca). Fragments from medieval buildings are exhibited in the Lapidary situated in the northern tower of the Fishermen's Bastion, while other relics, especially documents dealing with modern times (from 1686 on), are displayed in the Kiscell Museum (108 Kiscelli utca).

The Agricultural Museum, located at the Vajdahunyad Castle in the City Park, has a highly valuable and interesting collection. The Petőfi Literary Museum (16 Károlyi utca) arranges documentary exhibits dealing with great Hungarian poets. Data pertaining to other museums can be found in the Appendix, page 269.

LIBRARIES

The National Széchényi Library (14-16 Múzeum körút), located in the building of the Hungarian National Museum, is the major collection of books in Hungary. It is the national library, which contains all books, periodicals and newspapers published in Hungary. The University Library (10 Károlyi utca) and the Library of the Academy (9 Roosevelt tér) are next in importance, while the Szabó Ervin Municipal Library (1 Szabó Ervin tér), aside from its rich collection of books dealing with social sciences, has a large network of branches, which also function as lending libraries to meet the great demand of the reading population.

Other important libraries to be mentioned are the Parliamentary Library (1-3 Kossuth Lajos tér), the National Technical Library (17 Múzeum utca), and the Central Library of the Budapest Technical University (4-6 Budafoki út). There are many other special libraries in Budapest, some attached to various institutions.

BUDAPEST — CITY OF SPAS

The history of the utilisation of medicinal waters in the Budapest area goes back practically to the same period as the history of the settlement proper. The excavated relics from the four centuries of Roman rule contain undisputed proof of an advanced bathing culture in Aquincum. The use of these waters must have continued after the Roman era, but the great upheavals of subsequent history obliterated its traces. The oldest documentary proof of the medicinal use of springs and waters goes back to the 12th century. In 1178 the knights of St. John devoted to the healing of the sick, obtained the area of the present-day Lukács and Császár Baths for the building of a hospital and a bath. Documents from the era of King Sigismund refer to a *balneum regium* in the area of the present Imre Baths. The town was occupied for 150 years by the Turks, who built baths in a style reflecting the Byzantine traditions brought from Asia Minor. The Rudas, Császár, Király and Imre Baths contain several halls and pools which are original Turkish constructions and have been preserved in their original form.

One can find many references to the healing effects of the Buda waters in old medical descriptions, but real progress in exploiting these resources began during the second half of the last century. Spa-hotels under medical supervision began operating at the beginning of this century, in the wake of the scientific disclosure of the effects of the baths, and a research institute was established, attached to the University Pathological Institute. This later became the National Rheumathological and Balneological Institute. There are a number of sanatoriums linked with medicinal baths and fully equipped for the diagnosis and cure of rheumatic diseases. The thermal springs also supply water to open-air baths used for recreation, amusement and the recovery of health.

It is indeed exceptional when the capital of a country, its cultural and economic centre, is at the same time a spa and health resort. Budapest is the only big city in the world to have the natural endowments for the development of a health resort.

The characteristic rock and crystal formations at the site of the hot springs indicate that in the previous geological periods these springs were located at a much higher altitude than at present or any time in recorded history. The Romans and later the Magyar settlers of the country found the thermal springs in their present location. Hot mineral water is provided at present also by deep-sunk wells.

Large volumes of hot water gush forth at 123 spots in Budapest. Approximately 40 million litres of hot water and 30 million litres of lukewarm water are provided daily by the springs and wells.

The occurrence and composition of the hot springs is determined by the geological structure of the soil. Owing to repeated tectonic movements towards the end of the Mesozoic era, the different strata broke up and some of them were displaced vertically to a depth of several hundred metres. This is the explanation, for instance, to why dolomitic rocks making up Gellért Hill were found, during the drilling of the artesian well No. 1 of the Széchenyi Baths in the City Park, at a depth of 917 m.

When the rocks of the Buda hills broke up under the impact of orogenic pressures, these fissures helped surface waters to seep in and circulate inside the earth. The water containing carbon dioxide caused the fissures and crevices to develop into a system of caves, holes and pits. The surface formations underwent a gradual abrasion, and later the sunken regions were filled with dense sediments of subsequent seas. The succession of sediments 900 metres in depth consist mainly of layers of clay, which are about 800 metres thick. While the Buda hills consist of rocks which allow the water to filter through, on the Pest side an extensive clay barrier had developed, which does not let the water pass through, thus also regulating the course of the waters.

In the Buda hills a part of the precipitation seeps downward into deeper and warmer layers. This mixes with water of a lower temperature which moves from the Plain towards the Danube. A third type of water joins this mixture: moisture "sweated out" at a great depth by the rocks under the effect of high temperatures. This latter is called profundal water which finds its way to the surface through deep crevices. These three different kinds of water are affected by the internal warmth of the earth and break out as hot springs (above 50°C), warm springs (30° to 50°C) or lukewarm springs (below 30°C).

The temperature of the springs depends on the mixing ratio of these three kinds of water. The temperature of the karstic water moving from the Buda hills towards the Danube is 14° to 16°C. This is the most abundant. On spots where the crevices resulting from the movements of the earth's crust are not deep, hardly any or very little water from the depth is added to the cold karstic water. This is how the lukewarm springs of various temperatures are formed. The rock fissures under the earth are interconnected, while in other regions they are independent of each other. This explains why waters of different temperatures come to the surface in close proximity. Thus on a small area, like that of the Lukács and Császár Baths, there are a number of adjacent springs with water temperatures varying between 21° and 64°C.

Not only the temperature of the waters gushing forth from the earth depends on geological factors, but their chemical composition as well. This is because the substances dissolved by the water come from strata of earth in which the water is stored and moves around. The calcium and magnesium usually found in the Budapest springs originate in the layers of limestone, while the radium salt, radium emanation and sulphur content shows that part of the water comes from a very great depth.

The formation of wells containing Epsom salt was also due to geological factors. In the southern part of Buda, where sloping valleys and basins were formed by crustal movements, the ground water fed by precipitation moves very slowly and runs into obstacles at certain places. In the meantime it decomposes the pyrite contained in the clay, leading to the formation of diluted sulphuric acid. This attacks the dolomitic rubble, sand and various feldspars, leading to the formation of what is called bitter water. The Hunyadi János, Ferenc József and Apenta bitter waters are well known. They were widely exported before the Second World War.

The Epsom salt springs are of little interest to the average tourist, their water is sold in bottles for medicinal use. The situation is different regarding the thermal springs which form the basis of large bathing establishments.

The temperature of the springs covers quite a large scale. The hottest water of artesian wells comes from well No. 2 of the Széchenyi Baths (76°C), while the hottest of the natural springs is the St. Stephen spring of the Császár Baths (50°C). These springs are so hot that their water can be used for bathing only when cooled. The great majority of the thermal baths, however, are of such a temperature that they can be used for bathing without any cooling. The difference in temperature of the various springs makes it possible to use the kind of water most suitable for the bather's system.

Sulphur, which plays a prominent role in the human body, is an essential constituent of the Budapest thermal waters. Biochemical studies of recent years have shown the indispensable part played by sulphur in the functioning of the joints. Part of the sulphur is present in the form of carbonyl sulphide which releases hydrogen sulphide through relatively slow decomposition. As a result of this slow process the sulphur content does not evaporate as fast as in case of waters containing only hydrogen sulphide.

Radioactivity is another important characteristic of our thermal waters. The considerable amount of radium emanation, present in gaseous form, is absorbed not only through the skin, but also by breathing it in with the air. The effect of radioactive matters is based on the radiation they emit which has a definite influence on the functioning of the cells. However, radiotherapy, like many other methods of medicinal treatment, is harmful if given in large amounts. The content of radioactive substances of the Budapest medicinal waters is too minute to cause radiation troubles, but quite sufficient to have a stimulating effect on the life processes, to enhance the activities of the endocrine glands and help heal inflammations and alleviate pains.

The ways and means of utilising thermal waters are determined by their chemical composition. Highly specialised physicians relying on several decades of experiences are at work in the Budapest sanatoriums.

The medical use of the Budapest thermal waters has a very wide scope. They are primarily applied in the treatment of rheumatic conditions, of diseases of the organs of locomotion. Arthritis, locomotory ailments resulting therefrom, diseases due to the wearing out and decay of the articular cartileges, the inflammatory and degenerative diseases of the spine react, as a rule, favourably to thermal bath therapy. Treatment by stretching and pulling the spine is utilised the world over in certain stages of sciatica and the neuralgia of the brachial nerves. This stretching is far less strenuous and more effective in a hot bath than when applied dry. The Budapest medicinal baths have up-to-date facilities for traction bathing in basins. Locomotory difficulties and rigidity of the joints are overcome far more quickly with thermal baths, combined with massage and gymnastics. Thermal baths are also prescribed for the treatment of conditions following chronic inflammation, e.g. in a large number of gynaecological diseases.

Mud cure is an important supplement of thermal baths. In most of Budapest's baths the patients are packed in warm medicinal mud. The Lukács Baths have also a warm outdoor mud lake. Mud cure is applied to achieve a highly stimulative reaction. For this reason it must be used with caution lest it result in renewed inflammation and excessive blood circulation.

Massage, gymnastic and electric treatment are integral parts of the thermal bath cures. The majority of the Budapest baths has the most up-to-date facilities for these supplementary treatments.

The Budapest thermal waters are also used for drinking cures, partly as a complement of baths for rheumatic conditions. They are also quite effective in the treatment of some of the diseases of the digestive system and for the prevention of kidney and bladder stones. Drinking cures should be undertaken on medical advice only, as excessive fluid intake may be detrimental for some.

Thanks to the large amount of thermal water available, the Budapest medicinal springs supply water also for open-air baths and swimming pools. Most of Budapest's outdoor baths contain, in addition to warm water basins, swimming pools with cold water. These outdoor and indoor swimming pools, maintaining an even temperature all year round, have produced many famous swimming champions, but, what is still more important, they provide healthy sporting facilities for tens of thousands of people, young and old. Some of the bathing establishments are very impressive sights and are much frequented.

The open-air baths and swimming pools are supplied with thermal water in the Gellért, Rudas, Lukács, Császár and Széchenyi Baths, on Margaret Island, in the area of the Béke Forrás (Peace Springs) at Dagály utca, the Árpád Springs at Csillaghegy, and at Pünkösdfürdő.

CITY OF SPORTS

Budapest is not only the administrative centre of Hungary, but also the main stronghold of a thriving sports movement. Most of the different branches of sport developed first in the capital, resulting in splendid achievements and many world records during encounters between great athletes assembled from various countries in the excellent stadiums of Budapest.

There is hardly a branch of sport in Hungary which did not get its start in Budapest. Quite often sports followed the examples set in foreign lands but sometimes they were directly initiated by foreigners who lived in the capital. Thus the Englishman Arthur Yolland was a trailblazer of soccer (he later became professor of the English language and literature at the University of Budapest), while table tennis found an enthusiastic supporter in Edward Shires, a salesman, who later became the general representative of a British typewriter concern in Budapest. Jean Dupuis of France opened a wrestling school in Budapest early in the 19th century and turned wrestling into a sport. Foreign fencing masters, such as the German Friedrich, the Frenchmen Clair and Chappon, the Italians Bissini and Santelli, and hosts of others left their mark in the introduction and development of sports in Hungary.

Some of the sports were introduced by Hungarian youths after their return home from abroad. Thus athletics and boxing were established by Miksa Esterházy (1875), rowing and horse-racing by István Széchenyi (1820). Károly Löwenrosen, a worker who had spent many years in British factories, became a promoter of soccer (1895). Basketball was introduced by Géza Kuncze, a teacher, skiing by ornithologist István Chernel, who had been to Norway (1891), bowling by Professor Sámuel Gyarmathy (1797), etc.

The history of the sport organisations also bears out

Budapest's leading role. All Hungarian sports federations were established in Budapest by the clubs concerned—with two exceptions: the Cycling Federation was formed in Szombathely, and the chess players organised in Győr. Of all sports only yachting has its centre outside of Budapest, at the major resorts of Balatonfüred and Siófok, at Lake Balaton. It must be stated, however, that even in yachting the way was paved by the Budapest Rowing and Sailing Club, established in 1862.

The sport grounds and stadiums of Budapest are up to European standards. The Millenáris (Millenary) grounds, the first of the modern sports grounds, was opened in 1896. It has been remodelled several times and is used now for cycle races and ice hockey. The growing interest in soccer called for the establishment of large-size stadiums. The FTC (Ferencvárosi Torna Club) stadium in Üllői út, with a capacity of 35,000, was opened in 1910, followed one year later by the MTK (Magyar Testgyakorlók Köre) stadium of similar size in Hungária körút. In 1925 the UTE (Újpesti Torna Egyesület) stadium of a greater capacity was opened. The other large stadiums, that of the Vasas (Iron Workers) Sport Club in Béke út, the Kispest stadium of the Honvéd Sport Club and the Sport utca stadium of the transport enterprises were all opened primarily with an eye to soccer. There are other stadiums which cater to different sports with mass participation. They include the group of sport grounds in the People's Park (Népliget)—among them the stadium of the Építők (Building Workers) Sport Club, the sport grounds at Csepel, the Tüzér utca establishment of the Honvéd and the Szőnyi utca sport grounds of the railway workers. The Tüzér utca grounds include a pool for swimming competitions, while the "sport paradise" of the railwaymen contains five warm-water pools, fed by the thermal springs of the City Park (Városliget) with a new indoor pool for swimming competitions.

The Nemzeti Sportuszoda (National Sport Swimming Pool) on Margaret Island is the most prominent of the numerous indoor and outdoor pools of the capital. The hall containing the indoor pool was built in 1930, with a large outdoor pool and another for springboard diving added in 1937 and a special pool for water-polo in 1956.

The first swimming competition was held in the Lukács Baths in 1890. The pool of the Rudas Baths with a 20-metre basin was built in 1894 and became the centre for swimming at the time. The much larger pool of the Császár Baths was completed in 1903. This was in 1926 the scene of the first European Swimming Championships.

The Nemzeti Torna Csarnok (National Gymnastics Hall) for indoor sports was opened in 1870, the large Nemzeti Sportcsarnok (National Sports Hall) in 1942.

Among all the sports establishments the Népstadion (People's Stadium) is, of course, the pride of Budapest sport enthusiasts. Its construction was started on March 15, 1948, and the opening took place on August 20, 1953. Its seating capacity is close to 100,000 with 25,000 more seats to be constructed.

Following the country's liberation in 1945, Budapest's sport activities were based on the enterprises, factories, offices, secondary schools and universities. The sport organisations of long standing merged with the existing or newly established sport clubs of enterprises, factories and offices. This was how the great sport organisations of Budapest came into existence such as the Honvéd (Army), Dózsa (Ministry of Home Affairs), Vasas (Iron Workers' Union), Vasutas (Railwaymen's), Építők (Building Trades), Előre (Transport Workers' Union), the reorganised FTC— Ferencváros (sponsored by the Food Workers' Union), the MTK (Textile and Leather Workers' Union), etc.

These organisations and sport affairs in general are directed in Hungary by the Magyar Testnevelési és Sport Tanács = MTS (Hungarian Council of Physical Education and Sport), almost a kind of sport's parliament. The MTS has its local bodies in charge of the various areas. Thus the Budapest TST is the central body for the capital, with locals in each district.

Sports activities in Hungary are under constant medical supervision. This is carried out, together with scientific research in sport medicine, by the OTSI = Országos Testnevelési és Sportegészségügyi Intézet (National Health Institute of Physical Education and Sport), whose Budapest branch (BTSI) is located at Kossuth Lajos tér. The treatment of accidents and sickness due to sport is administered by the Sportkórház (Sport Hospital) at 46 Alkotás utca. This is also the headquarters of the OTSI. Scientific development is ensured by the Testnevelési Tudományos Tanács (Scientific Council of Physical Education) and the Testnevelési Tudományos Kutató Intézet (Scientific Research Institute of Physical Education).

Several exhibitions, arranged according to branches of

sport and organisations, laid the groundwork for the Hungarian Sport Museum. At present this museum is located in the building of the Artificial Skating Rink in the City Park. The College of Physical Education is also in Budapest. Offering four-year courses, it trains 80 to 100 sports teachers annually. Training courses are provided for coaches as well as sports managers by the teaching staff of the College. The Budapest College of Physical Education has a large enrolment of foreign students who are expected to play a leading role in the sports life of their countries. The college's sport library is the best of its kind in Hungary.

To give a statistical summary of the sport facilities in Budapest: There are 10 stadiums, 158 sports grounds (all containing football fields, 80 of which are covered with lawn), 50 football fields, 80 grounds for track and field events, 100 courts for basketball, 250 for volleyball, 170 for handball, 340 outdoor tennis courts, 70 bowling alleys, 350 halls for gymnastics and fencing, 15 swimming pools, 70 boat-houses, 3 ski-jumps (the largest one is covered with plastic and can be used all the year round), and 3 indoor tennis grounds (with several courts). All told, apart from many smaller sport fields and playgrounds, there are nearly 1,600 sport establishments under the jurisdiction and supervision of the BTST.

There are roughly 1,000 sport clubs in Budapest. The registered and medically supervised sportsmen who train systematically include over 21,000 football players, 11,000 hikers, 8,500 table-tennis players, as many track-and-field athletes, almost 8,000 chess players, 7,000 each of handball players and anglers, 5,000 gymnasts and as many basketball players, 4,000 swimmers, 3,900 tennis players and 3,500 rowers who participate in competitive sports.

Budapest is also the centre of Hungarian sport publications. The daily Népsport (People's Sport) and the weekly Képes Sport (Sports Illustrated) are published here, as well as the monthly Sport és Tudomány (Sport and Science) furthering scientific research and popularising its results, and the periodicals Labdarúgás (Football), Magyar Sakkélet (Hungarian Chess) and various other sport reviews put out by the different sport federations.

PUBLIC HEALTH AND WELFARE

Budapest has always been the health centre of Hungary, the seat of the national public health and welfare organisations, the headquarters of social insurance and of the leading bodies of the health network covering the entire country.

Outstanding progress has been made in this field since the Second World War. An extensive and comprehensive system of social insurance has been established during the past 15 years. A network of panel doctors and district health centres cover the entire city. Hospitals and health institutions have been modernised and new hospitals built. A system of factory medical care is being developed in the industrial enterprises.

There are about 6,500 physicians in Budapest, 718 of them functioning as panel doctors. Medically the capital is one of the best provided big cities in the world, with about 36 physicians for each 10,000 inhabitants.

The city is divided into 162 health districts, each with a health centre where panel doctors provide care for patients all day. There are 26 large polyclinics with diagnosis and treatment by specialists (in addition to those of the large factories and the medical university), 24 T.B. dispensaries, 9 centres for nervous disorders, 26 clinics for venereal and skin diseases, 13 oncological clinics and 76 centres for maternity and infant care. Roughly 20,000 thorough medical check-ups are carried out annually in the kindergartens, 180,000 in primary schools and 40,000 in secondary and technical schools.

The hospitals and health institutions of Budapest have undergone great changes since liberation, and their technical equipment is up-to-date. The development in the health service for the working people, however, is far more significant. Practically the whole population of Budapest receives medical care and medicines through the social insurance scheme. There is an extensive and modern network of hospitals with close to 27,000 beds.

Progress since the war has affected, above and beyond the health and medical services, the other social and welfare institutions as well.

Children receive special attention, beginning with pre-natal care, up to the end of their school studies. Expectant mothers are under the constant supervision of the specialised visiting nurses attached to the district councils. Besides the 76 centres for the care of mothers and infants, there are 26 mother's milk banks and 11 nursing homes for infants. Working mothers can take their children to one of the 300 crèches and 500 kindergartens. Modern, sanitary crèches and kindergartens are attached to all large enterprises, offices and factories. Nurses and kindergarten teachers are given thorough training. Each kindergarten teacher cares for 16 children, on an average.

Budapest has 28 homes for the aged, run by the City Council, with room for 4,455 people. Similar homes are maintained in Budapest also by the government. There are 300 people in the institutions for the blind and 120 in the homes for war invalids. Many day-care centres are attached to the primary schools. They number over 300, and care for some 40,000 school children.

A tourist guide cannot give a comprehensive picture of the health and welfare conditions of a big city. The few data given here are meant only to convey an idea of the great achievements of the past few years.

CATERING TRADE

One can read in old chronicles about professional wine-coopers who lived in Óbuda and Pestújhely in the 13th century. Their example was followed by the establishment of taverns in Pest and Buda. Later on the famous Buda inns served, in addition to their own wines, home-made meals. The guild system greatly contributed to the development of catering, since these inns were the favourite meeting places of the guildsmen.

The advance of commerce led to the appearance of hostelries and hotels. Pest had seven hotels in 1690 with a total of 27 rooms for guests. The catering trade developed primarily at the highway junctions.

The growth of the national economy and the introduction of up-to-date means of communication (steamboat and railway travel) gave the catering trade a big boost. The famous Fehér Hajó (White Boat) hotel in Budapest was followed by the construction of many inns and hotels, such as the Hét Választó Fejedelem (The Seven Electors) which, until the building of the Vigadó (Concert Hall), was the most exclusive dancing place in Pest. Other establishments were the Fehér Farkas (White Wolf), the Bádog Kalap (Tin Hat), the Arany Borz (Golden Badger), the Arany Sas (Golden Eagle), the Magyar Király (Hungarian King), the Vadászkürt (Hunting Horn), the Tigris (Tiger), the Nádor (Palatine), the Angol Királynő (English Queen), the István Főherceg (Archduke Stephen) and the Európa (Europe), etc.

During the first quarter of the 19th century, when the great European wars came to an end and relatively peaceful conditions prevailed, a general desire arose to visit those areas which up to then had appeared inaccessible. A great upswing in tourist trade followed, which demanded hotels with home-like comforts and varied dining facilities of a high standard. This requirement led to a swift growth in the Hungarian catering trade, especially the system of hotels and restaurants established in Pest-Buda, the heart of Hungary.

As a result of increased tourism there was a rapid rise in the number of various catering establishments, such as inns, coffee shops, wine- and beer-houses, followed by many new cafés, restaurants and night clubs. The old cafés differed considerably from those we know at present. They had an intimate, home-like atmosphere. Many establishments even stored the pipes of their patrons. There were some 500 of them about the middle of the 19th century, each having its own permanent clientele attracted by the particular atmosphere of the place.

The cafés played an important role in the development of literary life in Hungary. The present-day Hungária (formerly New York) has been the meeting place of Hungarian writers and artists. The Paradicsom (Paradise) located on the ground floor of the Fehér Hajó Hotel, which was situated at the present Kristóf tér, was also considered a literary café. Then there was the Kávéforrás (Coffee Spring), quite popular among the writers of later generations, too. Especially famous and significant among the last century's literary cafés was the Renaissance which from 1843 on was named Pilvax Café after its lessee. This was where the greatest Hungarian poet, Sándor Petőfi, spoke in the spring of 1848 to the representatives of the revolutionary Hungarian youth, this was where their "12 points" embodying the revolutionary demands were drafted.

The upswing in the confectionery trade began also in the 19th century. Many old chronicles dealt with the sugar-makers, confectioners and pretzel bakers of the period. János Kertsok was a famous pastry baker whose confectionery shop was located on the present Kristóf tér. The famous master Neugebohren in the one-time Sebestyén utca had a combination coffee house and pastry shop. The renowned Russwurm opened his confectionery shop in the residential section of the Castle Hill area, while Kugler kept his fancy shop on Színház tér (Theatre Square), now Vörösmarty tér. This was taken over later and developed into a world-famous institution by Gerbeaud, a Swiss confectioner.

The music halls and night clubs of Budapest also have a quaint and long history. There is little information available on their early antecedents, but we have far richer sources concerning night life in Pest from the sixties of the last century onwards. The Új Világ (New World) night club operated at the site of the present-day Comedy Theatre. The Kormos-redoute (Smoky Redoubt) and the Blaue Katze (Blue Cat) in Király utca were also famous night spots. The Berger cellar at the corner of Király utca and Laudon utca was also very popular, together with the other night clubs, the Beleznay Garden, at the corner of present-day Rákóczi út and Puskin utca, the Nepauer Hall in Lövőház utca, the Három Nyúl (Three Rabbits), the Nagy Pipa (Large Pipe) and the Két Török (Two Turks), the amusement places of the ordinary people. The Széna-piac (Haymarket) music hall was on the present-day Calvin tér, and the Fehér Ló (White Horse) was built at the Hatvan Gate.

The most popular night clubs at the turn of the century were the Folies Caprices in Gerlóczy utca, the Oroszy Caprice in the building of the present Uránia Cinema, and most famous of all, the Somossy Orfeum, occupying the premises of the present Operetta Theatre. The most popular music halls between the two world wars were the Arizona and Moulin Rouge, facing each other on either side of Nagymező utca.

The Budapest catering trade suffered severely from the Second World War. The Ritz-Dunapalota, the Hungária, and the Carlton, this row of world-famous luxury hotels along the Danube, was destroyed by bombs and so were many cafés, restaurants, Buda inns and pastry shops. Most of the catering establishments which had remained standing had to be used temporarily for other, more urgent purposes.

Thanks to persistent, devoted work, sacrifice and resourcefulness, the catering industry of Budapest succeeded in rebuilding itself and winning back its international reputation. The reorganisation of the catering trade had a double objective. Hotels, restaurants and cafés had to be restored, modernised and expanded for the sake of tourism. Simultaneously a new network of catering places had to be established to meet the constantly growing demands of the general public. There are 2,700 catering establishments in Budapest, including 368 restaurants and dining places, and 391 pastry shops and espressos.

There has been considerable progress recently in the building of hotels. The reconstruction of the Gellért Hotel, the most representative and most beautiful in Budapest, was completed in 1960. The picturesque environment, the famous thermal baths and the high standard of catering at the Gellért makes it very popular among foreign visitors. The reconstruction of the Grand Hotel Royal in the heart of Budapest, in Lenin körút, has also been completed; with its 340 rooms and various catering establishments it enjoys a very high reputation.

The Szabadság (Liberty) Hotel (formerly Imperial), rebuilt and enlarged to 460 rooms, is expected to reopen in 1965. The Debrecen Restaurant, with its traditionally outstanding cuisine, next to the Szabadság Hotel, will be an added attraction for visitors in Budapest.

Only one hotel remained of the once famous row facing the Danube, the Duna (Danube, formerly Bristol), completely rebuilt and modernised with an espresso and pastry shop. The Duna-kert (Danube Garden) summer restaurant, espresso and dancing place, adjoining the southern part of the hotel, was opened after liberation. The reconstruction of the row of Danube hotels is planned and is to be completed by 1970.

The well-known hotels in down-town Budapest, the Astoria, the Palace and the Béke (Peace, formerly Britannia), were considered second rate between the two wars, but their standards have greatly risen owing to reconstruction and modernisation. The Astoria, with its excellent cuisine, grill-room, café and buffet for gourmets, is one of Budapest's most popular amusement places. The new restaurant of the Palace Hotel in Rákóczi út is one of the fanciest in Budapest, while the Béke Hotel in Lenin körút, with its huge dining room, domed hall and the Székely wine cellar, beer garden and pastry shop, is way above the pre-war standards. The Metropol Hotel with its new-type dining room in the classic traditions of Hungarian catering, has been rebuilt and enlarged. The Park Hotel has also been restored and modernised.

The rebuilt Grand Hotel on Margaret Island continues to maintain its leading role. Its guest rooms and suites, dining hall and other facilities, especially its large, shaded garden restaurant, still are an attraction for foreign visitors and the Budapest public alike. The Vörös Csillag (Red Star) Hotel on Liberty Hill was also modernised and is an excellent resort-restaurant all the year round.

Speaking of restaurants, the Gundel in the City Park, by the Zoo, has maintained its traditional reputation. Its cuisine, representing the best in Hungarian cooking, com-

73

bined with excellent service, luxurious dining halls and a garden restaurant accommodating 2,000 guests, is a great attraction for tourists. There are many other famous dining places like the Mátyás Pince (Matthias Cellar), noted for its fish dishes and good music, the Apostolok (Apostles) Restaurant, patronised between meals by beer drinkers, and the Kis Royal (Little Royal), popular with foreigners for its cuisine, wines and enchanting gipsy music.

Special mention should be made of the Berlin Restaurant with its attractive dining rooms serving Hungarian and German specialities, and also the modern Európa Restaurant, famed for its meals and drinks. The Fortuna Restaurant in the romantic Castle District attracts visitors with its fine gipsy music, while the bar adjoining it offers entertainment for people who prefer modern dance music.

Those who like to dine in hilly, wooded surroundings may choose among the Budagyöngye (Pearl of Buda), Erdei-lak (Forest Cottage), Fenyőgyöngye (Pearl of the Pines), and Veronika, all with shaded outdoor dining facilities. Mention should also be made of the Százéves (Hundred-Year-Old) Restaurant, the Moszkva and the Szófia dining rooms, the latter offering both Hungarian and Bulgarian specialities.

The Ezerjó (Thousand Boons) Restaurant, with its indoor and outdoor dining rooms in the heart of the City Park, is known for its excellent gipsy music. The Kék Duna (Blue Danube), a floating restaurant on the Danube, the rebuilt Emke Café, the Tengerszem (Tarn) Restaurant in the Kőbánya district, and the Balázs Restaurant in the Hűvösvölgy area, are also very popular. The Citadella Wine House on Gellért Hill offers a splendid panorama to its guests, who can also barbecue their bacon right on the spot if they like. The Panorama Restaurant and Espresso and the Búsuló Juhász (Sad Shepherd) Restaurant also have picturesque locations.

The tourist has a wide choice of dining places, hundreds of which are listed in the classified telephone directory. The names like Márványmenyasszony (Marble Bride), Három Diófa (Three Walnut Trees), Kakukk (Cuckoo), Két Kupa (Two Cups), Arany Fácán (Golden Pheasant), Diófa (Walnut Tree), Kulacs (Flask), Vén Betyár (Old Outlaw), Bagolyvár (Owl Fort), Víg Hajós (Merry Sailor), Gödör (The Pit), etc. have a traditional ring. Espressos have taken on names of flowers and one can sip the popular Hungarian strong coffee in the Narcissus, Lilac, Violet, Tulip,

Hyacinth, Forget-me-not, Wild Rose, and other shops bearing similar names.

There are many famous old pastry shops in Budapest, like the Gerbeaud (now Vörösmarty) on Vörösmarty tér, and the Russwurm on Castle Hill, but the new confectionery shops and espressos are successful competitors. Snack bars of a new type called the Mackó (Teddy Bear) have appeared in Budapest, specialising in cold buffet, grilled foods, cold fruit and milk drinks and delicious pastries.

When dealing with our catering trade mention should be made of the world-wide reputation of Hungarian cuisine, both past and present.

The earliest references go back to the period of King Matthias whose biographers describe the fine and varied meals served at his table. His wife, Beatrix, introduced Italian elements into cooking which were also reflected in the aristocratic households. From the middle of the 17th century onwards the influence of French cooking grew ever more noticeable, and under Maria Theresa and Joseph II, French cuisine predominated in the imperial household, consequently in that of the Austrian and Hungarian aristocracy too. Cookery books published in the German and French languages testify to this. Present-day Hungarian cooking, while maintaining its original features, reflects the influence of the best of foreign cuisine.

Hungarian cooking owes its reputation to the special methods of preparing the meals. These are quite different from those used in other countries. Most of our dishes are thickened and flavoured with a roux made of hot lard and highly glutenous domestic flour. The flour is browned in the hot lard, with spices added, giving a special flavour to Hungarian dishes. The use of pork fat accounts for the more extensive use of spices, especially of paprika.

The Budapest catering trade employs many chefs and pastry bakers whose international experience adds a special touch to Hungarian cooking. Our foremost chefs participate in international exhibitions and fairs and achieve outstanding results. The Brussels Universal Exposition in 1958 was the scene of a paramount success for Hungarian cuisine. Gourmets of all nations visited the Hungarian restaurant there, which was awarded the Grand Prix, and "Bravo, Hungary!" was a recurrent entry in the visitor's book, bearing many illustrious signatures. Some guests from overseas took home Hungarian paprika chicken and cheese strudel in vacuum containers by airplane.

Several Budapest restaurants are famous for their special dishes. Suffice to mention the fish specialities of the Sípos Halászkert (Fishermen's Inn) and the Mátyás Pince or the pork en brochette and the mixed grill of the Kis Royal Restaurant, the shellfish cream soup and paprika chicken at Gundel's or the freshly prepared pork with sausages and cabbage of the Palace Restaurant. The Aranyszarvas (Golden Stag) Inn has a century-old reputation in preparing game for the table.

The main attraction of Hungarian cuisine is its variety, with many original dishes to pick from. Brillat Savarin once said that "the discovery of a new dish contributes more to the betterment of the human race than the discovery of a new star by astronomy". This statement, of course, reflects a good deal of professional chauvinism, but the truth is that this is one of the most savoury and exciting ways to "discovery".

Last but not least, mention should be made of Hungarian wines. There is no need for historical retrospection, since it is known that the reputation of Hungarian wine grew with each century. Let us mention but a few instances, known to our generation. At the Paris World Exposition in 1900, Tokay wines won the prize away from the French Sauternes: an "aszú" (raisin wine) of Sárospatak, 1889 vintage, was judged the best white wine. The Grand Prix of the Brussels Universal Exposition in 1958 was also won by Tokay sweet wine. And what about the other famous vintages of Badacsony, Eger, Szekszárd, Pécs, Somló, Mór, etc.?

Serving wine calls for artistry. A good waiter always brings the proper wine, for he knows that the enjoyment of a good meal can be improved with the selection of the right kind of wine, and that a poorly selected drink spoils the effect. He knows that white fish calls for a light, dry white wine and not red wine. Entrées go with light, white, full-bodied table wine, such as the Balatonmelléki rizling or the Egri leányka, while roast veal or pork should be accompanied by stronger, dry, full-bodied wine, such as the Olaszrizling of Csopak. Paprika stews and stews in general, are best with light, dry table wine, like the rizling of Bácsalmás, while rare steaks should be enjoyed with heavy red wines, rich in tannin, such as the Egri bikavér (Bull's Blood of Eger) or the Nagyburgundi of Villány. Poultry and roast piglet demand high-quality white wine, like the Olaszrizling of Badacsony, the Szürkebarát (Grey

Friar) or the Dry Szamorodni of Tokaj. Pastry tastes best with Sweet Szamorodni of Tokaj, Zöldszilváni of Badacsony or Muskotály of Akali.

For aperitif and hard drinks, pure apricot and cherry brandies distilled from fermented fruit juices are recommended. Hungarian barmen are quite adapt in making the well-known Martini, Bacardi, and other cocktails while calling the guest's attention to the Hungarian speciality, the Puszta cocktail (made out of three parts of Kecskemét apricot brandy, two parts of Mecseki bitters and three parts of dry Szamorodni wine).

And finally, apricot or sour cherry liqueur, or the well-known Hungarian bitters, the Hubertus, Mecseki or Unicum, go well with the after-meal coffee.

TOURIST TRAFFIC — AMUSEMENTS

As a rule, capitals and big cities attract tourists the world over. Budapest is not only a capital, a big city, but from the point of view of its natural setting it is one of the loveliest cities in the world. It is also of interest to tourists as a traffic junction: whoever travels in Hungary must pass through Budapest, since every region of the country can be reached directly from here.

Between the two world wars the city administration began to deal with the question of tourist trade with increasing interest. Exact figures cannot be given, however, because comprehensive statistics on the tourist traffic of the time are not available.

The Central Statistical Office has been giving data systematically on the tourist trade of Hungarian hotels. The following figures illustrate the part played by Budapest.

1963	Hungary	Budapest	In percentage
Number of foreign tourists	319,264	194,125	61%
Number of days spent by foreign tourists	1,021,600	663,900	65%

Thus somewhat less than two-thirds of Hungary's tourist trade, both from the point of view of visitors and the number of days they spent here, was concentrated in Budapest. Budapest offers numerous opportunities for entertainment. People who enjoy dancing can do so in the larger hotels and restaurants both in the afternoons and evenings. Five-o'clock teas with dancing are quite popular in many confectionery shops. Of a number of night clubs we shall mention only three: the Budapest Dance Palace

(17 Nagymező utca), Pipacs (5 Aranykéz utca) and Jereván (5 Semmelweis utca).

The Grand Circus in the City Park, featuring international shows, is a favourite amusement place for tourists. The Gaiety Park is only a stone's throw away. Its merry-go-round, Ferris wheel, and a galaxy of other amusing games and competitions are a source of enjoyment for both young and old.

These are but a few tips for fun-loving visitors from abroad.

PART II

SIGHTSEEING IN BUDAPEST

REMEMBER:

domb	hill
Duna	Danube
fasor	alley
fürdő	baths
hegy	hill
híd	bridge
körút	boulevard
körtér	circus
liget	park
pályaudvar	railway terminal
rakpart	embankment
sétány	promenade
sziget	island
színház	theatre
tér, tere	square
út, útja	avenue
utca	street
város	town

NOTE—In Hungarian usage the family name precedes the Christian name. In the case of streets named after persons this practice has been retained: Kossuth Lajos utca.

ORIENTATION IN BUDAPEST

Budapest is an extensive city. It is divided in 22 districts and spreads over an area of some 52,500 hectares. Its inhabitants, numbering about two million, make up nearly one-fifth of the country's population. The geographical position of the town enables the visitor to find his way about with comparative ease. The Danube divides the town into two parts. Looking downstream, on the right bank we see Buda, a hilly area, and on the left is the plain of Pest.

If we want to find our way about Budapest we should stop at some central point of the town, let us say, at the Suspension Bridge (Lánchíd). From here we can soon locate the prominent landmarks, which will always help us find our way in Buda. To the south, Gellért Hill (Gellérthegy) overlooks the town. This landmark is easy to recognise with its Liberation Monument and the Citadel on top. In front of us lies Castle Hill (Vár-hegy) with the former royal castle, now under reconstruction, the Matthias Church (Mátyás-templom) with its Gothic spire and the white walls of the Fishermen's Bastion (Halászbástya). To the north we find the Hill of Roses (Rózsadomb) which reaches down to the Margaret Bridge (Margit-híd). Farther to the north we see the Hill of Three Boundaries (Hármashatár-hegy) and next to it Linden Hill (Hárs-hegy) as well as János Hill (János-hegy) topped by a lookout tower. János Hill extends to Liberty Hill (Szabadság-hegy).

On the left bank in Pest, owing to the flat land, the structure of the streets is much simpler than on the Buda side. Its basic scheme consists of three semicircular boulevards running from Danube to Danube and crossed by a number of wide avenues. The first important line is the Kiskörút (Inner or Little Boulevard), which partly follows the line of the ancient city walls and consists of Tolbuhin körút, Múzeum körút, Tanács körút and Bajcsy Zsilinszky út.

The Nagykörút (Great Boulevard) similarly forms a semi-circle. It begins at Boráros tér and ends at the Pest abutment of Margaret Bridge (Margit-híd).

The streets of the outer boulevards running parallel with the former are Könyves Kálmán körút, Hungária körút and Róbert Károly körút. The more important thoroughfares crossing these boulevards are Üllői út, Baross utca, Rákóczi út and Népköztársaság útja.

Other important landmarks to help in orientation are the Budapest bridges. From north to south they are: the Újpest Railway Bridge, Árpád Bridge, Margaret Bridge, Suspension Bridge, Elizabeth Bridge, Liberty Bridge, Petőfi Bridge and the Southern Railway Bridge.

The main traffic junctions also help the foreigner to find his way about. Some of these are the crossing of Rákóczi út and the Great Boulevard, the intersections of Kossuth Lajos utca, Rákóczi út and the Inner Boulevard, and the Great Boulevard at Népköztársaság útja. Among the important squares we might mention Felszabadulás tér, Szabadság tér, Vörösmarty tér, Roosevelt tér, Engels tér, Kossuth Lajos tér, Baross tér, Calvin tér, the Körönd and Marx tér in Pest, and Moszkva tér and Móricz Zsigmond körtér in Buda.

Large buildings are often helpful in orientation. Some of these are the Parliament Building, the National Theatre, the Opera House, the Erkel Theatre, the People's Stadium, the Hungarian Academy of Sciences, the Hungarian National Bank, the Hungarian National Museum, the Museum of Fine Arts, the Millenary Monument, the Basilica and the Gellért Baths.

THE MAIN THOROUGHFARES
OF THE PEST SIDE

1. THE INNER BOULEVARD

The visitor who wants to get a clear picture of Budapest should begin by taking a walk along the Kiskörút (Inner Boulevard) which surrounds the Inner City in a four-kilometre flat arc. This walk will show him the development of the city in a "longitudinal" section. The section from Liberty Bridge (Szabadság-híd) to Deák Ferenc tér, running first towards the east and then north and north-west, follows the line of the medieval city walls. This part of the city was built towards the end of the 18th and at the beginning of the 19th centuries, at a time when Pest burst its ancient stone wall boundaries in a surge of rapid expansion. A great number of buildings were erected in the neoclassic style. At many places the remains of the old city walls can still be seen in the courtyards of some of the houses or embedded in their walls.

At Deák Ferenc tér we reach the end of the old Inner City (Belváros). Bajcsy Zsilinszky út which starts here is, strictly speaking, not a part of the semicircle around the Inner City, still it is regarded as a section of the Inner Boulevard. In fact, it links the Inner Boulevard with the Great Boulevard. The quarter of the town beginning here originated in the second half of the 19th century. The apartment houses and business buildings are designed in an eclectic style, the St. Stephen Basilica is built in the neo-Renaissance style. At bustling Marx tér the Inner Boulevard joins the Nagykörút (Great Boulevard), which took shape at the beginning of the 20th century. Running in western direction, it takes us back to the Danube at the head of Margaret Bridge.

Dimitrov tér, which offers a breathtaking sight of the rocks on Gellért Hill on the other side of the Danube, is an important traffic junction. In the northern part of this square, which forms a park, stands a **bust of Georgi Dimitrov,** the hero of the Bulgarian and European labour movement (made by J. *Kratchmarov*, 1954). This bust was a present of the Bulgarian People's Republic to Hungary. In the south the square is bordered by the building of the **Karl Marx University of Economic Sciences** (No. 7-8), which was erected according to the designs of the Hungarian architect Miklós *Ybl* between 1870 and 1874. Originally this building was the Central Customs Office, and in 1950-51 it was converted into a University. The ten allegoric statues decorating the façade are the work of August *Sommer*.

Tolbuhin körút has been named after Marshal *Tolbukhin*, commander of Soviet army units which played a decisive role in the liberation of Budapest. In this comparatively short section of the Inner Boulevard stand quite a number of buildings built in the neoclassic style, among them the **Gabler House** (No. 2) which was the Nádor Hotel in the 19th century. The partition wall in the back of the two-storied house at **No. 16** still preserves part of the old city walls. Tolbuhin körút is a lively business street, on the other side (No. 1-3) is the largest **Market Hall** of the capital.

Tolbuhin körút leads into a polygonal square: Calvin tér (often spelt as Kálvin according to the Hungarian way of writing John Calvin's name), which is a traffic junction connecting the Inner City with the southeastern districts of the town. Among the pedestrians we notice many students. Calvin tér lies right in the heart of the university quarter.

The most important sight in Calvin tér is the **Calvinist church.** The building with its neoclassic façade and spire in the middle was erected between 1818 and 1830 and designed by József *Hofrichter* and József *Hild*. The portico occupies the centre of the front and is supported by four Corinthian columns, over which is a semicircular window and parapet. In the interior of the church which constitutes a single hall, is the sepulchre of Countess M. Zichy (the work of the Paris sculptor Raymond *Gaiard*). The organ dates back to the year 1829 and was made in the Vienna workshop of Jakob *Deutschmann*. Among the treasures kept there, let us mention a goblet with the coat of arms of Zsigmond Rákóczi, Prince of Transylvania, from the year 1600, an Augsburg chalice from 1611, an Augsburg paten from the middle of the 17th century and a paten made by the Pest goldsmith Lipót *Fischer* in 1796. A baptismal font and a can, by József *Szentpétery* (1829), belong to the masterpieces of Hungarian goldsmith's work.

The house at **9 Calvin tér** is an interesting building. Two stone lions on the façade remind us that from the end of the 18th century up to 1881 the hostelry "Two Lions" was located here, just outside the city walls of Pest. Just when the house was built is unknown, at any rate in 1775 it already existed. In the years 1816 to 1818 it was reconstructed by Mátyás *Zitterbarth*, the elder. At the corner of Calvin tér and Kecskeméti utca, on the wall over the garden premises of the Városkapu (City Gate) Espresso a design showing the outlines of the **City Gate** with the former city walls is set out in mosaic form. A commemorative tablet on the wall of the garden premises indicates the exact position of the city gate that was demolished long ago.

Leaving Calvin tér behind we turn into Múzeum körút. To the right (No. 14-16) rises the **Hungarian National Museum** (Magyar Nemzeti Múzeum).

This building in neoclassic style was built between 1837 and 1847 to the designs of architect Mihály *Pollack*. A commemorative tablet on the abutment of the wide flight of steps reminds us that in the afternoon of March 15, 1848, the poet Sándor Petőfi recited his stirring poem "Nemzeti Dal" (National Song) to the great crowd gathered in front of this building. Also here, from the plinth of the museum, the manifesto was read, which contained in twelve points demands of the revolutionary youth pressing for the liquidation of Hapsburg absolutism and the introduction of reforms.

Above the flight of steps of the museum is a central projection. The huge pediment is supported by a row of Corinthian columns, and the composition of figures on the tympanum was done by Rafael *Monti* on the basis of the designs of Ludwig *Schaller*, a Munich sculptor. The interior staircase is decorated with **frescoes** by Mór *Than* and Károly *Lotz*. The first parliament elected by the people held its sessions in 1848 in the stateroom on the first floor, next to the domed hall, and later on, in the second half of the 19th century, the Upper House of Parliament met here, too, until the completion of the present Parliament Building by the Danube. The National Assembly of 1945 also held its first session here. In the course of the last hundred years the collections of the Hungarian National Museum have accumulated to such a great extent that only a small portion of the vast material is kept in the central building. Consequently the institutions belonging to the museum as well as some of the collections had to be accommodated in other districts of the town. Part of the material relating to history and natural science can be found in the central building. It houses also the **Széchényi Library,** the largest national library of the country (some 1.5 million volumes).

Several busts and statues stand in the well-kept garden of the museum. In front of the main entrance is a **bronze statue of János Arany** (1817-1882), master of epic, lyric and ballad poetry (designed by Alajos *Stróbl*, 1893). The secondary figures of the monument represent the heroes of his masterpiece, the Toldi Trilogy: Miklós Toldi, the robust young man, and his sweetheart, Piroska. Beside the flight of steps stands an original column from the Roman Forum, and at some distance away a Roman sarcophagus can be seen. To the right stands the **bust of Giuseppe Garibaldi.** Scattered around the sides and behind the building, there are statues raised in honour of many other outstanding personalities of Hungarian cultural history, among them the writer **Ferenc Kazinczy** (1759-1831), the leader of the Hungarian language reform at the turn of the 18th and 19th centuries; the naturalist and ethnographer **Ottó Herman** (1835-1914), the founder of the National Museum **Ferenc Széchényi,** who, in 1802, bestowed on the nation his library consisting of 15,000 volumes and 12,000 manuscripts and maps, as well as his collection of coins, thus laying the foundation for the museum. The **bust of Károly Kisfaludy** (1788-1830), poet and dramatist, and the **statue of Dániel Berzsenyi** (1776-1836), also a poet, enhance the beauty of this garden. Farther along Múzeum körút, at No. 2-8, we come to a group of buildings of the **Faculty of Natural Sciences of the Loránd Eötvös University** (the main building was built in the neo-Renaissance style by Imre *Steindl*, 1880-1883). Through this group of buildings a longish courtyard, nicely laid out with turf, leads to Puskin utca. This passage is popularly called "Storks' Garden", "Stork" being the nickname in Hungarian for fresher at the university.

On the opposite side of Múzeum körút we find the Pest replica of the Paris "bouquinistes", a number of **secondhand bookshops** (in the houses at Nos. 15, 17, 21 and 35). Three fine works of the outstanding Budapest architect Miklós *Ybl* stand in this section of the street. In the partition wall of the romantic style house at **No. 5** part of the ancient city wall is still visible. The architectonic attractions of **No. 7** are seven little balconies supported by winged lions. The sculptural ornamentation and the fountain in the courtyard of **No. 19** are well worth seeing.

The crossing of Múzeum körút, Rákóczi út and Kossuth Lajos utca, where in 1963 an underground passage was opened for pedestrian traffic, is one of the junctions of busy traffic in Budapest. Right here, in the throbbing centre of the modern city, on a little grassy plot stands a Corinthian column which reminds us that in bygone days the first permanent Hungarian stone theatre of Pest stood on this spot. It was the old National Theatre, which was built with the proceeds of a public subscription, and had its festive opening on August 22, 1837. The theatre played a prominent role in strengthening and promoting Hungarian national culture during the period of the germanising Hapsburg regime. The building was torn down in 1913, and since that time the National Theatre has been located in a building on Blaha Lujza tér.

Beyond the crossing at Rákóczi út the next section of the Inner Boulevard making its course towards the north is called Tanács körút (Council Boulevard). This section begins with a modern block of houses and farther on it widens considerably. Several narrow, busy by-streets join the boulevard here, handling the traffic of the Erzsébetváros district: Dohány utca, Wesselényi utca and Dob utca.

In the big apartment house built on the side where Dohány utca joins Tanács körút is the Film Museum, a cinema showing the classics of screen art. Across from it (No. 2-8) stands the Byzantine-Moorish building of the **Synagogue** (built between 1855 and 1859) which was designed by architect Ludwig *Förster*. Alongside it is the **Memorial Temple** commemorating the Jewish victims of the Second World War, and the **Hungarian Jewish Museum** (Magyar Zsidó Múzeum).

A row of business premises now replaces the former back wing of the Budapest City Hall, which was destroyed by bombs during the last war. On the opposite side we see a block of modern apartment houses which is interrupted by Madách Imre tér, a small square bordered by arcades all around it.

In the period between the two world wars, a group of enthusiastic architects endeavoured to break through

89

the narrow streets of the Erzsébetváros district with the construction of a broad avenue which was to have its starting point at this small square, named after the poet and dramatist Imre *Madách* (1823-1864). (Imre Madách is the author of the dramatic poem "The Tragedy of Man".) The construction of Madách Imre út was prevented by the outbreak of the Second World War. 6 Madách Imre tér houses the **Repertory Theatre of the Madách Theatre.** A short distance from here are the headquarters of the **Déryné Színház** (Mrs. Déry Theatre), a modern "itinerant theatre" with about a dozen companies constantly touring provincial towns and small villages. The Déryné Színház was founded in 1949.

Deák Ferenc tér—named after Ferenc Deák (1803-1876), a leading politician of the 19th century, who brought about the Compromise with the Hapsburg dynasty in 1867—once constituted the northern border of old Pest. The ancient city walls came to an end here, turning at this point to meet the Danube again. This was the starting point of the highway leading to Vác, a town north of Budapest. Today the square is an important traffic junction. The **Lutheran church** on this square (No. 1-3) was built by Mihály *Pollack*, after designs by Johann *Kraus*, between 1799 and 1809. The façade was transformed by József *Hild*, and in 1867 Károly *Benkő* made further alterations. The main altar was designed by Mihály *Pollack*, the neoclassic pulpit by Lőrinc *Dunaiszky*. Among the treasures kept in the church we mention an artistic silver jar, the work of master Erasmus *Bergmann* of Besztercebánya (now Banská Bystrica, Czechoslovakia) from the 17th century, and a gilt chalice in the style of Louis XVI made in the workshop of József *Paschberger*, a Pest goldsmith of note at that time (1783). The last section of the Inner Boulevard, Bajcsy Zsilinszky út, starts at Deák Ferenc tér and takes us northward. The street is named after Endre Bajcsy Zsilinszky (1886-1944), the militant anti-fascist political leader who was executed by the Hungarian fascists in 1944. (A memorial tablet was placed on the wall of the house at **No. 12**, in 1945.)

Somewhat to the north, close to the spot where Népköztársaság útja (People's Republic Avenue) joins the Inner Boulevard, rises **St. Stephen's Basilica** facing in the direction of the Danube. With its vast proportions, lofty dome and spires it is one of the most characteristic sights of the capital.

Its construction was begun to the designs and under the guidance of József *Hild*, in 1851. After his death, Miklós *Ybl* was commissioned to continue it in 1867. In the course of building the cupola collapsed one day, which induced Ybl to modify Hild's original design in an eclectic style. As a result of this intervention the Basilica was completed in 1905 in the neo-Renaissance style instead of the originally planned neoclassic style.

The dome of the church which can hold 8,500 persons is 96 metres high, the ground-plan is 86 by 55 metres, covering a total area of 4,147 sq. metres. The reliefs, murals and statues are the work of the best artists of the period.

Bajcsy Zsilinszky út leads into spacious and bustling Marx tér. Here the Inner Boulevard comes to an end, and from this point the Nagykörút (Great Boulevard) continues its semicircle in the direction of the Danube.

2. THE GREAT BOULEVARD

The Nagykörút (Great Boulevard) is one of the longest and busiest thoroughfares of Budapest. Forming a four-kilometre-long semicircle, it crosses various districts of Pest.

The designation "Great Boulevard" refers only to the section passing through the Pest side which consists of four large segments: Ferenc körút, József körút, Lenin körút, and Szent István körút. Many shops, hotels, cafés, espresso bars and public buildings line the Great Boulevard.

The greater part of the Boulevard was built in the late decades of the last century, according to a uniform plan. The only square on the Great Boulevard laid out as a kind of park is Rákóczi tér.

Before beginning our walk, let us give a short survey of the history of the Great Boulevard. At the time when the old Inner City was still surrounded by walls, the so-called "Great Ditch" passed along the stretch which now forms the Great Boulevard. At flood time the Danube filled it up completely. Some historical sources mentioned the Great Ditch as a little arm of the Danube. Etchings dating from the time of the Turkish occupation clearly show this narrow channel flowing outside the town.

In the 18th century the inhabitants of Pest within the city walls numbered scarcely more than 12,000. Beyond the walls were fields, pastures, and livestock markets. However, soon the town proved to be too small, and outside the walls the outer districts of József-, Ferenc-, Lipót-, Teréz- and Erzsébetváros came into existence. And not long afterwards the walls, too, were pulled down. Rivalry began at that time between the two settlements, the rapidly developing Pest and dignified old Buda. In 1803 the Embellishment Commission was set up with the Palatine József as chairman. The construction of new streets became a civic affair, and owing to its swift growth, Pest soon won out in the rivalry. New streets, squares, blocks and rows of houses came into being, and year after year the face of the town changed. It gained its present-day appearance about the turn of the century. The former Great Ditch was replaced by the Great Boulevard.

Ferenc körút, the first section of the Great Boulevard, begins close to Petőfi Bridge, at Boráros tér. Five tram lines converge upon this point and several bus lines also start or end their routes here. This square is named after János Boráros, one-time alderman and judge of Pest.

Three to five-storied houses border the square, and all along Ferenc körút we find similar buildings. They were built in the early years of this century. Some of them are remarkable for their fine, ornate oaken or wrought-iron front doors (e.g. the house at **No. 35**).

At the crossing of Üllői út, on the right side, stands the former **Kilián György Barracks** (earlier called the Maria Theresa Barracks). During the counter-revolution of 1956 the building was badly damaged. Since its restoration it has become a residential house and also a students' hostel. This building was erected in 1844-45, and represents one of the most remarkable architectural monuments of the capital. It was designed by Miksa *Pauer*, and built by Ferenc *Kasselik*. The modern apartment house across the street with its arcades has already been built in accordance with the new plan of town development with regard to the widening of Üllői út.

The Great Boulevard and Üllői út intersection is a very busy one. To the left, Üllői út takes us to Calvin tér, and on the left hand side of Üllői út the **Museum of Industrial Arts** can be seen. In the opposite direction the road runs to Kispest and Pestlőrinc. At 78 József körút, Nap utca and Pál utca meet at the Boulevard. Here was the plot of land in former times where the "Paul Street Boys"—the heroes of Ferenc *Molnár*'s novel of the same name—played.

The next important crossing is at Baross utca. Toward the left this street ends at Calvin tér, and on the right is Harminckettesek tere with the **monument of the one-time local regiment of Budapest**. The straight line of Baross utca is interrupted by the building of the **Józsefváros Parish Church,** some distance from the Boulevard.

Rákóczi tér is on the right side of József körút. Here we can see a group of statues, entitled **Fishing Scene,** by Károly Senyei.

The editorial offices of the central organ of the Hungarian Socialist Workers' Party, Népszabadság (People's Freedom), as well as Esti Hírlap (Evening News), Nők Lapja (Women's Journal), Magyar Ifjúság (Hungarian Youth) are located at **5** József körút. The front facing the Boulevard is decorated with a **Relief,** three storeys high, the work of András Beck, Jenő Kerényi and Sándor Mikus. The main façade of the building is in the direction of Blaha Lujza tér. **Corvin,** one of the largest department stores of Budapest, is not far away from here, also facing Blaha Lujza tér.

Before József körút reaches Rákóczi út, on the right side, Népszínház utca opens from the Boulevard. At the corner of this street stands a building remarkable for its façade of red bricks with terracotta ornamentation. It was built in 1887 to the designs of Alajos Hauszmann. Close by is the Nemzeti (National) Hotel with 65 rooms. The corner building at **No. 2** houses the finest chemist's shop of Budapest.

The corner of the Great Boulevard and Rákóczi út is the busiest point of Budapest. The **National Theatre** (Nemzeti Színház) is located on the left side of the intersection. It is the work of Ferdinánd Fellner and Hermann Helmer, built between 1872 and 1875. Over the windows of the first floor stand the **busts of Károly Kisfaludy, Béni Egressy** and **József Gaál**. In front of the right wing stands the **statue of the actor Márton Lendvay** by László Dunaiszky made of zinc. The National Theatre opened its doors to the public on October 15, 1875. During the Second World War it was badly damaged, but in 1949 the restoration of the building was completed. Opposite the National Theatre is the **Emke Café** with its bar. It is a much frequented place of amusement.

Opposite to the Emke Café, in the house at **1** Lenin körút, on the ground floor of the building with the onion-shaped cupola, we find the largest food store of the capital.

Intersection of Great Boulevard and Rákóczi út

The building at **3-5** Lenin körút belongs to the Athenaeum Printing House. On the ground floor is a folk-art shop, and also a bookshop selling technical books. Walking past the Lucullus Restaurant, we reach the **New York Palace,** which is one of the finest buildings on the Great Boulevard. Today it is becoming known more and more as the Palace of the Press. The building was erected between 1891 and 1895 after the designs of Alajos *Hauszmann*. The Hungária Café and Restaurant, formerly known as the New York Café, occupies the ground floor. Many writers, poets, artists and musicians are among its regular customers. The valuable frescoes on the ceiling are worth noting.

94

Facing the Hungária Café is the **Newsreel Cinema** (Hír-adó Mozi), which was opened in 1939.

A little farther on the crossing of Wesselényi utca is a newly remodelled, modern theatre of Budapest, **Madách Theatre**. It was reopened in 1961. Walking along the Great Boulevard we reach the **Grand Hotel Royal** which is one of the largest and most comfortable hotels of the capital. It is connected with restaurants, a café, a bar, an espresso and a beer-house.

Making our way along Lenin körút, leaving the crossing of Majakovszkij utca behind, we come to November 7. tér. This intersection of the Boulevard and Népköztársaság útja forms a large square, which in the past was called the Octagon.

The house on Lenin körút next to November 7. tér **(No. 67)** was built by Alajos *Hauszmann*. It is the replica of the Strozzi Palace in Florence. On the ground floor is the **Central Marriage Registry Office** of the Budapest City Council. Nearby, at November 7. tér, is the booking office of the **IBUSZ tourist agency,** and next door, on the ground floor of the corner house at Népköztársaság útja, is the **philatelist shop.** The Abbazia Café, favourite meeting place of many Hungarian artists at the turn of the century, is located on the left side of the square. On the other side is the Savoy Café and Restaurant. The **electric newspaper** on the roof of the house at No. 7 carries the latest news every evening.

At the corner of Lenin körút and Szondy utca is the **Béke (Peace) Hotel** with its popular confectionery shop, bar, dancing and tea-room. The corner of the hotel building bears a coloured mosaic by Jenő *Haranghy*, which represents György *Szondy*, a legendary fortress captain of the time of the Turkish wars. The valuable frescoes in the hotel, with scenes from Shakespeare's dramas, are cared for by the Museum of Fine Arts. They are the work of Jenő *Haranghy*. A few steps farther on we come to the crossing of Rudas László utca, and then to the **Western Railway Terminal.** The first train departed from here on July 15, 1846, for Vác, and it took an hour to cover the distance of 35 kilometres.

In front of the Western Railway Terminal lies Marx tér, an important traffic junction.

On Szent István körút (St. Stephen Boulevard) one finds many espressos, pastry-shops, and it is also a shopping centre. On our right we soon come to the **Comedy**

Theatre (Vígszínház). It was built by the Viennese firm *Fellner and Helmer*, and gave its first performance on May 1, 1896. In the Second World War the theatre burnt down. It was restored in 1951. At the main entrance we see the bronze **busts of Petőfi** and **Miklós Zrínyi**, a poet and general in the Turkish wars.

Szent István körút ends at Jászai Mari tér. This square was named after the famous actress of the National Theatre (1850-1926).

To the left of the square runs Balassi Bálint utca. Here is the terminus of tram line No. 2, which follows the course of the Danube to the Petőfi Bridge. At the corner of Balassi Bálint utca stands the modern building of the **Central Committee of the Hungarian Socialist Workers' Party.**

Szent István körút takes us on to Margaret Bridge. At this point the Pest side of the Great Boulevard comes to an end. On the other side of the bridge begins the so-called "Buda Boulevard". This thoroughfare too describes a semicircle and ends at the Buda abutment of Petőfi Bridge.

3. NÉPKÖZTÁRSASÁG ÚTJA

Népköztársaság útja (People's Republic Avenue) is the loveliest road of Budapest. The laying out of the two-and-a-half-kilometre-long avenue gave Budapest a big city character in the second half of the last century.

The impressive houses on both sides of the road give it a uniform architectonic effect. This historic road, which always carries heavy traffic, is the "fastest" thoroughfare of the town, because it is closed to all vehicles but motorcars. At the same time it is a delightful promenade with numerous benches between its rows of trees. With its espressos, restaurants, pastry-shops and beer-gardens, Népköztársaság útja is a popular meeting-place of the Budapest people. This lovely avenue is also important in the cultural life of Budapest. Nine theatres, two academies, several exhibition halls and other institutions of art and culture are to be found here, or close by. Despite the mainly representative character of this road, it is significant in Hungary's trade, too.

The construction of this road was decided by an act of Parliament in 1870. This was an area of vineyards and scattered country cottages, and the present-day Hősök tere

(Heroes' Square) was a green field. In the first year some 107 plots were expropriated. The Council of Municipal Public Works soon realised that it could not cope with this immense enterprise, and looked for partners. In 1872 it concluded a contract with several banks which committed themselves to taking over the plots at purchase price, and to laying out the avenue in five years and its side streets in ten years.

Work began, and the road was inaugurated with due ceremony on August 20, 1876. On many plots, however, construction had not started yet, and public opinion grew impatient with the slow pace of the work. In 1885 the last plot was built over. On this occasion the road was named after its promoter, Gyula Andrássy, the foreign minister of that time. The famous architect Miklós *Ybl* shaped the architectural features of the road. He was considered the top-ranking advisor of Andrássy, and he directed the construction from the artistic point of view. The splendid buildings were soon handed over to their new owners. Aristocrats, bankers, landowners, speculators in grain and stocks, families with great names and upstarts rivalled one another sparing nothing to display greatest luxury. At that time elegant coaches drove along the roadway, and on the bridle-paths on both sides gentleman-riders rode with their grooms into the City Park (Városliget).

During the Second World War many of these houses were badly damaged. Three smaller houses had to be torn down. On the whole, however, the damage was repaired in the years of post-war reconstruction. The restoration of the doorways, courtyards, and frescoes is still going on.

The road as a whole is now under the protection of the Committee of Historic Monuments. Some of the buildings have been renovated, and the stores modernised. The roadway has to cope with many times the traffic of former times. The Radial Avenue, as it was originally called, has become the finest street of the city which now numbers close to two million inhabitants. Each of the houses along here conceals a wealth of historic relics, tradition and points of interest.

An especially interesting feature of Népköztársaság útja lies beneath the surface of the road. It is the **underground railway,** the first to be built on the Continent. The inauguration ceremony took place in 1896, in connection with the millennium of Hungary. The construction began in August 1894 and was ended 20 months later, so that the

7   97

public was able to ride on the new underground railway to attend the Millenary Exhibition in the City Park (Város-liget). The length of the whole track is 3.7 kilometres, of which 0.5 kilometre runs above ground.

From Bajcsy-Zsilinszky út to the Opera House we find many houses of architectural interest of which we shall mention only a few. The house at **No. 2** is a richly deco-rated palace. The **Zrínyi Bookshop** as well as a **foreign-language bookshop** are located on the ground floor. Many foreign customers enter the attractive premises. Next door we find the **show rooms** of the Ministry of Metallurgy and Machine Industry, where **models of in-struments** are displayed.

The house at **No. 3** was designed by Győző *Czigler* in the eighties of the last century. Frescoes painted by Károly *Lotz* decorate the walls of the staircase. The great Hun-garian artist painted them in the years when he created the ceiling frescoes of the Opera House. The mural paint-ings depict a Roman Bacchanalia. Apart from minor damage, they are in good condition, only the colours have faded to some extent. The entrance of the basement is a master-piece of wrought-iron work. The **Association of Hun-garian Philatelists** as well as the editorial offices of the Philatelist Review occupy the first floor.

Behind the beautifully carved door of the house at **No. 5** reliefs and friezes, statues, marble columns and a ceiling fresco decorate the entrance. In the courtyard we can see statues, wall ornaments and a fountain made of red marble. Fountains, by the way, can be found in nearly all the houses.

The most sumptuous fountain stands in the courtyard of **No. 12,** the most luxurious palace on the avenue. The fountain, built in 1885, is the work of György *Donáth*.

Rich murals and frescoes decorate the interior and the exterior of the houses at **Nos. 8** and **13.**

Negro Espresso is on the opposite side of the road, it is a popular meeting-place of artists.

Also the next building at the corner of Dalszínház utca **(No. 23)** is worth noting. In front of the doorway stand two female figures, the most beautiful caryatides of Népköz-társaság útja.

The **State Opera House** is one of the most imposing sights of the capital. It was built by Miklós *Ybl* in Italian Renaissance style between 1875 and 1884. The huge cen-tral projection interrupts the quiet lines of the façade

The Opera in Népköztársaság útja

which is decorated with a row of statues. The main hall contains statues of sixteen composers. In the niches of the first floor stand the Muses of dancing, lyric poetry, comedy and tragedy. The **statues of Ferenc Erkel** and **Ferenc Liszt,** on the ground floor, are the work of Alajos *Stróbl*, and the others were made by the sculptors Béla *Brestyánszky*, Gyula *Donáth*, György *Kiss*, Adolf *Huszár*, Gyula *Szász* and Leó *Fessler*. The most attractive sections of the Opera House are the staircase, the foyer and the auditorium. The frescoes in the staircase, painted by Mór *Than*, represent the birth and triumph of music, the stories of Apollo and Marsyas, of Orpheus and Amphion, and the punishment of the Sirens by the Muses. Murals of Károly *Lotz* decorate the great foyer, and other lovely murals by Árpád *Feszty* and Róbert *Scholtz* embellish the upper part of the walls.

Two small frescoes and a large one, painted by Gyula *Vastagh*, decorate the ceiling: the birth, education and triumphal march of Bacchus. Paintings by Mihály *Kovács*, Róbert *Scholtz*, Gyula *Bezerédi* and Gyula *Agghtázy* decorate the side entrances. The paintings in the box of honour depict dancing figures, they are the work of Gyula *Donáth*. Behind the box of honour is a large salon with mural paintings by Mór *Than*, which represent the Judgement of Paris, the Three Graces, Amor and Psyche, Ceres and Luna. The striking ceiling painting in the auditorium is a masterpiece of Károly *Lotz* and represents Olympus with the gods, the Muses and the Fates.

The palace across from the State Opera House **(No. 25)** was designed by Ödön *Lechner* and Gyula *Pártos*. When the Opera House was opened the construction of this palace had already been completed. Today it houses the State Ballet Institute.

On the house at **No. 24** a memorial tablet bearing the inscription "Fly, my little boat" can be read, marking the site of the former **Three Ravens Restaurant,** where Endre *Ady*, the great Hungarian lyric poet, wrote many of his poems. In the house at **No. 29** is the Művész (Artists') Espresso frequented, as the name suggests, mostly by artists, and chiefly by the members of the Opera House. Formerly it was a branch establishment of Gerbeaud, the famous Budapest confectioner of Swiss descent.

On our way along Népköztársaság útja we come to Nagymező utca. Here we find the theatre quarter: the **Literary Stage** (Irodalmi Színpad), the **Petőfi Theatre** and the **Municipal Operetta Theatre** (Fővárosi Operettszínház), and in Paulay Ede utca the **Thália Theatre** and in Révay utca the **Variety Stage** (Vidám Színpad). Then we come to two smaller squares facing each other: Jókai tér and Liszt Ferenc tér.

In Jókai tér stands the **statue of Mór Jókai,** the great story-teller and novelist. The statue is the work of Alajos *Stróbl*. On the far side of the square we find the building of the **Little Stage** (Kis Színpad). In the neighbourhood are two much-frequented shops: the renowned Opera Restaurant and the Rozmaring Espresso.

At the corner of Liszt Ferenc tér and Majakovszkij utca is the **Academy of Music.** The **statue of Endre Ady** (by Géza *Csorba*, 1960) stands in the square close to Népköztársaság útja. At one corner of this square we find the finest and most up-to-date bookshop of the capital.

Leaving these two squares behind, Népköztársaság útja reaches one of the largest squares: November 7. tér.

At November 7. tér begins the second section of Népköztársaság útja. Here the roadway is split into three parallel running parts.

At 67 Népköztársaság útja stands the **old Academy of Music** founded by Ferenc Liszt, which was the centre of Hungarian musical life in the past century. On the wall is a commemorative tablet with a relief portrait of Ferenc Liszt bearing the inscription: "To Ferenc Liszt, Founder and President of our Academy of Music", and signed: "the Ferenc Liszt Society, 1934". Over the windows of the second floor a row of locket-like **relief ornaments** can be seen with the portraits of Bach, Haydn, Liszt, Erkel, Mozart and Beethoven. As the director of the institute, the master himself lived in this house. This part of the town is the centre of fine arts, and on Népköztársaság útja we find the old Art Gallery, the Academy of Fine Arts, the Museum of Fine Arts and the new Art Gallery (Műcsarnok). The streets of the area bear the names of various painters and sculptors, such as Pál Szinyei Merse, Mihály Munkácsy, Bertalan Székely and József Rippl-Rónai.

The house at No. 69 is the building of the **old Art Gallery.** It was designed by Adolf *Láng.* The entrance hall and the gallery of the first floor are decorated with frescoes by Károly *Lotz.* This building also houses the **State Puppet Theatre.** The building of the **Academy of Fine Arts** (No. 71) was designed by the architect and painter Lajos *Rauscher.* The popular **Confectionery Shop of Specialities,** established in 1956, is located across the street (No. 70).

At the Körönd (Circus) the third section of Népköztársaság útja begins. The architects decided to break up the monotonous continuity of the avenue by inserting two large squares: the Octagon and the circular Körönd. In the little garden plots of this circus stand four **statues:** the legendary Kuruc general of Ferenc Rákóczi, **Vak Botytyán** (Bottyán the Blind), by Gyula *Kis-Kovács;* the heroic leader of victorious battle against the Turks, and commander of the Fortress of Szigetvár, **Miklós Zrínyi,** by József *Róna;* **György Szondy,** another legendary fortress captain at the time of the Turkish wars, by László *Marton,* and **Bálint Balassi,** poet and outstanding soldier in the second half of the 16th century, by Pál *Pátzay.*

Between the Körönd and Hősök tere the character of

the road again changes: the road seems to be wider owing to the front-gardens, which are laid out before the houses here. This is the diplomatic quarter, where embassies of a number of countries can be found. In this street and in the neighbourhood are the embassies of the Soviet Union, Albania, Bulgaria, the People's Republic of China, the Democratic People's Republic of Korea, the German Democratic Republic, Yugoslavia and also of Austria and France.

The corner building (No. 101) is the headquarters of the **Association of Hungarian Journalists** and the **Journalists' Club,** the meeting-place of the representatives of the domestic and foreign press.

The **Museum of Eastern Asiatic Arts** (Kelet-ázsiai Múzeum) founded by Ferenc *Hopp,* is housed in the building next door (No. 103).

After the First World War Ferenc Hopp bestowed his valuable East Asian collection and his house to the state on the condition that the East Asian material from the other museums would be united here. There is also a **Chinese Museum** in Gorkij fasor with its own material, thanks chiefly to contributions received from China and India.

From the Museum of Eastern Asiatic Arts a few minutes' walk takes us to the crossing of Népköztársaság útja and Dózsa György út. At this intersection lies Hősök tere (Heroes' Square).

Three architectural masterpieces stand on this spacious square: the Millenary Monument, the Museum of Fine Arts, and the new Art Gallery.

The **Millenary Monument** was erected to commemorate the millennium of Hungary. The construction was begun in 1896, and the work planned for a period of five years lasted 33 years. In the centre of the 85-metre-wide monument, proportionately distributed by a semi-elliptic open colonnade, rises a 33-metre-high column, surmounted by the bronze statue of the archangel Gabriel. The group of statues at the base, the work of the sculptor György *Zala,* represent the seven Magyar tribal chiefs. In front of the monument is a symbolic tomb of the soldiers who fell in action for their country.

The monument is surrounded by the open semi-elliptic colonnade, which is surmounted, on the left wing, by the statues representing Work and Well-being, and the galloping Chariot of War, and on the right wing, by the statues

Hősök tere and the Museum of Fine Arts

of the Chariot of Peace, and of Knowledge and Glory. Between the columns stand the **statues** of the great rulers and national leaders of Hungarian history: **Stephen I** (the first king of Hungary, 1001-1038), **Ladislas I** (1077-1095), **Könyves Kálmán** (Coloman Beauclerc, 1095-1116), **Andrew II** (1205-1235), **Béla IV** (the rebuilder of the country after the Mongol invasion, 1235-1270), **Charles Robert** (1308-1342), **Louis I the Great** (1342-1382), **János Hunyadi** (the great military leader who defeated the Turks, died in 1456), his son **King Matthias Corvinus, the Just** (1458-1490), **Gábor Bethlen** (Prince of Transylvania, King of Hungary, leader of the Reformation, 1580-1629), **István Bocskai** (Prince of Transylvania, organiser of a fight for freedom, 1557-1606), **Imre Thököly** (Prince of Hungary, leader of a war of independence, 1657-1705), **Ferenc Rákóczi II** (Prince of Transylvania and Hungary, leader of an extensive war of independence, 1676-1735), and **Lajos Kossuth** (leader of the 1848-49 War of Independence, 1802-1894).

On the left side of the square stands the impressive building of the **Museum of Fine Arts,** designed by Albert
Schickedanz and Fülöp *Herzog* in 1900. On the central
projection over the monumental flight of steps a row of
columns supports a tympanum in relief. The **Art Gallery**
on the opposite side of the square was built also to the
designs of *Schickedanz* and *Herzog*, in 1895. (For more details on museums see page 269.)

4. RÁKÓCZI ÚT

Rákóczi út is four kilometres long and begins at the border of the Inner City, being the continuation of Kossuth
Lajos utca. It runs between the Erzsébetváros and Józsefváros districts straight to the Eastern Railway Terminal.
There this thoroughfare branches into two parts: to the
left as Thököly út and to the right as Kerepesi út connect-

ing two outer districts. At the beginning of Rákóczi út (No. 4-6) we find the **Extra Áruház,** a **department store** selling ready-made garments with odd measurements (undersized and oversized). On the opposite side is the building of the former **Pannonia Hotel.** The house at No. 15 was the former **White Horse Hotel,** the scene of much merriment in the 19th century. The building has remained faithful to its traditions, because today it houses an espresso with music and entertainment programmes. Its garden premises are very popular in summer. In the house at No. 12 is a renowned outfitting department store, **Verseny Áruház.**

Characteristic of Rákóczi út are the numerous espressos which are interspersed among fashionable business premises and department stores. While the espressos in Buda and in the Inner City of Pest are more suited for a longer stay, here people take their black coffee in rather a hurry, standing at the bar. A popular coffee shop of this

105

sort is the Mackó (Teddy Bear) on the corner of Puskin utca.

One of the oldest cinemas of Budapest, erected some fifty years ago, is the **Uránia**, now a first-run cinema. It is located at 21 Rákóczi út. The Moorish style of its interior is especially worth noting.

About a hundred metres on past the Uránia Cinema the road becomes narrower: the old building of the **Semmelweis Hospital** (formerly called St. Roch Hospital) as well as the adjoining **St. Rosalie Chapel** jut out into the street. The **statue of Ignác Semmelweis**, the "Saviour of Mothers", stands in front of the doorway of the hospital. Semmelweis (1818-1865), eminent Hungarian physician, and later on head-physician in the old St. Roch Hospital, discovered the cause of puerperal fever and also the way to prevent it. The hospital's history goes back to the beginning of the 18th century. It was erected by the Pest City Council in 1711, at the time when the country was plague-stricken. When the epidemic subsided, the hospital remained and was enlarged several times. The building in its present form was designed by Mihály *Pollack* in 1837.

The origin of the baroque chapel also goes back to the year 1711. Its original size corresponds to its present-day chancel and it gained its present form in 1740. To the right of the main entrance stands a stone crucifix, and next to it the statue of the Blessed Virgin mounted on a marble column. Close by is the doorway of the hospital, in Louis XVI style. The relief over the doorway bears the inscription: *Pestanum calamitosorum domicilium* (Home of the helpless of Pest). The marble tablet on the wall facing Rákóczi út indicates the water level of the great flood of 1838. In the shade of this wall the peasant women of Mezőkövesd and Kiskunhalas display and sell their world-famous embroideries, dolls and laces of the Matyó and Halas regions. Many foreigners come to this spot to buy gifts and souvenirs.

On the other side modern arcades line Rákóczi út. They were built between 1958 and 1960 to allow for an expansion of the sidewalk.

Behind the block of the Semmelweis Hospital, Rákóczi út broadens into a square, which is named after Lujza Blaha (1850-1926), the famous operetta singer, the "Hungarian Nightingale". The **Corvin Department Store** stands in this square (No. 1-2), occupying a whole block of build-

Rákóczi út

ngs. Close by (No. 3) is the **Népszabadság House**, a
block of buildings which houses the editorial offices and
printing shop of the central organ of the Hungarian Socialist Workers' Party (Magyar Szocialista Munkás Párt—
MSZMP) and other dailies and periodicals. On the eastern
side the **National Theatre** (Nemzeti Színház, 35-37 Rákóczi út) completes the group of buildings in Blaha Lujza
tér. It was built according to the designs of Ferdinánd
Fellner and Hermann *Helmer*, between 1872 and 1875, and
originally its purpose was to present "popular plays", ro-
mances about outlaws accompanied by the music of gipsy
orchestras—a genre of theatre performances that has now
become extinct. Later on, in 1913, when the building of
the old National Theatre was torn down, the leading theatre of the country was moved here. (As a matter of fact,
this building too is to be torn down in 1965. The National
Theatre will move into a new building of modern construction in another part of the city.) Since then the finest
traditions of the theatre have become associated with its
name. The varied programme embraces classical and mod-

The National Theatre

ern works of both Hungarian and world literature. The members of its ensemble are the foremost actors of the country. At the right side of the building stands the **statue of Márton Lendvay** (1807-1858), who was one of the most outstanding actors of the National Theatre in his time. Over the windows of the first floor are the **busts of Károly Kisfaludy** (1788-1830), poet and dramatist; of the writer **József Gaál** (1811-1866), and the composer and playwright **Béni Egressy** (1808-1866).

The two busiest thoroughfares of Budapest meet at the corner of the National Theatre: Rákóczi út and Nagykörút (Great Boulevard). The electric clock by the street island at the side entrance of the National Theatre is a rendezvous of young people and the theme of many songs, poems, cartoons and jokes. Opposite we find the **Emke Café,** popular amusement spot, which has been reconstructed and modernised. An espresso and a snack bar are on the ground floor with the restaurant and the bar on the first floor. On another corner of the Great Boulevard

(50 Rákóczi út) is the largest food store in Budapest, and just opposite (39 Rákóczi út), a chemist's shop occupies the corner premises, where day-and-night service and special medicaments from abroad are available.

In the section extending between the Great Boulevard and the Eastern Railway Terminal past the building of **Népszava** (Voice of the People), the daily paper of the Trade Union Centre (54 Rákóczi út), we find several hotels in Rákóczi út: **Metropol Hotel** (No. 58), with a quick-service restaurant on the ground floor, **Palace Hotel** (No. 43), and **Szabadság** (Liberty) **Hotel** (No. 90). Adjoining is the **Debrecen Restaurant,** well known for its excellent Hungarian cuisine (No. 88). (At present the new buildings of both the Szabadság Hotel and the Debrecen Restaurant are under construction.)

An interesting monument is located in the courtyard of No. 57: the **Lutheran church** for members **of the Slovak community,** built by József *Diescher* between 1857 and 1867. The altarpiece is by Mór *Than.* At the corner of this building Luther utca branches off from Rákóczi út and leads to the **Erkel Theatre,** the second opera house of Budapest.

Rákóczi út leads into an oval square, Baross tér, which is named after **Gábor Baross** (1848-1892), who as a statesman and cabinet minister rendered great services in developing the Hungarian railway system. His statue (by Antal *Széchy,* 1908) stands in the centre of the square.

At the farther end of Baross tér is the **Eastern Railway Terminal** (Keleti pályaudvar). Its main building was designed by Gyula *Rochlitz* and it was opened to traffic in 1884. The **statues of Stephenson** and **Watt** decorate the façade, and the murals of Mór *Than* and Károly *Lotz* the entrance-hall.

With the Eastern Railway Terminal, Rákóczi út comes to an end. At this point the thoroughfare splits up: the southern branch, Kerepesi út, leads to the arrival platform and to the terminal of the suburban tram line which connects Budapest with Gödöllő and passes by the **National Riding School** and the **trotting race course** (No. 11). The **gallop race course** (57 Kerepesi út) can be reached best by tram or by bus. Near the race course are the grounds where **agricultural exhibitions, cattle shows** and **fairs** are held.

Thököly út, named after Imre Thököly (1657-1705), the Kuruc leader of the war of independence against Hapsburg

109

oppression at the turn of the 17th to the 18th century, leads from the departure platform of the Eastern Railway Terminal to the outer district of Zugló and ends at Bosnyák tér. The "sports quarter" of Budapest begins at the intersection of Thököly út and Dózsa György út. Particulars about the People's Stadium, which can hold nearly 100,000 spectators, the Sports Hall and the Millenáris Sport Ground will be given on page 277.

5. ÜLLŐI ÚT

Üllői út begins in the centre of the town and is the longest road in Budapest. It extends from Calvin tér to Pestlőrinc, a southeastern suburb of the capital, thus running through Budapest in a length of 5.5 kilometres. Its first section beginning at Calvin tér gives the impression of old Pest of the 19th century with its houses in neoclassic style, then the Museum of Industrial Arts shows a fine example of the modern-style architecture which was much in use at the turn of the century. Farther on there are residential areas where the sunny flats, business premises, day nurseries and schools are already achievements of socialism. Afterwards we see family houses and groves, and Üllői út finally passes through factory areas and leaves the town on its way towards the Great Hungarian Plain. Coming from Calvin tér, the first building worth mentioning is **No. 7,** a single-storied apartment house in neoclassic style designed by Ferenc *Kasselik* in 1839. Two well-known architects took part in building the house at **No. 17.** Originally it was built by the master of classicism, Mihály *Pollack,* and later on, in the second half of the 19th century, Miklós *Ybl* added another storey. Erkel utca, which runs into Üllői út, bears the name of the famous Hungarian composer who lived here for many years. In the 19th century, Ferenc Erkel (1810-1893) was—in addition to Ferenc Liszt—a leading personality of Hungarian musical life. He was the founder of Hungarian national opera. Among his works based on historical themes let us mention "Bánk Bán", "Hunyadi László" and "Brankovics György", which are part of the repertoire of the Opera House. He also composed the music of the Hungarian national anthem.

Beyond the houses in neoclassic style, a group of buildings, the **clinics and institutes of the University of Medi-**

cine, comes into view, filling in the block abutting on Szentkirályi utca, Baross utca and Mária utca. Farther on the building of the **Museum of Industrial Arts** (No. 33-37) with its characteristically coloured cupola catches our eye. The construction of the central building dates from 1893 to 1896 and is the work of Ödön *Lechner* and Gyula *Pártos*, who were intent on developing a specific, Hungarian architectural style. The façade of the museum is decorated chiefly with ceramics composed of Hindu-Islamic and Hungarian folk decorative elements. The **Institute for Artistic Designs in Industry** is housed in the same building.

After the Museum of Industrial Arts, at the corner of Üllői út and the Great Boulevard, we find a huge block of apartments at No. 45-51, the former **Maria Theresa Barracks**, erected according to the plans of József *Hild*.

Proceeding along Üllői út, on the right side, we come to the **Church of Perpetual Adoration** flanked by two wings built in the neo-Gothic style. The building was designed by Mihály *Pollack*. A home for boys has been established in its residence. The streets in this vicinity bear the names of famous personalities of Hungarian medical history. János Bókay was a professor of pediatrics, and in the street named after him is the pediatrics clinic of the University of Medicine. In Korányi Sándor utca, named after the famous scientist of internal medicine at the turn of the century, we find the university's clinic for internal diseases. The whole area here is a complex of medical institutes comprising research laboratories and clinics of surgery, ophthalmology, urology and gynaecology.

Reaching the clinics, Üllői út broadens into a square forming Kun Béla tér. It bears the name of a leading statesman of the Hungarian Republic of Councils of 1919, who was an outstanding leader of the communist movement in Hungary (1886-1938). In the centre of the square stands a **monument** raised in honour **of the soldiers of the Soviet Army** who lost their lives in the battle that liberated Budapest. To the east, the group of buildings of the former military academy completes this square. The **Alfa Cinema** is located in the former military building erected by Mihály *Pollack* in the neoclassic style between 1830 and 1836. At present it is the largest cinema in Budapest. The other buildings house the Bem József secondary school and a factory manufacturing goods for the light industry.

A new housing estate along Üllői út

After Kun Béla tér we reach Nagyvárad tér, which ends the inner section of Üllői út. The square is an intersection of several busy thoroughfares, an important junction of tram and bus lines. At Nagyvárad tér and close by we find several health institutions: the **István Hospital**, the **László Hospital**, the **Institute for Experimental Medicine** now under construction and belonging to the **Scientific Institute of Food and Nutrition**, the **National Institute of Public Health** and the **National Institute of Labour Hygiene.**

A less densely built outer section of Üllői út follows after Nagyvárad tér. Here are the **football field** and **athletic grounds** of one of the oldest sports clubs, the **FTC** (Ferencvárosi Torna Club), at No. 129. Opposite to it is the building of the **State Mint.** At this point Üllői út crosses the outer boulevard of the capital. This section of the boulevard is Könyves Kálmán körút. King Kálmán (Coloman, 1095-1116) introduced, among his many reforms, the use of writing in the administration of justice. Here we find the **Ethnographical Museum** and the **Budapest Film Studios.**

Then Üllői út passes along the People's Park (Népliget), which covers an area of over 110 hectares. Numerous statues and monuments decorate the promenades—among others the **statue** of the poet and chronicler **Sebestyén Tinódi Lantos** (1505-1556), and the **monument of the Polish Legionaries** of the Hungarian War of Independence of 1848-49. Beyond the People's Park is a modern housing estate which was built in the years after the liberation in the place of the former slum area that had been demolished. This is already an achievement of socialist construction. After the Express Highway to the Ferihegy Airport of Budapest branches off from it, Üllői út continues through an area of family houses and large factories to the suburban districts of Kispest and Pestlőrinc.

THE INNER DISTRICTS OF PEST

1. THE INNER CITY

The Inner City (Belváros) is the heart of Budapest. This is where the life of the town pulsates with the greatest activity. An unforgettable experience for all visitors is the Danube Promenade (Duna-korzó) with its splendid panorama. The visitor can never see enough of the beauty that the embankment of the Danube has to offer at whatever time of the year he may come to Budapest.

Looking towards the south from the Danube Promenade, we can see as far down as the Southern Railway Bridge. Then, moving up the river, follows the Petőfi Bridge, the Technical University, the Gellért Hotel and the Liberation Monument on Gellért Hill. Overlooking the town, on top of Gellért Hill, is the Citadel, whose grey walls today house a restaurant, a beer-house, an espresso and a tourist hostel. Then as we look further north Castle Hill (Vár-hegy) comes into sight, with its one-time royal castle which burnt down in the Second World War. Its restoration has been under way for over a decade. On Castle Hill prominent landmarks are the Fishermen's Bastion and the Matthias Church. Further upstream are the Suspension Bridge (Lánchíd), the Margaret Bridge (Margithíd) and Margaret Island (Margitsziget) and the Hill of Roses (Rózsadomb) and in the distance the Hill of Three Boundaries (Hármashatár-hegy) and the northern foothills of the Buda mountains.

The Inner City is the busiest shopping centre of the capital. From early morning till evening a flood of people streams along Kossuth Lajos utca, Petőfi Sándor utca, Váci utca and the larger squares. In the late afternoon hours when offices, ministries and shops close, thousands of people come into the streets to make their way home. Only late in the evening does the noise subside, and the night life of the city begin in espressos and other places of amusement.

Let us look at this district more closely now and set out, say, from the Duna (Danube) Hotel, turn in towards Felszabadulás tér (Liberation Square). Here we hardly find any traces of the old Inner City with its tiny houses, its narrow passages and zigzagging, winding little lanes. Only the marble tablet and the relief on the wall of the old Franciscan Church reminds us of the great flood that devastated half the town in 1838.

Let us stop at the corner of Felszabadulás tér and Petőfi Sándor utca. From here we can see one of the finest and largest delicatessen shops of the capital. In front of it stands the **Franciscan Church** which was built between 1727 and 1743 in the baroque style. Many of the frescoes that decorate the interior of the church were painted by Károly *Lotz*. On the outside wall a bronze relief by Barnabás *Holló* shows Miklós Wesselényi, the "Boatman of the Floods", making his way along the streets in his barge. On March 13, 1838 the muddy waves of the Danube flooded the whole Inner City within minutes, devastating hundreds of houses, and endangering the lives of thousands of people. Miklós Wesselényi was the bravest among the many who came to the assistance of the desperate population; he alone saved the lives of many hundreds.

A few steps past the church we reach the **Kárpátia Restaurant,** and then the building of the **University Library,** built between 1873 and 1876. It contains half a million volumes, among them 150 valuable codices and over a thousand incunabula.

Our walk takes us into Károlyi utca, to the old **Károlyi Palace.** It was built in 1696, and about fifty years later it was reconstructed in the baroque style. Further reconstruction followed in the 19th century. There is a story that the owner of that time, when he came to Budapest to have a look at his new palace, did not even get out of his carriage because he was not pleased with the work. He at once engaged Mihály *Pollack* to have it reconstructed in the form it now has. A memorial tablet on the side wall facing Egyetem tér (University Square) reminds us that Lajos Batthyány, the first constitutional prime minister of Hungary, who was executed later by the Hapsburg authorities, was arrested in this house on January 8, 1849. In the grounds of the palace open-air concerts, often featuring well-known artists from abroad, are given in summer. The building houses the **Petőfi Sándor Literary Museum.**

At the corner of the building is Egyetem tér with the block of buildings forming the centre of today's **Eötvös Loránd University.** The university, which was founded by Cardinal Péter Pázmány in 1635, originally at Nagyszombat (now Trnava, Czechoslovakia), had only a faculty of theology and philosophy. The faculty of law was added in 1667, and the faculty of medicine in 1770. In 1777, its seat was transferred to the Buda Castle, and in 1784 to its present location. In 1949 the university was renamed after the great Hungarian physicist and scientist, Loránd Eötvös. At the corner of the building facing Eötvös Loránd utca stands the **University Church,** which was restored a short time ago. This church was built on the basis of plans by András *Mayerhoffer* between 1722 and 1742. Its frescoes are the work of Johann Baptist *Bergl.* The richly carved pulpit and benches are of particular interest.

The Central Seminary is located close by the University Church. The building which was erected between 1715 and 1744 was originally a monastery of the Order of the Paulites. Its beautiful baroque library contains 16,000 volumes. The other side of the university faces Szerb utca. At the corner of Királyi Pál utca, in Szerb utca, stands a building erected in 1733, which was originally a convent. Later, however, it was converted into a hospital, and then it was occupied by the faculty of economic sciences of the university. Today it houses some chairs of the Technical University.

If we return to Felszabadulás tér and stop in front of the Franciscan Church we see on the opposite side the **head office of the IBUSZ Travel Agency** and below, on the ground floor, the Jégbüfé (Ice Buffet) confectionery shop. A few steps farther on, in Kígyó utca, is the Mézes Mackó (Honey Bear) snack bar. The short street leading to the Danube is Szabadsajtó útja (Free Press Avenue) with the Belvárosi Café at the corner. This street ends in Március 15. tér, where we reach the Pest abutment of the former Elizabeth Bridge, whose successor is actually under construction. Here stands the **Inner City Parish Church,** the oldest monument of Pest. It was built in 1046 and at the time of the Mongol invasion it was completely destroyed. A Romanesque church was built in its place and in the 15th century it was reconstructed in the Gothic style. During the Turkish occupation it remained for some time a Christian church, but was later converted into a mosque. The Turkish praying

Felszabadulás tér

niche next to the sanctuary is a reminder of that time. The façade was demolished by the Turks. It was rebuilt in the baroque style between 1725 and 1740.

The church possesses many relics and art treasures. Among these the tabernacles in the fourth side chapel, both on the right and left side, dating from the years 1507 and 1510, are worth mentioning. Nineteen niches with seats in the Gothic style occupy the space below the chancel windows, at the end of which is a Turkish praying niche, known as a *mihrab*. The **Florian Statue** at the outside wall, in the rear, is the work of *Hörger*, a Buda sculptor. The modern high altar is by László *Gerő*, the triptychs were painted by C. Pál *Molnár*.

When the sightseer arrives at Petőfi tér the **statue of Sándor Petőfi,** the poet and hero of the Hungarian War of Independence of 1848-49, is the first thing to catch his eye. The bronze figure is the work of the sculptors Miklós *Izsó* and Adolf *Huszár* and the pedestal that of Miklós *Ybl*. The carved stones on Március 15. tér lead to the **Underground Museum.** The tombstones that can be seen at the entrance were brought here from the National Museum and are relics from the old Roman fort of Contra-Aquincum, which was situated on the Pest side. The *castrum* was built during the reign of Emperor Diocletian, in 294 A.D., and was of great strategic importance, similarly to the forts built on the Buda side. Its foundation walls were excavated in 1932. In 1944 further remains of the Roman wall were unearthed when excavations were carried out near the sanctuary of the Inner City Parish Church.

A short distance away from here stands the **Greek Orthodox Church,** which was built by József *Jung* between 1791 and 1801. The spires, designed by Miklós *Ybl*, were added in 1873. One of the spires was destroyed in the Second World War. Behind the Inner City Parish Church we find the building of the **Faculty of Arts of the Eötvös Loránd University.** The main entrance of the building faces Pesti Barnabás utca. On the side of the building along Váci utca we find the **Gorky Foreign-language Bookshop.** In the **Csók István Gallery,** at the corner of Váci utca and Pesti Barnabás utca, paintingr and ceramics of contemporary Hungarian artists, and artistic furniture and upholstery material are on sale.

Among the buildings of the baroque Inner City, which had to be pulled down at the beginning of the century

The Hungarian Academy of Sciences

when the construction of the Elizabeth Bridge was started, only the so-called **Kriszt House,** at the corner of Pesti Barnabás utca and Galamb utca, has remained intact. The construction of the baroque palace was begun in 1756 and tells of living history. Since 1831 it has been a restaurant. At that time it was called "To the City of Buda", today it is called Százéves Étterem (Hundred-Year-Old Restaurant).

Now our path takes us back through Pesti Barnabás utca to the **Danube Promenade.** On our way we cross Apáczai Cseri János utca running parallel with the Danube, where we come to the **Duna Hotel.** This is the only remaining building of the once famous row of Danube hotels. Its popular garden restaurant is called the **Dunakert.** Past the Duna Hotel parks have been laid out and behind them, in Apáczai Cseri János utca, three fine old houses in the neoclassic empire style can be seen.

A short distance away lies Vigadó tér. In this square is a

memorial to Soviet airmen who fell in the battle for the liberation of Budapest, and the remains of the **Vigadó** (Concert Hall), built between 1859 and 1863 on the basis of designs by Frigyes *Feszl*. During the Second World War the building was almost completely destroyed. Today only the outer walls and part of the interior are standing. Its reconstruction has already begun. The façade fronting towards the Danube will be preserved in its original form. Behind it, on Vörösmarty tér, a concert hall with a seating capacity of 3,000 will be built.

The site of the Vigadó was formerly the place of the old Redoubt, part of the city walls of Pest. During the siege of Buda in 1849, before the Hungarian armies recaptured the Buda fortress, the Austrian general Hentzi shelled the buildings along the Pest embankment, among them the old Redoubt. In its place came the Vigadó, where many famous musicians of the past century gave concerts. Next to the Vigadó, at the corner of Apáczai Cseri János utca, is the **head office of MAHART** (Magyar Hajózási Rt. = **Hungarian Navigation Company).** On the lower embank-

120

...lding

ment is the **landing stage of the excursion boat,** which sets out every afternoon and evening for a two-hour cruise upstream to Szentendre Island. Farther along on the Danube embankment past the Soviet memorial we come to the Dunakorzó Café. The neighbouring lawn was the site of the one-time Ritz Hotel. In Eötvös tér, where the Danube Promenade ends, stands the **statue of József Eötvös,** writer, poet, publicist and statesman. It was modelled by Adolf *Huszár* in 1879. The **Kék Duna** (Blue Danube) **floating restaurant** lies at anchor on the lower embankment. Its terrace, beautifully laid out with flowers, affords a pleasant stay even in the hottest summer evening.

To some extent Eötvös tér forms part of neighbouring Roosevelt tér, named after Franklin Delano Roosevelt. This spacious square also forms the Pest abutment of the Suspension Bridge.

At the corner of the square and József Attila utca stands the **building of the Ministry of the Interior.** Its wall bears a **tablet commemorating Attila József,** the great

121

Hungarian proletarian poet. On the left side stands the **statue of Ferenc Deák,** prominent Hungarian political leader in the second half of the last century. It is the work of Adolf *Huszár*. The neighbouring building is the imposing **Gresham Palace.** The Municipal Tourist Office and a very popular snack bar occupy the ground floor. A bronze **statue of István Széchenyi** by József *Engel* stands on the northern edge of the square. Széchenyi was the initiator of great reforms in Hungary, and we are indebted to him also for founding the **Hungarian Academy of Sciences,** whose building stands in the square. It was designed by the Berlin architect Friedrich August *Stüler*, and built between 1860 and 1864. The **relief** on the side wall, by Barnabás *Holló*, depicts the scene where Széchenyi, on November 3, 1825, offered his one year's income amounting to 60,000 florins for the foundation of the "learned Academy". The library of the Academy consisting of about one million volumes, many valuable manuscripts and incunabula, is housed in this building. The great Hungarian poet, János Arany, general secretary of the Academy, resided in the building for a few years at that time.

Two houses dating from the years 1835 and 1836 stand in front of the Academy of Sciences. They both belong to the **Ministry of the Food Industry. A commemorative tablet** on the house at **1 Akadémia utca** tells us that József Bem, the legendary Polish general of the 1848-49 War of Independence, stayed there for a few days while in Pest.

Akadémia utca leads straight on to Kossuth Lajos tér, which is the finest square of Budapest. It can be reached easily from all parts of the town by tram, bus and trolley-bus. At the south end of the square stood the Kossuth Bridge, constructed in the winter of 1945-46, which first connected Pest and Buda after the liberation of the capital. Before its completion communication between the two banks of the Danube was confined to boats, small steamers and pontoon bridges. The Kossuth Bridge was designed as an emergency bridge, and it was removed after fulfilling its purpose.

The monumental building in the square is the **House of Parliament.** The splendid structure, 118 metres wide, extends to a length of 268 metres along the embankment of the Danube. Its dome rises 96 metres, and the area of construction totals 17,745 square metres. The architect of the building, which was erected between 1885 and 1904, was Imre *Steindl*.

The main entrance faces Kossuth Lajos tér and is flanked by two bronze lions modelled by Béla *Markup*. Two hundred and fifty allegorical statues ornament the building. Art historians employed by the Municipal Tourist Office (Fővárosi Idegenforgalmi Hivatal), 5 Roosevelt tér, regularly organise guided tours for visitors wishing to see the interior of the Parliament building. Doorway No. XII, next to the main entrance, leads to the marble staircase decorated with ceiling frescoes by Károly *Lotz*. The steps end at the Gothic domed hall, which is the scene of grand receptions on festive state occasions. From the northwest corner of the hall a door leads to the conference room which is decorated with a piece of gobelin tapestry of tremendous size, designed by the painter Gyula *Rudnay*. Another door on the northwest side of the domed hall opens into the Hunting Hall. Its name comes from the room's fine fresco "Buffalo Hunt" by Aladár *Körösfői-Kriesch*. The lounge of the Parliament building opens towards the south, with a corridor leading into the Chamber of Deputies. The Congress Room is in the north wing of the building.

In addition to Parliament, the **Presidential Council** and the **Council of Ministers of the Hungarian People's Republic** meet in the House of Parliament. The **Information Bureau of the Council of Ministers** also has its offices here. Free access to the library of Parliament is available to all. It contains over 400,000 volumes, chiefly reference books on politics, history and law. The façade of the Parliament building towards the Danube is richly ornamented. From the arcades there is a fine view of the Buda districts opposite, the Danube and Margaret Island.

After our visit to the House of Parliament let us return to Kossuth Lajos tér. To the right an equestrian **statue of Prince Ferenc Rákóczi II** comes into sight. It was done by János *Pásztor* in 1935. Ferenc Rákóczi II was the leader of the freedom struggle between 1703 to 1711 against Hapsburg rule. Opposite the House of Parliament rises the building of the **Ministry of Agriculture,** the splendid work of architect Gyula *Bukovits*, built between 1885 and 1887. The statue of the "Agronomist Girl", in front of the northern wing of the building, is by József *Somogyi*. Another vast structure on this side of the square is the **National Gallery** (Nemzeti

The Hungarian National Gallery

Galéria). The building was erected to the designs of Alajos *Hauszmann* in 1896. Originally it was meant to serve as the Supreme Court which, in fact, it was until the end of the Second World War. The frescoes in the entrance hall are the work of Károly *Lotz*. The large rooms of the palace house the collections of the National Gallery, the finest Hungarian art works of the last 150 years. In the park in front of the National Gallery stands the **statue of** the great Hungarian statesman **Lajos Kossuth.** The main figure is the work of Zsigmond *Kisfaludi Strobl*, the auxiliary figures are by Lajos *Ungváry* and András *Kocsis*.

Báthori utca starts beside the Ministry of Agriculture and broadens midway at the intersection with Rosenberg házaspár utca into a small square. A **perpetual light** in a bronze socket was set up here, a reminder that the tyranny of the Hapsburgs put to death Lajos Batthyány, the Hungarian prime minister at the time of the 1848-49 War of Independence.

Not far from the perpetual light a short street takes us to Szabadság tér (Liberty Square). Its whole western front is taken up by a single structure, the **House of Technology.** Formerly this building was the stock exchange.

Since 1957 it has been the home of scientific associations and it also houses the studios of the **Hungarian Television.** Across the square we find the building of the **National Bank of Hungary,** designed by Ignác *Alpár* and built in 1905. The **former Postal Savings Bank,** which now forms part of the National Bank, is also here. This latter building was erected by Ödön *Lechner* (1900-1901) who gained great distinction by developing a special Hungarian architectural style. The building is remarkable also for the coloured majolica tiles from the famous Zsolnay Factory at Pécs, that are used to ornament the walls.

The **Legation of the United States of America** (12 Szabadság tér) is also a fine building.

Szabadság tér—now protected under the Historical Monuments Act—forms a semicircle on the north side, where the **Soviet war memorial** stands. At the south end of the square, at the corner of Október 6. utca, stands the building of the **Ministry of Metallurgy and Machine Industry.**

One of the streets leading from Szabadság tér to the centre of the Inner City is Nádor utca. No. 7 in this street was the residence of Lajos Kossuth in 1844. The adjoining house is the former Tiger Inn. Another important building in this street is the **National Planning Office.**

Let us now go back to Felszabadulás tér and acquaint ourselves with the southern part of the Inner City, the area within the city walls in former times. This wall ran from Calvin tér to Deák Ferenc tér, and reached down to the Danube on both sides. Almost everywhere we still see remnants of the ancient little town.

Walking from Felszabadulás tér into Petőfi Sándor utca past the **Repertory Theatre of the National Theatre,** named after the great Hungarian dramatist József Katona, we turn into the first by-street on our left, Pilvax köz. Here stands the historic **Pilvax Café,** which was the meeting-place of the revolutionary youth of Pest in 1848, before the outbreak of the revolution. The modern café still preserves in its glass-cases old relics of the 19th-century revolutionary days: newspapers, posters, Honvéd pistols, and swords.

Having returned to Petőfi Sándor utca, we come to the building of **Post Office No. 4** and walk past a number of attractive shop windows to Martinelli tér. This square is named after the architect Anton Erhardt *Martinelli* who

The Ministry of Agriculture opposite the Parliament building

built the nearby palace of the Budapest City Council. In the centre of the square stands the slender column surmounted by the **statue of the Holy Virgin.** Behind it is the **Church of the Servites** which was originally built in the baroque style between 1725 and 1732. The façade is of later construction. Városház utca (Town Hall Street) begins here. Among the sights to be seen in this street we mention the palace of the **City Council of Budapest.** It was built between 1716 and 1735. Originally it was intended as a home for disabled soldiers, later it served as a barracks, and today it houses the offices of the executive committee of the Budapest City Council. In the courtyard of the building stands the **statue of Endre Ságvári,** a young communist leader who was killed fighting the fascists in 1944. At the corner of this building, Városház utca opens onto Kammermayer

Károly tér. In 1873, after the unification of the towns of Pest, Buda and Óbuda, Károly Kamermayer became the first mayor of Budapest. His **statue** stands in the square bearing his name. The short street behind the statue leads into Semmelweis utca, named after Ignác Semmelweis, the "Saviour of Mothers", who discovered how to prevent puerperal fever.

On the other corner of Kamermayer Károly tér stands the building of the **Pest County Council.** Its façade was built according to the designs of Mátyás *Zitterbarth* between 1838 and 1841. The front along Semmelweis utca was built earlier, in 1825. The library with a vaulted ceiling, in the interior of the building, which served as a county prison, is interesting to see.

Passing through Városház utca, Vármegyeház utca and Semmelweis utca we come to Kossuth Lajos utca. Formerly the street was called Hatvani utca, because a city gate once stood here, which was the starting point of the highway to Hatvan, a town northeast of Budapest. Kossuth Lajos utca is the busiest street of the Inner City. At the intersection of Kossuth Lajos utca and the Inner Boulevard an underground passage serves pedestrian traffic. On the site of today's **Astoria Hotel** was the Köbler House where Sándor Petőfi resided in 1844. In the house at 9 Kossuth Lajos utca is the **Pioneer Department Store.** Opposite is **Pushkin Cinema.** Not far away from the Astoria Hotel is the **commission shop for period furniture.**

Through Kossuth Lajos utca, Felszabadulás tér and Szabadsajtó útja we come to Váci utca, the most famous street of the Inner City. On entering the street, to the left we find the **House of the Officers of the Hungarian People's Army.** A **commemorative tablet** on the wall of the building at the corner of Irányi utca tells us that in 1714, while crossing Pest on his ride from Constantinople to Stralsund, King Charles XII of Sweden stopped for a short rest in this house. The **baroque church** (No. 47) belonged formerly to the Order of Mary Ward Nuns. It was built by András *Mayerhoffer* between 1747 and 1749. In the Middle Ages a Dominican church stood on its site. The building at No. 62-64 is the so-called **New City Hall,** which now houses several departments of the Budapest City Council. It was erected in the period from 1870 to 1875, according to the designs of Imre *Steindl.* The staircase and the conference rooms are of special interest because they are decorated with frescoes by Károly *Lotz.* A little farther on Váci utca leads into Dimitrov tér.

And now coming from Szabadsajtó útja let us turn to the right. This part of Váci utca is the finest shopping street of Budapest. Here are shops of some of the best Hungarian dress designers, milliners, tailors and furriers, also book-shops, cosmetic shops and the largest folk-art shop in the town. In the daytime, with the people gazing at the shop-windows, it is difficult to make one's way through the crowded sidewalk of the street. A few steps from the corner of nearby Türr István utca is the **Bartók Béla Concert Hall.** The famous inn "The Seven Electors" was once located here. The building was erected by József *Hild* in 1840. At that time the famous balls of Pest were held here. The offices of the **Aeroflot** Soviet air transport company are located in the house at 4 Váci utca, and opposite are the offices of the **Sabena** Belgian airline company. As a matter of fact, Váci utca begins at attract-ive Vörösmarty tér. Here we find the terminus of the underground railway, the booking office of MALÉV (Hungarian Air Transport Company) at No. 5 and the of-fices of the **KLM** Dutch airline company and that of **CSA.** In the centre of the square stands the **statue of Mihály Vörösmarty,** one of the greatest of Hungarian poets. He was born in 1800 and died at the age of 55. His statue, a work of Ede *Kallós* and Ede *Telcs,* dates from 1908. In front of it stood the Haas Palace, which suffered such heavy damage in the Second World War that it had to be torn down. In former times this was also the site of the German theatre of Pest. Beethoven composed an overture in 1812 for its formal opening. At the corner of Vörös-marty tér and Vigadó utca is the **Ministry of Home Trade** with the central booking agency of **MALÉV** on the ground floor. The buses start from here to take passen-gers to Ferihegy Airport. The Aero Espresso has been opened in front of the booking office. Dorottya utca be-gins here and the offices of several foreign trade enter-prises and the **Institute for Cultural Relations** are located in this street which leads to Roosevelt tér. The **international sea and air transport booking of-fice of IBUSZ** as well as the **office for hotel reser-vations** are in the building at 5 Vörösmarty tér. The **Vörösmarty Café,** formerly **Gerbeaud,** a Budapest café and pastry shop of long standing, occupies the ground floor at No. 7. István Türr, Garibaldi's Hungarian general the builder of the Corinth Canal and initiator of the Panama Canal, lived in this house.

Right in front of this building is the **terminus of the underground railway,** which runs under Népköztársaság útja to the City Park. It was opened in 1896, and it was the first subway on the Continent. The length of its track is just over three and a half kilometres.

From the northeast corner of Vörösmarty tér we come to József nádor tér. Archduke Joseph (1776-1847), the seventh son of the Austrian Emperor and Hungarian King Leopold II (1790-1792), who was elected palatine of the country in 1796 and retained this dignity for the rest of his life, rendered great services to the country by remodelling the old city of Pest. His **statue** standing in the centre of the square is the work of Johann *Halbig*. It was unveiled in 1869. Several other monuments can also be seen in this square. The house at **No. 1** was built by József *Hild*, the house at **No. 5-6** was designed by Hugó *Máltás* (1852), the neoclassic building at **No. 7** by Lőrinc *Zofahl* (1833) and the house at **No. 12** was also erected according to designs by József *Hild* (1833). The building at No. 2-4 dates from the early part of this century and at present houses the **Ministry of Finance.** No. 7 is the **Museum of Modern History.** The **Central Propaganda Bureau of Museums** has its headquarters in this house.

Turning round the corner of the square to the right, through József Attila utca, we reach Engels tér. This is the largest park of the Inner City, and here we also find the **Central Bus Terminal** for long-distance buses. Nearby is the **statue of Mrs. Pál Veres** who pioneered education for Hungarian women. It was made of red Carrara marble by the sculptor György *Kiss*, and was unveiled in 1906. In 1929 the **statue** entitled **Folk Song** by János *Horvay* was erected in the park. The **fountain** of Miklós *Ybl*, which once stood in Calvin tér, has been set up here. During the war it was badly damaged, but since its restoration it has been the pride of the square. The statues of the fountain are the work of Leó *Feszler*.

Bécsi utca which leads into Engels tér, is another busy shopping street of the Inner City. In Harmincad utca, a short street that takes us back to Vörösmarty tér, is the **British Embassy** with its consular, commercial and press sections.

There are many architectural monuments in the old streets

of the southern part of the Inner City between Kossuth Lajos utca and Dimitrov tér. In Szerb utca, next to the university, stands an interesting old **Greek Orthodox Church,** enclosed by walls. In neighbouring Molnár utca and Veres Pálné utca a number of old houses are historical monuments. At the corner of little Kéményseprő utca and Március 15. tér is **Mátyás Pince** (Matthias Cellar), a restaurant with famous cuisine. The names of the streets in the northern part of the district between Váci utca and the Danube embankment such as Régiposta utca (Old Post Office Street), Párizsi utca (Paris Street), Galamb utca (Dove Street) and Fehérhajó utca (White Boat Street), remind us of old Pest.

2. TERÉZVÁROS

Terézváros extends over an area of only 2.75 sq. km., but with its inhabitants numbering over 90,000 it is one of the most densely populated districts of Budapest. It is a district of interesting contrasts. The residential area in and around Majakovszkij utca (formerly Király utca) has preserved the memory of the Pest of two hundred years ago.

The narrow streets, the former business houses with many courtyards recall the late 18th century. On the other hand, Terézváros has a thoroughfare which originated in the second half of the 19th century, in the era of large-scale and rapid town development. It is Népköztársaság útja (People's Republic Avenue) and it rivals those of any modern big city.

The part of District 6 which resembles most of a big city is the neighbourhood of Nagymező utca between Bajcsy-Zsilinszky út and Majakovszkij utca. This is the quarter of theatres, cinemas and amusement spots with musical programmes, also called the "Broadway of Pest", where entertainment ranges from operettas to literary satire, from cabarets with the usual sharp humour of Pest to night clubs with dancing.

Majakovszkij utca, which starts from the Inner Boulevard at Deák Ferenc tér, was, till the end of the 19th century, one of the most important thoroughfares of Pest. After the construction of today's Népköztársaság útja, for some time it retained its importance as a leading business street of the town, and it was only later that it had to cede this role to Rákóczi út. The atmosphere of the past hundred years is truly reflected also in the architectural monuments of Majakovszkij utca, since the buildings are mainly in the neoclassic style of the early 19th century.

Right at the beginning of the street (**No. 6**) stands a three-storied neoclassic house from 1830. Its arched doorway is surmounted by an interesting Mercury head. Noteworthy is the two-storied house at **No. 12**, which was built by Mihály *Pollack* in 1812. The three-storied house at **No. 16** also dates back to the 19th century. Its courtyards are worth seeing for their rich neo-Renaissance architecture. In the courtyard of the house at **No. 20** stands a graceful fountain made of red marble, with railings of fine iron work. This reminds us of the time when there was no water-conduit system in the district and the population was dependent on the wells in the courtyards or had to cart water from the Danube.

The houses at **Nos. 26, 32, 36** and **38** were built in neoclassic style, and were designed by József *Hofrichter*, in 1818. The fine railings of the latter's landings are worth noting. At the turn of the present century this building housed a famous inn. Another house in neoclassic style, **No. 44**, was built by Ágoston *Pollack* in 1839. A contemporary relief can be seen below the windows of the first floor.

On the other side of Majakovszkij utca we find, in addition to houses in neoclassic style, several buildings in romantic and late baroque styles. The wing of the single-storied house at **No. 9** facing the courtyard was built between 1800 and 1805. This is the only monument in Pest of the Louis XVI style palace architecture. The neoclassic building at **No. 11** was designed by Mihály *Pollack*, in 1812, as was the house at **No. 12** which borders on a building in romantic style (built in 1833). The house at **No. 25** was erected in 1810, in the early classicist style, and the house at **No. 27** was built about the year 1840 in neoclassic style. Over the doorway is a wide balcony with wrought-iron railings and with the inscription in German "Zur Stadt Pest" (to the city of Pest). The façade of the building was rebuilt about 1910. Among the numerous architectural monuments the corner building at **No. 47** is worth mentioning. This is the so-called Pekáry House, built in the neo-Gothic—romantic style by Ágoston *Pollack* in 1847-48 for the one-time city vice-captain, Imre Pekáry. The well-known writer Gyula Krúdy (1878-1933) lived in this house. At the corner of the house at **No. 49** stands a **statue of St. Theresa,** with a book in her hands, on the level of the first floor under a canopy. The neoclassic buildings at **Nos. 55** and **57** were designed by József *Hild,* the renowned architect of his time. In the courtyard of the house at **No. 99** built in the romantic style stands a fine neoclassic fountain.

After crossing Nagymező utca, Majakovszkij utca reaches Liszt Ferenc tér. Here in the building at No. 8 on the square is the **Academy of Music** named after Ferenc Liszt, where students receive their highest education in music, and where concerts for the public are held. The great hall of the academy has been the scene of concerts by some of the foremost artists of the world for generations. The building was erected between 1904 and 1907 under the direction of architects Flóris *Korb* and Kálmán *Giergl.* Over the main entrance stands a tall **statue of Ferenc Liszt,** the work of Alajos *Stróbl.* In the lobby, on the ground floor of the concert hall which seats 1,200 persons, there is a bronze **statue of Béla Bartók** by András *Beck.* A **museum** containing many of the personal effects of **Ferenc Liszt,** the founder and first president of the Academy of Music, is located on the second floor. The building houses a large **music library** consisting of some 50,000 volumes. The largest collection of scores in the country is also to be found here.

Beyond the Great Boulevard the character of Majakovszkij utca changes. Here there are fine apartment houses, three to four storeys high, built in the first decades of the 20th century, when the booming town practically "swallowed up" its ancient districts. At that time the houses of former Király utca were pulled down and more modern and larger apartment houses took their places. In the course of reconstruction the famous Pest shooting range was demolished, and now only the name of the square reminds us of the building that stood here at Lövölde tér (Shooting Range Square).

A broad avenue lined with magnificent trees leads from Lövölde tér to the City Park (Városliget). Gorkij fasor—although being the direct continuation of Majakovszkij utca—has a character entirely different from the previous section of this thoroughfare. Here we find villas in gardens enclosed by wrought-iron fences, like the eclectic house at **No. 12,** which was built by Emil *Unger* for György *Ráth,* the famous art collector and founder of the Budapest

Museum of Industrial Arts, in 1880. György Ráth bestowed his collections and his house on the state, and now the **Chinese Museum of the Eastern Asiatic Museum** is exhibited in the building. Close to the museum (No. 5) stands a **Calvinist church** which was designed by Aladár Árkay and built between 1911 and 1913. The **Lutheran church** (No. 17) built by Samu Petz, stands a little farther down the street. Its altarpiece is the work of Gyula Benczúr.

Gorkij fasor which extends to the City Park forms a part of the diplomatic quarter. In the villas of the avenue we find the **Polish Embassy** (No. 16) and the **Legation of Israel** (No. 37). The headquarters of the **Hungarian Writers' Association** is located in the building that forms the corner of Gorkij fasor and Bajza utca (18 Bajza utca). The Library of the Writers' Association is in the house at 10 Gorkij fasor, while No. 45 houses a public library, a branch establishment of the Gorky Library.

At the end of the avenue we find the headquarters of various trade unions: the **Union of Workers of the Food Industry** (No. 44), the **Miners' Union** (No. 46-48), **Building Workers' Union,** whose main façade is on Dózsa György út (No. 84/a) and the **Central Council of Trade Unions** (No. 84/b). The **Foundry Workers' Union** is in the same building. The house in nearby Bajza utca, No. 43, is the headquarters of the **Trade Union of the Workers of Local Industries** and the **Workers of Communal Management.**

Near Gorkij fasor, Dózsa György út broadens into a spacious and lengthy square. It was planned in 1949 as a site large enough to hold mass processions and parades on festive occasions. Proceeding on Dózsa György út we cross Hősök tere, and then the thoroughfare leads along the northwest wall of the Zoo and through an underground passage into District 13 of the capital.

The thoroughfare running along the northernmost border of Terézváros is Rudas László utca named after the Marxist philosopher László Rudas (1885-1950), who was a professor of economics at the Budapest University. The street begins at Bajcsy Zsilinszky út, crosses the Great Boulevard and runs parallel with the railway tracks of the Western Terminal as far as Dózsa György út. About midway a bridge, Élmunkás-híd, leading over the rail system of the railway terminal offers quick communication between Districts 6 and 13. Near the end of this street (No. 111), we come to the **Hospital of the Hungarian State Railways** and its **Central Clinic.**

Near the Great Boulevard, and running parallel with it, is Nagymező utca, a busy thoroughfare. It starts at Bajcsy Zsilinszky út as a narrow business street and broadens shortly before reaching Népköztársaság útja. The places of amusement along this street are the **Municipal Operetta Theatre** (Fővárosi Operettszínház) mentioned earlier (No. 6), the popular **Budapest Dance Palace** (No. 17) with variety shows, on the opposite side (No. 22-24) the **Petőfi Theatre,** the "home of musical comedy", and beyond Népköztársaság útja, the **Literary Stage** (Irodalmi Színpad, No. 11), which performs Hungarian and foreign works in prose and verse and entertaining literary caricatures. The **Ernst Museum** (8 Nagymező utca) was founded by the art collector Lajos *Ernst* at the beginning of this century as an exhibition hall for his paintings and graphics. Nowadays it is used for temporary exhibitions. The beautifully coloured windows above the entrance hall are by József **Rippl-Rónai,** the "Hungarian Nabi" (1861-1921). In the house at No. 1 is the **Bartók Béla High School of Music.** In connection with this part of Terézváros several other cultural institutions are worth noting which are only a few hundred yards away from Nagymező utca, but belong to this neighbourhood.

In Paulay Ede utca, named after a former manager of the National Theatre, is the **Thália Theatre** (No. 35). Beyond Népköztársaság útja, in Révay utca running parallel to Paulay Ede utca, is the popular cabaret **Variety Stage** (Vidám Színpad) at No. 18. The **State Opera House** (22 Népköztársaság útja) has been mentioned already among the sights of that street. A number of restaurants, pastry shops, cafés chantants, espressos contribute to the attractions of this part of Budapest.

A characteristic building of Terézváros is the **Parish Church** at the corner of Nagymező utca and Majakovszkij utca. It was built by Ferenc *Kasselik* between 1801 to 1811, originally in the Louis XVI style, and was remodelled later with baroque elements. Its spire is by Miklós *Ybl* (1871), the stone statue of St. Theresa at the façade is the work of Lőrinc *Dunaiszky* (1811). The high altar was designed by Mihály *Pollack,* the altarpiece by József Ágost *Schoefft,* and the organ comes from the Vienna workshop of Jakob *Deutschmann* (1834).

3. ERZSÉBETVÁROS

Erzsébetváros is District 7 of Budapest, bordered by Tanács körút, Majakovszkij utca with its continuation Gorkij fasor, Dózsa György út, Thököly út and Rákóczi út. This is the smallest, but at the same time the most densely populated district of the capital. Its most important streets running in west-east direction are Dohány utca, Wesselényi utca and Dob utca. The oblong district is almost bisected by the Great Boulevard. Among the other transversal by-streets Rottenbiller utca, Szövetség utca, Csengery utca and Akácfa utca are worth mentioning. The most important squares of the district are Rózsák tere, Izabella tér, Bethlen Gábor tér, Almásy tér and Klauzál tér.

In 1944 the inner area of Erzsébetváros suffered a dreadful fate when in the last months of the Second World War the German occupation forces and the Hungarian fascists crowded together tens of thousands of Jewish citizens in a ghetto they had marked out here.

This district, by the way, has three **synagogues.** The principal synagogue in Dohány utca has already been mentioned in connection with the Inner Boulevard. The second synagogue is located in Kazinczy utca, and the third in Rumbach Sebestyén utca, a street running parallel with Kazinczy utca. The latter synagogue was erected in romantic style by the Vienna architect Otto *Wagner* in 1872.

There are two noteworthy buildings in Dohány utca. The building at No. 42-44 houses a **revue theatre** which was formerly a cinema, and the **Continental Hotel.** Beyond the Great Boulevard the street broadens into a square, Rózsák tere. Here stands a neo-Gothic Catholic **Parish Church** with three aisles, which was built between 1893 and 1897 after the designs of Imre *Steindl*. The **statue of St. Elizabeth** of the Árpád dynasty of Hungary stands in the centre of the square. It is the work of József *Damkó*, and was erected in 1932.

In nearby Rottenbiller utca we find the **University of Veterinary Sciences.** Up to 1962 when this institution obtained the rank of a university, it was a college. Its area is bounded by several streets, the main entrance being in Landler Jenő utca. Rottenbiller utca obtained its name from Lipót Rottenbiller, a one-time mayor of the town of Pest. Near the university lies the **Playing-card Factory**

and Printing Shop as well as the **Dairy Enterprise of Erzsébetváros.**

No. 75-81 Dob utca is as large modern building with white walls, housing the **Ministry of Communications and Postal Services.** This building decorated with seven statues by Gábor *Boda* was erected in the late 1930s. On the ground floor is the **Philatelic Museum** with its world-famous stamp collection open to the public every day except Mondays.

In Izabella tér stands the **former Magyar Színház.** This theatre was opened in 1897. Since its reconstruction frescoes painted by Béla *Kádár* decorate the interior. At present it is the temporary home of the Petőfi Theatre. The statue **Dancing Girl** standing in the square is by Ferenc *Medgyessy.*

In Akácfa utca we find the headquarters of the **Municipal Tram Company,** the "Kis Pipa" (Little Pipe) restaurant, and the **Gorky Cinema.** In neighbouring Kertész utca is the **House of the Artists' Associations** (Művészeti Szövetségek Háza) with the **Artists' Fészek Club.** (Fészek means nest.)

4. JÓZSEFVÁROS

Józsefváros lies east of the centre of the town. The Inner Boulevard separates it from the Inner City. Rákóczi út forms its border in the north, and Üllői út in the south. In the inner area of Józsefváros we find a number of quiet little streets with old monuments, museums and cultural institutions. Further out we find bustling, busy streets and an important factory area.

This is District 8, a comparatively young part of the town. At the beginning of the 19th century straggling settlements, gardens and fields extended over the present-day streets. The greater part of the cottages built in the next few decades were destroyed by the icy floods of 1838. In the second half of the 19th century construction boomed in Józsefváros. Rákóczi út and Üllői út, the two main thoroughfares of Józsefváros, have already been described under their own heading. Noteworthy among the other main streets of the district are: Baross utca and its continuation, Kőbányai út, Népszínház utca and József körút, as well as Mező Imre út. Less important but just as busy are Bródy Sándor utca and József utca. There are also a few large squares in this district where parks have been laid out. We may mention Köztársaság tér (Republic Square), Teleki László tér, Kulich Gyula tér, the Museum Gardens extending round the National Museum, Kun Béla tér and in its neighbourhood the Orczy Gardens.

In Bródy Sándor utca (Sándor Bródy was a significant Hungarian writer and journalist, 1863-1924) the two-storied house at **No. 4** is interesting to note. This house in the neo-Renaissance style was erected in 1875-76, and was designed by Antal *Weber*. The **frescoes of the loggia** on the first floor are worth seeing: they were painted by Károly *Lotz*. The building at **No. 8** was built also in the neo-Renaissance style, by Miklós *Ybl*, in 1865-66. For several decades, from April 1866, the Hungarian House of Representatives held its sessions here (the Upper House at that time met in the National Museum near by). When the House of Parliament on the Danube embankment was completed, Parliament moved into the new palace. Today the Italian Cultural Institute resides in the "Old House of Representatives". The house at No. 16 is the centre of the Society for the Dissemination of Popular Scientific Information (Tudományos Ismeretterjesztő Társulat). In front of it (No. 5-7) lies a block of buildings which is now the headquarters of the **Hungarian Radio and Television.** From the studios in Bródy Sándor utca the programmes are transmitted to the wireless tower at Lakihegy, on Csepel Island, and are broadcast from there.

The one-storied building at **No. 15** bears the statue of a chimney-sweep at the level of the first floor. This reminds us that the house, which was built between 1851 and 1855, was the property of Mihály Devecis, master chimney-sweep of Pest.

In Puskin utca which crosses Bródy Sándor utca, the house at **No. 6** in neoclassic style is worth visiting. It was built about 1810, and it is noteworthy because between 1839 and 1846 it housed the first Hungarian pediatric hospital. The house at **No. 38** Puskin utca, in neo-Renaissance style, was built by Miklós *Ybl*. The buildings and gardens of the faculty of sciences of the Eötvös Loránd University face Puskin utca. South of Bródy Sándor utca, Puskin utca broadens into a square, which bears the name of Mihály Pollack, the classicist architect of the 19th century, the builder of the National Museum and many other significant buildings in Budapest. The building in the neo-Renaissance style at 3 Pollack Mihály tér was erected to the designs of Miklós *Ybl* between 1863 and 1865. The palace at **No. 8** in eclectic style was built by Alois *Baumgarten* about 1865. From 1946 to 1949 it was the residence of the president of the Hungarian Republic. At present it belongs to the block of buildings of the Radio. The palace at **No. 10** was also built to the designs of Miklós *Ybl* in 1862.

Beyond Pollack Mihály tér, at the corner of Múzeum utca, is a palace (26 Puskin utca) which houses the **Association of Hungarian Architects.** The club premises are decorated with interesting reliefs composed of ceramics by Margit *Kovács.*

In Múzeum utca (No. 11) is the central organisation of Hunga ian tourism, the **National Council of Tourism** (Országos Idegenforgalmi Tanács),the **Managing Committee of Lake Balaton** (Balatoni Intéző Bizottság), and No. 17 is the home of the **National Technical Library** (Országos Műszaki Könyvtár). The house at No. 7 is another building belonging to the **Society for the Dissemination of Popular Scientific Information** and the Kossuth Club, the club of Hungarian intellectuals. The one-storied building in the neo-baroque—rococo style, at 1 Szabó Ervin tér, was built as a private palace after the designs of Arthur *Meinig* in 1887. At the turn of the century it was converted into the **Municipal Library,** and in 1946 it was named after Ervin Szabó. The development of the library is closely connected with the name of Ervin Szabó, its first director. Today the library has branches all over Budapest and disposes of some 370,000 volumes. A little farther on, at 23-25 Baross utca, is the University of Medicine with its clinics, surgery and gynaecology. The next block of houses in Baross utca already touches on the Great Boulevard.

Crossing the Great Boulevard, Baross utca broadens into a square named Harminckettesek tere after the one-time 32nd Infantry Regiment, which was the local regiment of Budapest. The **memorial of the soldiers of the 32nd regiment** who died for their country in the First World War stands in the centre of the square. A short distance away lies Horváth Mihály tér, named after the outstanding historian and minister of education of the time of the 1848-49 War of Independence.

In the centre stands the twin-spired **Józseváros Parish Church** which was erected in 1797-98 to the designs of József *Tallherr*. The statue of St. Joseph, at the side of the church, is by Lőrinc *Dunaiszky*, the high altar is the work of József *Hild* (1835-1837), the figures are by Michael *Bauer*. The monumental painting over the high altar portraying the glorification of St. Joseph, as well as the altarpiece of the Madonna, are the work of the Viennese master Leopold *Kupelwieser*. In front of the church stands the **statue of Péter Pázmány** (1570-1737), archbishop of Esztergom, a leading personality of the Counter-Reformation period in Hungary.

The next square in Baross utca is named after Gyula Kulich (1914-1944), a martyr of the Hungarian young workers' movement. Then Baross utca leads into Orczy tér. Kőbányai út, which begins at the far end of the square, belongs to the industrial area of Józsefváros and leads to the boundaries of the district.

Running eastwards from the Great Boulevard is Népszínház utca, a busy street, which touches Köztársaság tér (Republic Square), the largest square of the capital (with an area of 66,000 sq. metres). On November 1, 1918, following the victory of the bourgeois revolution, a mass rally held in this square demanded the proclamation of the republic.

The **Erkel Theatre** with a seating capacity of 2,300 also lies in this square. It is the largest theatre of the capital. It was built according to the designs of Dezső *Jakab* and Géza *Márkus*, in 1911, and was reconstructed in 1961-62. The Erkel Theatre is under the management of the State Opera House and is the second opera house of Budapest. The **house of the Greater Budapest Party Committee** of the Hungarian Socialist Workers' Party is at No. 26-27. The tablet on the wall commemorates the communists who were murdered in the party building during the counter-revolution of October 1956. In Köztársaság tér stands a monument by Viktor *Kalló* to those murdered during the counter-revolution.

From Köztársaság tér we soon reach Mező Imre út, which connects the neighbourhood of the Eastern Railway Terminal with the industrial area of Józsefváros. (Imre Mező was an outstanding member of the communist movement who lost his life in the battles during the counter-revolution.) The building at No. 19/a houses the **Social Insurance Centre of the Trade Unions** (Szakszervezeti Társadalombiztosítási Központ), a 20-storied building, the tallest edifice in Budapest. Next to it stands the block of houses of the Koltói Anna Traumatology Clinic. (Anna

Koltói was a leading member of the Hungarian labour movement in the period between the two world wars.)

The opposite side of this street is occupied almost entirely by the **Kerepesi Cemetery**. It is the final resting place of leading figures of Hungarian history, writers, poets, artists and martyrs of the labour movement. The tallest structure in the Kerepesi Cemetery is the mausoleum where Lajos Kossuth rests. There is a fine view from its terrace over the whole cemetery and the surrounding city area.

Mező Imre út leads us on to Teleki László tér. (László Teleki, 1811-1861, a writer and political leader at the time of the 1848-49 War of Independence, ambassador of the Hungarian government in Paris.) At the eastern edge of the district, in Százados út, are the houses of the **artists' colony**. A short distance away, at Hungária körút, are the athletic grounds and football field of the well-known **sports club MTK**.

At 25 Illés utca lies the **botanical garden** of the University, the oldest of its kind, founded in 1771, in Hungary.

5. FERENCVÁROS

Scarcely a hundred years ago District 9 of the capital was still a suburb. About the turn of the century it was looked upon as the district of milk-vending women and gipsy musicians. At that time and early in this century Ferencváros was a romantic place. In the rows of single-storied houses lived thousands of cabmen and milkwomen, side by side with whole gipsy dynasties. Wherever good fortune may have thrown a Hungarian gipsy musician, he always came back from the big towns of the world to his home, Budapest-Ferencváros.

In the course of the last fifty years this part of the town underwent enormous development. Its northern limit is today's Tolbuhin körút. In the west it borders on the Danube, in the south the district of Kispest and to the east Üllői út mark its boundaries.

In Soroksári út we find the most important flour mills of the capital, the **Ferencváros Flour Mill** and the **Hulling Mill**. Here are the **Slaughter-house for Cattle**, the Meat Packing Plant and a short distance away the Salami Factory. The **Budapest Distillery, Leaven and Liquor Factory** is located in Ipar utca, and in Illatos út lies the

Hungária Chemical Works. Other important plants are the **Budapest Chocolate Factory** in Vágóhíd utca, the **Central Repair Shop of the Postal Services** in Gyáli út, and the **Budapest Slaughter-house for Pigs,** in Gubacsi út.

Attila József, the great Hungarian proletarian poet, was born in Gát utca, also in this district.

Among the churches of this district we may mention the **Ferencváros Parish Church** in Bakács tér. It was erected in the neo-Romanesque style by Miklós Ybl between 1861 and 1879. Károly Lotz, Alajos Stróbl and Mór Than participated in the decoration of the interior. Another noteworthy church is the **Church of Perpetual Adoration** in Üllői út.

Important institutes of public health are the **Institutes for Microbiology, Pathology, Pharmaceutics and Organic Chemistry,** as well as the **University Pharmacy** in Hőgyes Endre utca. This street bears the name of the founder of the Hungarian Pasteur Institute, who was a celebrated professor of medicine. At 14 Knézits utca we find the **Schoepf-Merei Hospital for Premature Infants.** The street is named after the founder of Hungarian pediatrics. In Tűzoltó utca are **Children's Clinic No. 2** and the **Institutes of Anatomy, Histology, Embryology, Surgical Anatomy and Surgery.**

Balázs Béla utca has been named after Béla Balázs, the writer, poet and film aesthetician. In this district there is also a street named after Sebestyén Tinódi Lantos, a minstrel and poet in the 16th century, another named after Ferenc Erkel, the great Hungarian composer of the 19th century, and one bearing the name of Pál Kinizsi, a hero of the Turkish wars in the 16th and 17th centuries.

In conclusion mention should be made of Ráday utca, which has the name of the poet and art collector Gedeon Ráday. The **Theological Academy of the Calvinist Church** with a library consisting of about 100,000 volumes is in this street.

THE DANUBE

For centuries the Danube has been one of the most important waterways of Europe. It is the second largest river of the Continent, and an important link between East and West. Towboats, old-time paddle-wheel steamers and up-to-date motorships, water buses, barges and recently also hydrofoils are in service on the river. The seagoing Danube ships that put out from Csepel, making for distant ports in the East, are built in the shipyards of Óbuda and Újpest. The panorama of both Danube embankments, the kaleidoscope of life in the quays, the landing places and the bridges, presents a fascinating picture.

1. QUAYS AND LANDING STAGES

Danubian navigation can look back upon a great history. The Romans already possessed a "Danubian fleet".

The construction of the Danube embankment was begun, in 1851, by the Danubian Steamship Company at the Pest abutment of the Suspension Bridge. The twelve-kilometre-long embankment on the Pest and Buda sides was built by state and municipal funds towards the end of the last century. These walls are very significant as far as flood control is concerned.

Owing to the ever growing traffic and frequent high water levels the quays with their narrow steps are hardly suitable any longer for the unloading and landing of deep-draught barges and freighters. At best they are still significant in handling passenger traffic, and the bollards on the bank serve mostly as seats for anglers and young lovers.

Long-distance passenger boats dock at the Central Landing Stage at Belgrád rakpart, or at Bem József rakpart, on the Buda side. Excursion boats put out from Vigadó tér and Bem József tér. Water buses start from Gellért tér nd call at the landing-places of Petőfi tér, Bem József tér, Margaret Island–Casino, Margaret Island–Grand Hotel, Liberty Baths and Újpest–Árpád utca. In addition there are also a number of ferryboats crossing the Danube.

Unloading from railway cars takes place below Boráros tér on the one-kilometre-long quay of the freight yard by the Danube.

Traffic on the Danube grew steadily and soon the inner quays proved inadequate to cope with all the river traffic. The construction of a large international port was begun which was also connected with the railway network. In 1928 the National Free Port laid out on the right bank of the northern tip of Csepel Island was opened to traffic. It has three large basins directly communicating with the Danube. These basins are 2.6 metres deep, even when the water level is at the lowest. The wharfs are equipped with the most up-to-date machinery. The Free Port and the coaling dock are situated next to the upper basin. Then follows the grain wharf whose twelve-storey silo can hold 35,000 tons. In the south lie the petrol and oil wharfs. The basins are deep enough for seagoing Danube ships to cut in. At the time when the Free Port was constructed, the Budapest–Ferencváros Port—3.5 kilometres long, 120 metres wide and 3.5 metres deep—was built on the left bank of the island, in the Soroksár arm of the Danube. Ships of over thousand tons can enter its basins. The wharf of the left bank is suitable for direct railway car loading. In addition to the big ports, certain industrial plants such as the Gas Works in Óbuda, the Rolling Mill in Lágymányos, the Iron and Steel Works in Csepel and the Freight Railway Yard of Budafok have smaller wharfs.

The largest winter harbour of the capital is in Újpest. Built in 1863 with a basin area of 30 to 35 hectares, it is 2.5 kilometres long and two metres deep, and can receive 500 ships. At the left side entrance is the well-equipped drydock repair shop of the Újpest shipyard. The shipyard in Óbuda has two winter harbours and a repair shop.

2. BRIDGES

Several bridges link Buda and Pest, thus welding the two parts into a single town. From one end of the capital to the other ships have to pass under seven bridges. The eighth—at the site of the one-time Elizabeth Bridge—is actually under construction.

In the winter of 1944-45 all the bridges were blown up by the encircled fascist troops retreating towards Buda. In scarcely ten years six bridges were rebuilt again. And today they are more beautiful, wider and stronger than before, and are certainly among the most interesting sights of the town.

The first bridge in the north is the **Újpest Railway Bridge.** It was constructed in the years 1893 to 1896 and was reconstructed in its present form between 1952 and 1955. This bridge connects the industrial area of Újpest with Óbuda, and provides direct transportation for the coal of the mining district of Dorog. It also links the capital with Esztergom by rail. The total length of this 12-metre-wide bridge is 898 metres. Its left-bank section crosses People's Island (Népsziget). The bridge consists of seven arches, each of them 93 metres long.

The **Árpád Bridge,** the youngest Danube bridge of Budapest, spans the river at the northern tip of Margaret Island. With its total length of 982 metres over water it is the longest bridge in Central Europe. Together with the approach ramps the bridge is almost two kilometres long, with a breadth of 13 metres. The pillars are built so that the width of the bridge can be doubled. The Árpád Bridge was opened on November 7, 1950. At this place the Romans had already built a bridge, its stone arches linked Aquincum with the fortifications of Contra-Aquincum on the opposite river bank.

The **Margaret Bridge** connects the south end of Margaret Island with both river banks. It was built according to the designs of the French engineer Ernest *Gouin*, and the construction was carried out by the French firm *Pattignole* between 1872 and 1876. From the middle of the bridge a 70-metre-long branch leads to the island. The Margaret Bridge was restored in 1946-48. Its total length is 637.5 metres, and it is 25 metres wide. It is one of the broadest of all Budapest Danube bridges, carrying the greatest volume of traffic, and connects the Great Boulevard with the Buda Boulevard.

Suspension Bridge

The oldest bridge of the capital is the **Széchenyi Suspension Bridge** (Lánchíd), which through the generations has already become a symbol of Budapest. The construction of this bridge at that time was the first step towards the unification of the three towns: Buda, Pest and Óbuda. At the suggestion of István Széchenyi the English engineer William Tierney *Clark* was commissioned with the construction, and the building was completed by Adam *Clark*. The building of the bridge lasted eleven years and was opened to traffic on November 30, 1849. After the Second World War the bridge was rebuilt in 1948-49. It is 380 metres long and 15.7 metres wide.

The birth of the Suspension Bridge has an interesting story. Apart from all kinds of difficulties of a financial and legal character that preceded the construction proper, the builders of the bridge had to surmount two major technical dangers. Both main chains of the bridge were assembled with great ceremony in the summer of 1848. On this occasion a large crowd gathered at the river banks and on a large raft erected especially for this purpose. Suddenly one of the huge chains broke and the spectators on the crowded raft had a narrow escape from the crashing girders. Before completion during the War of Independence the Austrian commander of Buda, General Hentzi, issued an order to blow the bridge up. Adam Clark, however, who learned of this attempt, flooded the chain chambers, so that the gunpowder could not be packed there. The bridge, therefore, did not suffer any major damage. This event, however, claimed three victims: the officer and two of his men who carried out the order perished in the blast.

Four huge stone lions ornament the abutments of the bridge, they are the work of János *Marschalkó*. On the Buda side the bridge leads to the foot of the steep hillside of Castle Hill (Vár-hegy), but its roadway continues through a tunnel under Vár-hegy.

The **Elizabeth Bridge** was the direct continuation of Rákóczi út and Kossuth Lajos utca. It was built between 1897 and 1903 and formed a single span of 290 metres over the river; it was a technical wonder of the time. Its total length was 331 metres and its breadth 18.2 metres. The new bridge which is under construction will be a kind of suspension bridge.

The **Liberty Bridge** carries the traffic of the Inner Boulevard over to Gellért tér in Buda. This bridge was designed by János *Feketeházy*, and ranks among the finest cantilever bridges in the world. It is 331 metres long and 20.1 metres wide. After the Second World War it was the first to be rebuilt and opened to traffic (August 20, 1946).

The southernmost highway bridge within the Budapest area is the **Petőfi Bridge,** which was built in 1933-37, and was reconstructed between 1950 and 52. It is 514 metres long and 25.6 metres wide.

Before the Danube leaves the area of the capital, it is spanned by another bridge, the **Southern Railway Bridge.** This bridge was built by János *Feketeházy* in 1873-76. It is 477.3 metres long and 14.1 metres wide. It carries the international railway line which connects western Europe with the countries of southeastern Europe. The bridge obtained its present form during reconstruction between 1948 and 1953.

3. MARGARET ISLAND

Margaret Island (Margitsziget) is the "park" of Budapest. It covers an area of about a hundred hectares. It is about 2.5 kilometres long and at its broadest point it measures 500 metres. Its shape reminds one of a ship. The island is about 15,000 years old. In prehistoric times the Danube had approximately the same river bed it has today. Having liberated itself from the grip of the mountains in the Danube Bend, in the north of Hungary near Visegrád, the river slowed down its course and began to form shoals and islands with its alluvial deposits. Margaret Island, too, came about in this manner.

Originally it consisted of three, possibly four, shoals and later formed three or four islets. In the north was Bath Island, then Margaret Island proper, which then was called the "Island of Rabbits", and in the south was Painter's Island. The river current then constantly eroded the northern tips of the islands, washing them away, and depositing silt and gravel in the south. In the course of many thousands of years the island thus "wandered" slowly southwards, until it was stopped around the middle of the last century when the banks were fortified with walls.

At flood time the Danube inundated the islands and when the water receded and left its fertile mud behind, this sediment, rich in organic matter, formed excellent soil for vegetation, which then created the basic conditions for animal life.

The history of the island is about as old as the history of the town itself, which means about 2,000 years. Archaeological discoveries clearly show that at the time of the Romans a watch-tower stood on the island, forming part of the chain of fortifications that surrounded Aquincum. Research workers found stones in the area with inscriptions from which they concluded that here, on the island, a Roman patrician possessed a villa.

During excavations on the island the foundation walls of an 11th-century Gothic chapel were discovered. According to the songs of a French minstrel towards the end of the 12th century, the island was the residence of King Imre (Emerich, 1196-1204).

At the end of the 12th century the knights of St. John had a fortified monastery on the island. Early in the 13th century Ladomér, Archbishop of Esztergom, built a palace at

its northern end. In 1251, King Béla IV founded a Dominican convent where his daughter, the pious Princess Margaret, was educated. The island is named after her. The
Franciscans began the building of a church and a monastery in the central part of the island in 1272. Except for
the part which continued to belong to the royal game reserve—hence the later denomination "Island of Rabbits"
—the rest of the island remained for a long time the property of holy orders.

In the first half of the 16th century the monks and nuns
fled the island at the news of the approaching Turks, and
after the surrender of Buda (1541) the Turks used it for
military purposes. During the Turkish occupation which
lasted for 145 years nobody did anything about the renovation of the buildings. Finally, only ruins remained and
for centuries the island was desolated. No earlier than the
18th century did it regain significance, when the Hapsburg
archdukes built a castle and created a vast park close by
the ruins of the Franciscan monastery. At first it was private property, but after 1840 it was also opened to the
public. Later an inn and a bathing establishment were
added.

The present form of the island dates back to 1851, when
the upper Bath Island was dredged away and Margaret
Island proper was linked to Painter's Island by a stone
dyke. The engineer Vilmos *Zsigmondy* bored the first artesian wells in 1867, which yielded medicinal waters 43°C
in temperature. In 1870 the Margaret Medicinal Baths
were erected according to the plans of Miklós *Ybl.* Then
followed the Grand Hotel (Nagyszálló) and the beer garden, and in 1871 a horse tramway was put into service.
The Danube Steamship Company began to operate ferryboats to improve traffic, and in 1901 a direct line was
established with the mainland through the Margaret
Bridge.

After the First World War the island was turned into a
centre for tourists. The open-air theatre of the State Opera
House, the Palatinus Baths, and the National Sport Swimming Pool were built. A new artesian spring (No. 2) yields
water 70°C in temperature, and the water of spring No. 3
comes up at 43°C. Club houses and boat-houses as well as
luxurious amusement places were established. In the Second World War the island was destroyed almost completely. A great part of the buildings was demolished by shells,
and the trees and plants suffered much damage. After the

liberation of the capital everything was soon rebuilt, and newer and finer establishments helped Margaret Island to develop at an unprecedented pace. The island has grown into the loveliest recreation park of the capital.

The approach ramps of the Árpád Bridge at the northern tip, and of the Margaret Bridge at the southern tip, connect the outer and inner boulevards of the capital with a motor road that runs the length of the island. A bus starting from the Comedy Theatre (Vígszínház) on Szent István körút passes along this road, linking the Grand Hotel with the city. In addition, the interior of the island can be reached by water buses from both the Pest and Buda embankments.

If we take a walk from the Margaret Bridge to the island on our left we see the **boat-house of the Ministry of Communication and Postal Services.** Close by is the **Pioneers' Stadium** which was designed by Tivadar *Hübner*, in 1942, and reconstructed and enlarged in 1947. Its grandstand can seat 3,000. A football field, athletics track, handball, volleyball and basketball grounds, gymnasiums and tennis courts, bathing facilities and club rooms are at the disposal of the pioneers, members of a youth organisation.

To the right of the road, scarcely visible under concrete roofs, are the underground **engine houses of the wells** of the Municipal Waterworks. They pump water into the main conduits on the Pest side through pipes with a cross section of two metres located 28 metres deep.

At the end of the branch of the Margaret Bridge leading to the island a large circular flower bed greets the visitor. It resembles a round Persian carpet woven of colourful flowers. In the centre a monumental fountain spouts water high into the sky. In the evenings sixty coloured floodlights illuminate the fountain.

On the left side we see a red brick structure half hidden by trees. Here again we find an engine house of the water works. Artesian spring No. 2—the **Magda Spring**—sends up its medicinal water from a depth of 310 metres and the pumps pass it on into the National Sport Swimming Pool, into the gardens of the Municipal Horticultural Enterprise and into the central heating systems and bathrooms of the nearbly blocks of flats on the Pest and Buda embankments.

On the right side of the road a gravel walk takes us to the **Casino Restaurant and Night Club,** and in the other direction the motor road as well as a walk turn towards the National Sport Swimming Pool. The Casino is the biggest catering establishment on the island with room for 3,500 guests. It was built over the foundation walls of the ancient fortified monastery of the knights of St. John to the designs of Miklós *Ybl*, in 1870, and since that time it has been altered and modernised several times.

The broad promenade passing by the garden premises ends at the ferry-boat and water-bus landing stage on the bank facing the Pest side.

The **National Sport Swimming Pool** (Nemzeti Sportuszoda) is the stronghold of Hungarian competitive swimming. It was built in 1931 by Alfréd *Hajós*, Hungarian swimming champion at the first Modern Olympic Games held in Athens in 1896. A marble tablet in the entrance hall records the names of the Hungarian Olympic swimming champions. In summer and winter alike training goes on in six indoor and outdoor pools. There are dressing rooms for 4,000 people. The indoor stadium has a seating capacity of 2,500 and the grandstands of the outdoor pool can accommodate 6,000 spectators.

Behind the National Sport Swimming Pool, in a small building, the water of Margaret Spring No. 1, the popular aerated "Crystal water", is bottled by a plant belonging to the Municipal Soda Water Factory.

A children's playground comes next, and then a shaded narrow walk leads us to the **Vörösmarty Open-air Cinema** which can seat 2,500. To the right of the road near the bus stop are the **ruins of the Franciscan church** dating from the 13th century. The front wall, in comparatively good repair, and the entrance face the motor road. On the triangular pediment the door leading to the choir is still visible, and next to it is a Gothic rose window. The vestiges of the spire and spiral staircase on the northern side leading to the choir and the remains of a few consoles appear before the eye.

Leaving the ruins behind, on the left side of the road, we come up to the entrance of the **Palatinus Medicinal and Open-air Baths.** The "Female Nude" standing in front of the colonnade of the main building is the work of Emile *Guillaume*, a French sculptor. The open-air bath built in 1937 was designed by István *Janáki*. It lies in a park covering some 70,000 sq. metres and is equipped with the most up-to-date facilities. The dressing rooms can accommodate 15,000 bathers. The four pools with waters of various temperatures and serving different purposes are laid out amidst wide grassy plots. The large swimming pool and another with artificial waves are fed by water from the Margaret Spring, cooled down to 24°C. The shallow bathing pool in a covered colonnaded hall receives its medicinal water from Spring No. 3, cooled down to 36°C. This water is mildly sulphurous, containing also calcium hydrocarbonate.

In front of the Palatinus Baths, on the other side of the motor road, lies the island's extensive **flower garden**, more than a hectare in area. From early spring till late autumn visitors can delight in the fragrance and rich colours of the many hundred varieties of flowers. Here we come to the fascinating rose garden with its several thousand rose trees and about 25,000 rose bushes displaying over two hundred varieties.

Beyond the Palatinus Baths a promenade leads towards the Buda river bank. A short distance from here we find the **Dózsa Tennis Stadium**. The stands can seat 5,500 spectators. Not far from here is the **Petőfi Sándor Pioneer Camp**, the summer sport paradise of Budapest schoolchildren.

Here the road divides: one branch leads to the Árpád Bridge, the other to the rock garden and the "musical well" and ends at the northern tip of the island, at the **clay-pigeon shooting grounds.** The hot water of the Margaret Spring rushes down from the artificial rocks several metres high in the middle of the garden. The rocky walls in the garden are coated with a layer of glittering minerals and their surface is covered with algae. The water splashes down into a little **pond** at the foot of the rocks. Water lilies with dark green foliage float on the surface of the pond, while schools of goldfish with pale yellow, silvery, red and black spots frisk about under them.

The narrow little stream follows a meandering course to a second pond dotted with little islets. A tiny Japanese bridge leads over the stream, hence its name: Japanese Garden. Rare plants and flowers from distant countries grow in the artificial rock garden round the two ponds. The charming statue "Boy Catching Crayfish" is the work of Miklós *Ligeti*.

A few steps further, beyond the rock garden, a little domed structure resting on six columns catches our eyes: **the musical well.** Its original stood at one time in the main square of the town of Marosvásárhely (now Tîrgu

151

Musical Well on Margaret Island

Mureş, Rumania) and was designed by a Transylvanian artist, Péter *Bodor*, in 1820. This copy on the island was made in 1936. It was destroyed in the Second World War and rebuilt in 1954. The water organ with its special mechanism, however, is not in working order at present.

So we have reached the northern end of the island and are in front of the towering concrete pillars of the Árpád Bridge. From both sides an approach road and a footpath lead up to the bridge, and one can walk to the tip of the island through a tunnel. A clay-pigeon shooting ground has been formed here.

Coming back to the bifurcation of the motor road and walking in the direction of the bank facing Pest we encounter a spacious square with tall plane trees and beautiful flower beds. Here we find the bus terminus, a taxi stand, the landing stage of the ferry boat and, most important, the **Grand Hotel.**

Since its construction in 1872 by Miklós *Ybl*, this hotel has been altered and enlarged four times. With its 140 rooms and 14 apartments, it is one of the finest hotels of the capital. Thermal water heats the building and supplies it with hot water. The hotel is famous for its Hungarian and international cuisine. The garden terrace, the most fashionable in Budapest, can accommodate 2,500 guests. In front of the Grand Hotel stood the medicinal bathing establishment, mentioned earlier, which had been designed by Miklós *Ybl*. It suffered such heavy damage in the Second World War that it had to be torn down.

If we follow the footpath on our way back we come to the **water tower.** This tower, more than twelve stories high, supplies the island with drinking water, independently from the water system of the capital. It can be seen from any point of the island. Its designer was Szilárd *Zielinszky* and it was erected in 1911.

Close by, at the foot of the water tower, is the **Open-air Theatre of the State Opera House,** built to the designs of Péter *Kaffka* in 1921, and rebuilt by István *Kotsis* in 1937. For many years following the Second World War it was the scene of excellent operatic performances in the summer months. It is now under reconstruction.

A few steps away from the water tower towards the Pest side is the area of the ancient monuments of the island. Here stands the reconstructed **St. Michael Chapel** dating from the 12th century. Its foundation walls were unearthed in 1923. Under the floor of the interior of the chapel the foundation walls of a yet older chapel were discovered belonging in all probability to the 11th century. The ruins of the **monastery of the provostship** close by have been uncovered only in part. The reconstruction of the spire was carried out in 1931-32, according to the plans of Kálmán *Lux*. The oldest church bell of Hungary, originating from the 15th century, which was found among the roots of a decaying tree nearby in 1914, hangs in the belfry of the chapel. In the spacious garden of ruins extending to the south lie the remains of the **Dominican Church** and the convent dating from the Middle Ages. In those days the order of the Dominican monks was a powerful ecclesiastic institution in Hungary. It possessed enormous landed estates all over the country, especially in the region of Pest and Buda, and wielded considerable political influence. The monks founded the monastery on Margaret Island after the Mongol invasion of the year 1241.

In 1251, King Béla IV entrusted the Dominican nuns with the education of his nine-year-old daughter, Margaret. Soon afterwards the young princess took the veil and retired completely from secular life. Her virtue and gentle personality were already common talk in her lifetime, and when she died, at the age of 29, many legends about her life were circulated.

These ruins were discovered after the great floods of Pest in 1838. In the course of the excavation of the church the rich tomb of a prince was found under the sanctuary. With him were buried a costly gold crown with gems and a mantle of fine texture, woven with gold. Pearls, rings, and gold coins had been placed beside the body. First it was thought to be the sepulchre of the royal princess, but later it was established that this was the resting place of King Stephen V. Further excavations in 1914 opened up the sacristy south of the axis of the church, the chapter house, several passages, the kitchen, as well as the foundation walls of the cloisters surrounding the square monastery courtyard. The parts of the building round the courtyard were discovered in 1923. Further excavations in 1937 revealed an additional chapel to the west, and south of it the remains of the monastery and the arcades leading to it. In 1958 the excavations were continued and the brick floor of the chapter house, a section of the water conduits of the monastery and the remains of an interesting central heating system under the flooring of the refectory were unearthed. Bronze fittings and mounts like those used for book corners dating from the 15th century, Venetian glass jars and glazed earthenware vessels were brought to light. Systematic research work will continue and further interesting finds are expected.

The road leads southwards past the ruins to a clearing, where **busts** of two great poets stand: **of János Arany,** by Alajos *Stróbl,* dating from 1912, and **of Mihály Tompa** which was erected in 1940. On our way lies the **Rózsakert** (Rose Garden) **restaurant.** Beyond the summer restaurant, in an enclosure surrounded by a wire fence, we see **groups of deer, peafowl and pheasants.**

As we walk on the trees gradually thin out. We reach a clearing with a fountain in the middle, whose bronze figures represent the **"Two Chums":** a child with a dog, by Alice *Gosztonyi.*

And thus we come back to our starting point, to the Casino, and our walk has come to an end. From the huge round flower bed to the Grand Hotel, open microbuses take the visitors round the island, so that one may enjoy the sights while taking a comfortable ride.

4. CSEPEL

Another large island of Budapest is Csepel. Here in District 21 lies the heavy industry of the capital. Strictly speaking, only the northern part (over 26 sq. km.) of the 47-kilometre-long island belongs to the area of Budapest. This alone is an extensive district, with 60,000 inhabitants. It lives almost an independent life, and together with the Csepel Iron and Steel Works, it constitutes one of the most important industrial centres of Hungary.

Csepel was not incorporated in the capital until 1950. Before that it was a separate, independent suburb, lagging behind Budapest in every respect. Since its incorporation this district has developed immensely by building new housing estates, a road system and public utilities, and a whole series of cultural and health institutions. Gradually it grew into an organic part of the Hungarian capital.

The island looks back on a long history. The cemeteries discovered here, which date from the bronze and copper ages, show clearly that the island was inhabited in prehistoric times. Finds from the Roman period give ample evidence of construction by the one-time masters of Pannonia. After the conquest of the country by the Magyars, the leading tribe of chieftain Árpád took possession of the island which later on passed into the possession of the queens.

During the Turkish occupation in the 16th and 17th centuries, Csepel Island became entirely bare of inhabitants. No sooner than at the end of the 17th and the early 18th century was the island populated again with German and Serbian settlers. The industrialisation of this agricultural area began in the 1880s with the founding of the plants and enterprises of Manfréd Weiss. In spite of this the settlement retained its former rural character with its single-storied houses, until the township was incorporated in the capital city.

Csepel can be reached from the inner districts of Budapest in ten minutes by the fast electric railway built between 1949 and 1951, starting from Boráros tér. In addition, an express highway, bus lines and also ferry boats carry traffic to Csepel.

On the way to Csepel some of the interesting sights are the Central Market Hall of Budapest, located on the Danube embankment, the Kvassay sluice gate to close off the western Danube branch, and the National Free Port, an important central European junction for goods traffic. Apart from handling import and export traffic—as a free port—it is also an important transit station for East-West goods exchange. Beyond the tanks of the oil refinery the streets of Csepel come into view.

The main thoroughfares of Csepel take the form of a reversed Y. The northern stem of the Y is the Main Port Street and its continuation, Kossuth Lajos utca, leading straight south from the Danube bridge. Rákóczi út, one of the two southern branches, runs in the southwestern, and Kalamár József út in the southeastern direction. Kossuth Lajos utca takes us into the garden city. In Tanácsház tér (Town Hall Square) stands a **war memorial** set up after the First World War by Jenő *Homonnay*, and a **statue of Sándor Petőfi** by Sándor *Mikus*.

Modern apartment houses surround Béke tér (Peace Square). Close by we find one of the most up-to-date sports stadiums of the capital.

Between the residential area and the Danube extends one of Hungary's largest industrial estates, the Csepel Iron and Steel Works.

In 1882, Manfréd Weiss erected a cannery here. At the turn of the century he established an arms and ammunition factory. The large-scale armament of the Austro-Hungarian Monarchy and the First World War guaranteed him a practically unlimited market. The enterprise of Manfréd Weiss gradually grew into a powerful concern. In addition to war materials "WM" manufactured everything that was in line with the iron industry, "from horseshoenails to threshing machines". At that time the labour movement in this vast plant developed very swiftly. In 1919 the workers of the Csepel concern were first to take a stand in favour of proclaiming the Hungarian Republic of Councils. The first workers' battalion against the interventionist troops was formed among the Csepel workers. Since that time this area has been called "Red Csepel" in the Hungarian labour movement.

Between the two world wars production in the Csepel factories grew even more ramified. The manufacture of bicycles, motorcycles, sewing machines and precision instruments was begun. The products of the plant were exported to all parts of the world. In the course of the Second World War production was concentrated mainly on the manufacture of war materials. Towards the end of the war the nazis tried to dismantle the plant and carry away machinery and equipment, yet the workers of Csepel — the most militant of whom actually took part in guerilla battles—succeeded in preventing the destruction of the great plant.

After the liberation, in October 1946, the Iron Works of Csepel was placed under state supervision, and in December of the same year it was taken over by the state for good. Since that time life has changed radically in the Csepel Iron and Steel Works. With the setting up of new factory units (precision metallurgy, a rolling mill, a tube factory and transformer factory, etc.) the enterprise has been systematically expanded. At the same time by rational specialisation the former dissipation of productive resources has been eliminated. Many specialists are trained in various branches. Machine-tools, pumps, motorcycles and transformers of the Csepel plant are exported today to numerous countries of the world. The Csepel Iron and Steel Works produces 300,000 tons of steel, 200,000 bicycles, and close to 50,000 sewing machines a year. The Csepel open-hearth furnace yields 14 to 15 per cent, and the rolling mill 17 per cent of the total output of their respective branches of production in Hungary.

THE MAIN THOROUGHFARES
OF THE BUDA SIDE

The Buda side has the same system of avenues and boulevards as the Pest side, although it may not seem to
come out in such sharp relief as on the Pest side.

1. FRANKEL LEÓ ÚT

Frankel Leó út begins at the inner boulevard of Buda, at
Margaret Bridge, and runs to Zsigmond tér parallel with
the Danube, then continuing its course as Bécsi út (Vienna
Road) through Korvin Ottó út and Szentendrei út it
leads through the oldest parts of Buda. Via Óbuda and
Aquincum it reaches Római-part (Roman Beach), Budapest's largest resort centre along the Danube river.
This street bears the name of Leó Frankel (1844-1896),
a leading figure of the Hungarian and international labour
movements. Born in Óbuda, he joined the labour movement already as a youth. For his participation in organ-
ising and leading the 1871 Paris Commune he was sen-
tenced to death, but he managed to escape. He also
played an important role in the developing working-class
movement of Hungary.
Frankel Leó út might well have been named the "street
of medicinal baths". To the left of the street the most
abundant and warmest springs of the capital gush forth
at the foot of steep Joseph Hill (József-hegy). Their curative
power has been known for over two thousand years. The
Romans, the Hungarian religious orders, the Turkish pa-
shas had medicinal baths here. The street passes just over
the springs and this also determined its character. There
is hardly anything besides baths, hospitals and swimming
pools in this street.
At the beginning of the street, in the house at No. 17,

is the **Central Hospital and Clinic of the National Institute for Rheumatism and Balneology,** a hospital for the treatment of rheumatic and other diseases of the locomotive organs. Apart from balneotherapeutic treatments up-to-date electrotherapeutic installations are also at the disposal of the patients. This side of the road as far as Zsigmond tér is lined with the buildings of the Lukács and Császár Baths, and the Császár Swimming Pool.

The baths and hospitals are fed by 24 medicinal springs which yield 15 million litres of water a day at temperatures ranging from 25° to 64°C. The spring waters contain natural sulphur, calcium and magnesium hydrocarbonate. At the time of the Turkish occupation the finest bath here was that of Sokoli Mustafa Pasha. Remains of it are still visible in the Császár Baths.

The main building of the **Lukács Baths** was erected in 1924, over the walls and parts of buildings dating from the last century. The neoclassic building of the **Császár Baths** was erected to the designs of architect József *Hild*, in 1806, and in 1841-44 it was enlarged. The inner court with its Doric columns is an interesting sight. Thousands of people come here every year seeking cure for their ailments. All sections of the baths, thermal, steam, mud and individual baths, provide the most up-to-date medicinal and technical treatments. Both swimming pools of the Lukács Baths are very popular, they are used even in winter. Centrally heated corridors lead from the dressing rooms to the warm-water pools, which have a temperature of 25°C.

A **sanatorium** with 16 rooms is available to guests who come here for balneotherapeutic treatment. The reservation of rooms is handled by IBUSZ. The baths are indicated for patients suffering from rheumatic ailments of the joints, muscular rheumatism, neuralgia, neuritis, chronic exudations, as well as for the after-treatment of lesions, paralysis, atrophy, etc. In a separate building of the establishment, under the administration of the National Institute for Rheumatism and Balneology, there is a section for bed-patients and a hospital for rheumatism.

The drinking waters in the well room have a beneficial effect on intestinal activity, in cases of gastric catarrh, hyperacidity, gastric ulcer, kidney- and gallstones.

Both outdoor swimming pools of the Császár Baths are supplied with the water of medicinal springs, which is cooled down by a special installation. In this way it is possible for sportsmen to participate in swimming and water-polo training in the outdoor pools even in winter. In front of the two bathing establishments, on the left side of the street, is the **Mill Pond** (Malomtó) with its Egyptian lotus flowers and other subtropical plants. The pond obtained its name in the Turkish times when the water of its abundant springs was used to run the grain and gunpowder mills. At the southern end of the pond we find the remains of a domed **Turkish bath** which was built in the 16th century on the orders of Veli Bey. There is a modern snack bar at the northern end.

Among the buildings of this street it is worth mentioning the house at **No. 50-52,** another at No. 62 where the **Heine-Medin hospital for the treatment of infantile paralysis** is located, **St. Stephen Chapel** (No. 54) and also the houses at **Nos. 58** and **92** built in romantic and neoclassic styles respectively.

2. SZILÁGYI ERZSÉBET FASOR

This busy street which runs from Moszkva tér (Moscow Square), with a fine row of three to six-storied buildings on the right side, and a spacious park on the left side, bears the name of King Matthias Corvinus's mother. At the beginning of this row of houses we find the Fasor Pastry Shop (No. 13) and the Városmajor Restaurant (No. 33). The park called **Városmajor,** with its well-kept walks, lawns, children's playgrounds and an open-air stage, covers an area of about 100,000 sq. metres, and is one of the loveliest of its kind in Budapest.

In 1724, Heinrich Josef *Daun*, the commander of Buda, established a farm and a garden round it, hence its name (city farm). He later sold it to the council of Buda. For a long time the meadow around Daun's farm was called "Ecce Homo Meadow", named after a statue dating from the 18th century, which still stands in front of the János Hospital close by. At present a **statue of Beethoven** by János *Horvay* (1932), and the **statue of the "Tyrolese Sharpshooter"** by Zsigmond *Kisfaludi Strobl* (1940), ornament the park. Towards the end of the 18th century trees were planted in this area, and for a time it was the botanical garden of the University.

Cultural and literary traditions are also attached to Városmajor. The house at **No. 44** in neighbouring Városmajor utca was once the residence of Miklós Barabás, a noted portrait painter of the last century. The building at No. 47/b houses the **private museum** of Loránd *Basch*, now under state protection. The museum contains Greek and Roman pottery, objects of glass, clay and bronze figures, Pannonian jewellery, an archaeological collection originating from the Roman town of Brigetio, a collection of oil lamps and keys from the Roman period up to the 18th century, a collection of wooden statuettes, dating from the Middle Ages, Anatolian carpets from the 17th and 18th centuries, furniture from the Renaissance period and paintings of Hungarian and Dutch masters.

The house at No. 68 is a **Surgical Clinic.** Towards the west the park ends at the **terminus of the cogwheel railway,** which leads up to Liberty Hill (Szabadság-hegy) and Széchenyi Hill (Széchenyi-hegy).

Near the bifurcation of Szilágyi Erzsébet fasor and Kútvölgyi út is the **János Hospital,** the largest hospital of Budapest, which was founded in 1895. Not far from here, at 4 Kútvölgyi út, there is the eight-storied building of the **Central State Hospital** (Központi Állami Kórház).

3. VÖRÖSHADSEREG ÚTJA

At the point where the tram lines from Moszkva tér divide into two, the Szilágyi Erzsébet fasor also comes to an end. Its right-side continuation is Vöröshadsereg útja (Avenue of the Red Army), which leads over Lipótmező (Leopold's Meadow) in a northwestern direction to Hűvösvölgy (Cool Valley), and to a residential area. In documents from the 14th and 15th centuries present-day Lipótmező and Vadaskert (Game Garden) are mentioned by the name of Nyék. Near the one-time game reserve of the village of Nyék (78 Vöröshadsereg útja) towards the end of the 15th century there stood the famous hunting castle of King Matthias, whose foundation walls were unearthed in 1931-32. The game reserve was surrounded by a stone wall, parts of which are still visible. In the course of archaeological excavations the foundations of the old village church of Nyék were also discovered 150 metres north of the hunting seat.

In Vöröshadsereg útja there are several fine catering establishments. The Veronika Restaurant (No. 34) is one of the most delightful places in the Buda hills for a pleasant dinner. The **Budagyöngye** (Pearl of Buda) Garden Restaurant next door (No. 36-38) is also very popular. In the house at 132 Vöröshadsereg útja is the Hársfa (Linden Tree) Inn. Thus we reach the terminus of the tram and bus lines. Here, to the right, is the popular **Hűvösvölgyi Népkert** (Popular Garden), a favourite place of hikers, and to the left we find the **terminus of the Pioneer Railway** (Úttörővasút).

Hűvösvölgy has for generations been a much frequented excursion point. Groups of workers belonging to the underground labour movement camouflaged as various tourist associations held meetings in the large field of Hűvösvölgy called **Nagyrét** (Large Meadow), a short distance away from the terminus. To perpetuate the memory of these meetings the workers of the building industry still hold their traditional yearly celebrations there.

Kis Ördögárok (Little Devil's Ditch) crosses this spacious field, which is now an amusement park with all sorts of attractions for the youngsters, where games, sideshows, shooting galleries and merry-go-rounds can be found. A permanent **Pioneers' Camp** has been established near by.

4. BUDAKESZI ÚT

The rather steep, 5.5-kilometre-long road, which starts at the upper end of Szilágyi Erzsébet fasor and runs to the left, to the village of Budakeszi, takes its name from this village. Right at the beginning, at No. 5, there is a pastry shop, **Youth Confectionery,** in front of which Endre Ságvári, a leader of the Hungarian communist youth organisation met a hero's death on July 27, 1944.

This road reaches its highest point (350 metres above sea level) at **Ságvári Liget** (Grove). This little hill saddle on Great Linden Tree Hill (Nagyhárs-hegy) is a very popular spot in the Buda mountains, much favoured by hikers. At the **stations of the Pioneer Railway** which crosses the street here, there is a restaurant with a pleasant espresso.

5. ALKOTÁS UTCA

In front of the **Southern Railway Terminal** at Magyar Jakobinusok tere (Square of the Hungarian Jacobins) where Krisztina körút (Christina Boulevard) turns to the southeast, along the Vérmező (Meadow of Blood), a long and almost straight thoroughfare branches off from the line of the inner boulevard of Buda. It forms the continuation of the outer Buda boulevard, which begins at the Margaret Bridge, running south between the eastern slopes of Liberty Hill (Szabadság-hegy) and Sun Hill (Nap-hegy). This is Alkotás utca.

In neighbouring Márvány utca (Marble Street) is the **Kis Royal Restaurant** (No. 19), one of the most attractive places in Buda.

Not far from the corner of Márvány utca, on the left side of Alkotás utca, is the **College of Physical Education**. It was founded in 1900 as a gymnastics school and has since acquired international fame for modernising the teaching of Hungarian physical culture and sports.

The house at No. 48 is the **Sport Hospital** and the **Institute of Physical Education and Sport Hygiene**. Near Csörsz utca the factory buildings of the **Hungarian Optical Works** (Magyar Optikai Művek), founded in 1886, come into view. A short distance from here, alongside the railway line connecting the Southern Railway Terminal with the Kelenföld Railway Station, Alkotás utca splits into two forming Villányi út to the left, and Budaörsi út to the right. The latter joins the highway leading to Lake Balaton.

6. VILLÁNYI ÚT AND MÓRICZ ZSIGMOND KÖRTÉR

The third section of the Buda boulevard starts at the bifurcation of Budaörsi út and ends at Móricz Zsigmond körtér (Circus). Villányi út leads through an area of villas which came into existence between 1920 and 1930.

At the corner of Budaörsi út we find the **Víg hajós** (Merry Seaman) nightclub. No. 67 houses the **Institute of Kinesthetic Therapy**.

The new housing estate in Villányi út was built gradually between 1954 and 1959. The other side of the street is occupied by gardens of the **College of Horticulture and Viticulture**.

To the left of Villányi út several streets lead steeply up Gellért Hill. On the right side there is a large flat area with a **pond** in the middle, which covers an area of about one hectare. In olden times this was the site of a brickworks, but later subsoil water welled up flooding the clay pit. The **Park Espresso Restaurant** situated here at the edge of this flower-bordered pond, frequently referred to as the Bottomless Pond, is perhaps the finest and most up-to-date of its kind in the Budapest area. Swans and other water birds swim in the pond, and a fountain also adds to its beauty. A few steps from the restaurant are rows of tennis courts, and close by is the **open-air stage named after Béla Bartók,** which can seat 1,650 spectators.

Opposite the park stands the neo-baroque **St. Emerich Parish Church** (designed by Gyula *Wälder*). The adjoining building is **József Attila Gymnasium,** one of the most modern and best-equipped secondary schools of the capital.

A few minutes away from here we arrive at the most important junction of southern Buda: **Móricz Zsigmond körtér.** (Zsigmond Móricz, novelist, 1879-1942, was the greatest critical realist of Hungary.)

At the corner of the square and of Bartók Béla út is the largest motion picture theatre of southern Buda, the **Bartók Cinema. A statue of Prince Imre,** the son of King Stephen I (the work of Zsigmond *Kisfaludi Strobl,* 1930) stands in the little park in the northern part of the square.

The last section of the Buda boulevard is formed by Karinthy Frigyes út, which begins at Móricz Zsigmond körtér and leads to the Danube. (Frigyes Karinthy, 1888-1938, a great Hungarian satirist of the 20th century.) Here, in the Lágymányos quarter, one of the most up-to-date housing estates is in course of construction, and on the site beyond it exhibition buildings are being erected. This is where the annual Budapest International Fair will be held.

The **Lágymányos Tobacco Factory** is situated at the corner of Budafoki út. Further on to the left is the new group of buildings of the **Budapest Technical University.**

The last section of Karinthy Frigyes út slightly rises to the approach of the Petőfi Bridge, the southernmost highway bridge of Budapest over the Danube.

The open-air bath of the Gellért Hotel

7. BARTÓK BÉLA ÚT

The busiest street of southern Buda is Bartók Béla út. (Béla Bartók, 1881-1945, world-famous Hungarian composer.)

This thoroughfare with its lively traffic starts from Gellért tér, at the Buda abutment of the Liberty Bridge, and is flanked by four- to five-storied apartment houses with big stores, many restaurants and cafés. Gellért tér is an important traffic junction. The imposing buildings of the **Gellért Hotel** and the **Gellért Medicinal Baths** shape the character of the square. In the centre of a small park stands a **Soviet war memorial,** and behind it we see a group of buildings of the **Technical University.**

The first technical college in Budapest was founded in 1847. After the defeat of the 1848-49 War of Independence the Austrian authorities forbade the use of the Hungarian language in schools, and German was introduced instead and made compulsory in teaching. Lectures in Hungarian were not resumed until 1860 also at this college which at that time was called a technical school.

The main building of the Technical University facing the Danube was built by Alajos *Hauszmann*—the famous architect who also built the royal castle—between 1904 and 1909. The other buildings were designed and built by Győző *Czigler*.

Not far from the beginning of Bartók Béla út is the **Zalka Máté Barracks**. There is a relief on the wall, made in 1959 by sculptor György *Segesdi* to commemorate the legendary General Lukács, a Hungarian hero of the Great Socialist October Revolution and the Spanish civil war.

At this point Bartók Béla út turns in a slight arc, and in a little park here we can see a bronze **statue of Géza Gárdonyi** (an outstanding Hungarian novelist, 1863-1922). The statue, the work of János *Horvay*, was erected in 1933. The street then leads past the Borostyán (Ivy) Garden Restaurant to Móricz Zsigmond körtér. Here it widens into a large avenue, which is also flanked by three-to-five-storied houses, but already of more recent construction. On our way we come up to Kosztolányi Dezső tér. (Dezső Kosztolányi, writer and poet, 1885-1936.) Before reaching this square we pass by the **Bartók Cinema** and the **Budai Kis Mackó** (Little Teddy Bear) **snack-bar**.

Meanwhile Bartók Béla út continues its straight line, passes under a railway viaduct for the trains coming from the Eastern Railway Terminal to the Kelenföld Station, and then the street itself ends at the **Kelenföld Railway Station**.

THE INNER DISTRICTS OF BUDA

1. CASTLE HILL

On the right bank of the Danube, in the centre of the Buda side, rises Castle Hill (Vár-hegy) with the splendid Castle (Vár) at its top. This part of the city is a piece of Hungarian history carved in stone. From the 13th to the 18th century the purpose of the ramparts of the castle on the slopes of the hill was to protect the town. Today, together with the buildings and streets in this quarter, they are relics of the past. The plateau within the massive ramparts has been declared a protected area.

The Castle Hill area divides into two parts: the southern section comprises the former royal residence, the Castle proper, and the northern part, the larger part, was the civilian town, or, as it was called, the Castle quarter.

In the Second World War aerial bombardments and gun-fire devastated the buildings of Castle Hill. Yet, strange to say, the devastation caused not only terrible damage, but was also of some advantage to the ancient monuments, for it revealed the medieval Castle beneath the fallen plaster work and the torn walls. The royal castle and the civilian town were rebuilt many times in the course of bygone centuries, but now they lay bare in their original form. The work of rebuilding is going on very slowly and with painstaking care. The work that is in progress here is more than just reconstruction, because the Castle District will be restored to its original form.

This old part of the town stands in the middle of the modern city as a historic museum under the open sky. Not only historians come here, but also people who love romance and quiet, and are fascinated by the past. Artists, musicians, painters and writers like to stay here on Castle Hill, because the environment offers them inspiration.

Apart from its historic background, Castle Hill possesses

yet another attractive quality: the unique beautiful surroundings. Castle Hill stands in the centre of a semicircle formed by the Buda hills all around. This line begins in the north with the Hill of Three Boundaries (Hármashatár-hegy), then spreads over to the west, with János Hill (János-hegy) as the highest peak, then passes on to Eagle Hill (Sas-hegy) in the south, and finally ends with Gellért Hill (Gellérthegy). These hills form a more or less unbroken chain which, however, is separated from Castle Hill by mildly rolling plains. Standing there in the centre of the Buda hills, Castle Hill affords a picturesque view indeed.

Castle Hill is readily visible from all parts of the capital. From the lookout towers on the Buda hills and from even more distant places in Pest, which are at a higher level, it catches the viewer's eye at once.

There are promenades along the ramparts of Castle Hill. In the centre of the hill rises the Fishermen's Bastion (Halászbástya) providing a wonderful lookout point.

In outline Castle Hill is almond shaped. From northwest to southeast it is 1.5 kilometres long and its breadth measures 0.5 kilometre. Its longitudinal axis forms an acute angle with the course of the Danube, and its southern, narrower part reaches down almost to the river. The southern part rises 45 metres and the northern 60 to 62 metres above the Buda promenade along the river bank. Its highest point is Szentháromság tér (Trinity Square), 80 metres above the level of the Danube.

The hill is composed largely of Buda marl. The top is covered with a 10 to 11-metre-thick layer of lime, on which the Castle and the residential quarter are built. The entire area of Castle Hill, together with its slopes, forms a triangle whose angles are at Moszkva tér (Moscow Square) in the north, Batthyány tér in the east and Szarvas tér (Stag Square) in the south. Comparatively straight streets connect these squares, so that it is easy to walk around the hill.

Castle Hill is accessible from various sides. Here we mention three of the most convenient approaches. From the Buda abutment of the Suspension Bridge, at Clark Ádám tér, a serpentine road, Hunyadi János út, leads up to Dísz tér (Parade Square); on the southwestern side Palota út (Palace Avenue) climbs up the slopes of the hill winding up to Dísz tér; and finally on the north side Várfok utca and Ostrom utca lead up to Bécsikapu tér (Vienna Gate Square).

HISTORY OF CASTLE HILL

In the area of Castle Hill we find no monuments dating from times before the Magyar conquest of the land (896). In its surroundings, however, there are vestiges of settlements from prehistoric times that have remained intact, e.g. in the basin of Tabán, where in prehistoric times a ferry crossing must have existed. It does not seem likely that structures of major importance were built on Castle Hill at the time of the conquest of the country.

The first buildings of any significance originated in the period after the Mongol invasion, when King Béla IV decided to protect the country by building fortifications on a large scale. Thus, he had a fortress built in Buda. In all probability the line of the ramparts followed the sides of the hill. Medieval records speak of the Church of the Blessed Virgin (the present-day Matthias Church), of the Mary Magdalene Church and of the Royal Quarters built in the southern part of the hill.

During the reign of King Sigismund, in the 15th century, Castle Hill began to develop vigorously. Sigismund, being at the same time Emperor of the Holy Roman Empire, had a luxurious palace built on Castle Hill, the so-called "New Palace", which was praised in a number of contemporary reports. The civilian town and the houses of artisans, guilds, etc., were built round this palace.

Under the reign of Matthias Corvinus, the social picture of Castle Hill changed immensely. The strong concentration of royal power attracted the aristocrats of the country to the palace area. They drove the burghers out of the town by purchasing real estate. As a result of the influx of wealthy aristocrats the northern, larger, part of the castle area began to develop by leaps and bounds. This was the area of the present-day residential quarter. Buda was already at that time, towards the end of the 15th century, virtually the centre of the country, politically, economically and also culturally.

This Renaissance town of the Middle Ages numbered about 8,000 inhabitants. The defeat at Mohács (1526) sealed the fate of medieval Buda. After their victory the Turks pushed on to Buda, plundered Castle Hill and returned home with enormous booty. Fifteen years later, on August 29, 1541, Castle Hill came entirely under Turkish rule, and remained a part of the Ottoman Empire until 1686. The Hungarians residing in the city either fled, or were imprisoned in the Csonka Torony (Broken Tower). The Turks turned the churches into mosques. They did not bother much about the buildings, which thus gradually fell into ruin.

The Turks built only minarets and baths. They used the royal palace as a stable and as an ammunition store. They were busy, however, building ramparts and fortifications. Several parts of the fortifications of the hill which still stand originate from that period.

In 1686, following a siege lasting several months, the united Christian armies recaptured the fortress town, which, as a result of heavy and desperate fighting, was almost completely devastated. The decisive assault took place on September 2, 1686. The Christian army first succeeded in penetrating the Castle at the so-called Esztergom round bastion. At this place we find a commemorative tablet. Abdurrahman, Pasha of Buda, the defender of the fort, fell at present-day Hess András tér.

The Castle was reduced to ruins. In 1686 the number of inhabitants of one of the biggest towns of medieval Europe dwindled to 616. The reconstruction of the town began in the 18th century. In 1703 Leopold I issued a royal charter declaring Buda a town vested with special privileges. From that time on, Buda was ruled by a council of twelve, which was headed by a mayor.

Buda did not win back its former political significance at once. The Hapsburg kings no longer resided in the Buda Castle, and even the Diet held its sessions in Pozsony (now Bratislava, Czechoslovakia) until 1790. At that time the Castle area was inhabited by civil servants and officials of the empire, whose backwardness greatly hindered the town's development. The merchants and artisans lived in Pest, whose population towards the end of the 18th century outnumbered that of Buda, although at the beginning of the century it had no more than a quarter as many people. The area which was once a famed European centre now became a quiet, pleasant little baroque town.

At the time of the 1848-49 War of Independence, Buda did not yet play an important role. On May 21, the Hungarian Honvéds (the patriotic army of national guardsmen) took the Castle, but after the defeat of the War of Independence the Austrian armed forces again occupied it. Castle Hill was placed under Austrian administration.

When in 1872 Buda, Óbuda and Pest united to form Budapest, the capital, systematic town planning was begun

Buda Castle, now under reconstruction

which included the reconstruction of the royal castle. Towards the end of the century the Matthias Church was rebuilt and the Fishermen's Bastion was erected. From the beginning of our century till the end of the Second World War, Castle Hill remained almost unchanged.

As a consequence of the siege of Budapest in 1944-45, all the houses in the Castle District were damaged. The front and roofing of just one house alone remained intact. The royal palace lay in ruins. On February 12, 1945´ the fascist German troops encircled on Castle Hill surrendered.

All that has happened since that time already belongs to the history of our epoch. We shall give further information on reconstruction and rebuilding where our walk through the Castle quarter is described.

FROM BÉCSIKAPU TÉR TO SZENTHÁROMSÁG TÉR

Starting from Moszkva tér and Széna tér—Fiáth János utca, Ostrom utca and Várfok utca lead up to the northern entrance of Castle Hill, which is called the **Bécsi kapu** (Vienna Gate).

171

In 1541 the Turks overran the area and penetrated the Castle at this gate by stealth, while the feudal lords were visiting the camp of the sultan as his guests. This gate obtained the name Vienna Gate during the Turkish occupation, for it looked on the highroad leading to Vienna. The gate obtained its present form in 1936, when the 250th anniversary of the liberation of Buda was commemorated. On this occasion a **memorial tablet** and a **statue depicting a rushing angel** (by Béla *Ohmann*) were unveiled.

Through the gate we get to Bécsikapu tér, a traffic junction of the northern Castle District. From here Fortuna utca and Tárnok utca run lengthways along Castle Hill.

In the Middle Ages market days were held on Saturdays in this square and in adjoining Kapisztrán tér. On March 28, 1723 a great fire broke out and spread rapidly. Helped by a north wind it swept over the whole Castle area and blew up the ammunition store located close by the Fehérvári kapu.

In the centre of the square stands the **Kazinczy Ferenc Memorial Fountain** (by János *Pásztor*, 1936). Kazinczy was a pioneer of Hungarian enlightenment at the end of the 18th and early 19th centuries. The tallest building in this square is the **Hungarian National Archives** (Országos Levéltár, built between 1913 and 1917) containing a rich collection of medieval documents and many rare letters and papers bearing on affairs in Hungary. In front of the building of the National Archives stands a **Lutheran church** built in 1896.

The more significant sights of Castle Hill begin here. On the western side of this square there are four historic monuments comprising four houses (Nos. 5 to 8). The house at **No. 5** obtained its present-day form in 1780. It is interesting to note that in the 18th century only blacksmiths and their families lived in this house. The house at **No. 6** has a baroque façade, the wall of the ground floor, however, dates from the Middle Ages. The doorway and the barrel-vaulted premises next door belong to the same period. The two houses have a common roofing. The tradition attached to it says that one of the house-owners built the common roofing for the sake of his daughter, who loved the son of the neighbouring house-owner. Thus the conscientious father was intent not only on "bringing the house under roof", but also the love of the young people.

The house at **No. 7** was built in the 18th century from medieval ruins. It received its early classicist façade with allegorical figures representing the sciences and the arts in 1807. To the left, by the entrance, we see an ornamental tablet. It was put up by the archaeological committee of the Academy of Sciences and bears the year mark 1866. Tablets with similar inscriptions (A. M. T. A. R. B. 1866) can be found at many places on houses within the Castle District, although scientifically the data do not always tally. To the right of the entrance a modern oblong table, the likes of which can be seen on the walls of nearly all houses there, indicates the reliable data ascertained by present-day historical science.

The house at **No. 8** is more recent than its neighbours. It was built in the neoclassic style in the 19th century and was reconstructed in 1929-30.

Petermann bíró utca (Judge Petermann Street) leads from Bécsikapu tér to Kapisztrán tér. Once this street, too, formed part of the Saturday markets. When the Christian army entered the Castle by the Esztergom round bastions, the bulk of the Turkish army was squeezed together in this street, and a dreadful hand-to-hand battle ensued. According to contemporary descriptions blood flowed on the roadway staining everything red, hence its former name: Vér utca (Blood Street). In 1954 the street was renamed after a progressive-minded judge of the town of medieval Buda.

Kapisztrán tér lies in the northwestern corner of Castle Hill. The former market ended here. The Castle's longitudinal streets in the northwestern and southeastern direction ran from this point.

The **Capistranus Memorial** standing in the square is a work of József *Damkó*, dating from 1922. Capistranus was a general in the army of János Hunyadi, the victorious military leader who defeated the Turks in the 15th century, and with Hunyadi he participated in the defence of Nándorfehérvár (today's Belgrade) against the Turks in 1456. Later he was canonised. (In memory of the victory over the Turks at Nándorfehérvár, Pope Calixtus III ordered the bells to be rung every day at noon.)

In the north the square is flanked by the **State Printing Shop** and the former Ferdinand Barracks (today it is the War History Museum), in the south rises the Magdalene Tower, a survival of the **Mary Magdalene Church,** one of the oldest buildings on Castle Hill.

At first this was the church of the Hungarian population of Castle Hill, while the Matthias Church was frequented by the German-speaking population. Excavations of recent years also revealed parts of buildings from the 13th and 14th centuries. The tower was built in the second half of the 15th century. Its present-day form is Gothic. Between 1950 and 1952 it was renovated on the basis of designs of József *Csemegi*. Its spire has been rebuilt in the baroque style.

The streets of Castle Hill starting from Bécsikapu tér and Kapisztrán tér run almost parallel, only Táncsics Mihály utca follows the zigzagging course of the northeastern bastion line. Nearly all the houses in this street are valuable historic monuments. On the site of the building at **No. 7** were formerly two houses. Out of their remains a palace was built later on, which, however, was demolished in 1750, and the present palace was built according to the designs of Máté *Nepauer*. Beethoven stayed here in 1800. The relief on the pillars of the gate supposedly represents Máté Nepauer, the designer of the house.

A historically significant building in this street is the house at **No. 9**, a one-time prison. From 1837 to 1840 it was the place of confinement of Lajos Kossuth, the spiritual and political leader of the Hungarian War of Independence of 1848-49. Mihály Táncsics, the first Hungarian socialist publicist, was imprisoned there in 1847-48 and from 1860 to 1867. To the left of the entrance a white marble tablet displays a **relief of Kossuth** and to the right is a bronze **relief of Táncsics** (by Lajos *Berán*).

A popular place of amusement with dancing on Castle Hill is the Bécsikapu Espresso in the building at No. 25. It is furnished with period furniture and majolica pictures from the last century and a stove from the period of Maria Theresa.

Fortuna utca, the busiest street in this part of Castle Hill, also opens from Bécsikapu tér. It is one of the streets that suffered most in 1944-45. Gradually the street is being rebuilt. Restoration work here began in 1957. The house at **No. 3** is a simple building in the baroque style. The ground floor is occupied by the Pest-Buda Restaurant, a pleasant little place, which reflects the atmosphere of the Reform Age and the War of Independence period. A few steps further, the house at **No. 9** was originally built in the baroque style, but towards the middle of the 19th century it was given a romantic façade. In 1921 this was

Dwelling houses in Bécsikapu tér

simplified and the window on the upper floor was replaced by a **relief of the goddess Fortuna.** (As a matter of fact, on the walls over the entrance door quite a number of reliefs can be seen, mostly images of saints.)

Many houses in the north of this street were restored in 1958-59. Most of them are monuments dating from the Middle Ages. The house at **No. 14** is one of them. Today it houses an **antique shop.** Through the windows of the entrance door one can see the medieval doorway with its seating niches. These niches are remarkable architectural characteristics of the history of the Buda Castle District. They recall the times when Hungarian aristocrats flocked into the Castle area during the reign of King Matthias and, intent on transforming the burghers' houses into aristocratic palaces, drove out those living here.

The southern ends of Táncsics Mihály utca and Fortuna utca meet in a triangular square, Hess András tér. With its valuable art monuments this square of the Castle District reflects a very intimate atmosphere. One corner of it borders on Szentháromság tér. In the centre of Hess András tér stands the **statue of Pope Innocent XI,** who, in 1684, created an alliance to oust the Turks, and he supported this war generously with money. This statue is the work of József *Damkó.* The most significant monument stands on the east side of the square: the **St. Nicholas Church.** Parts of the spire were built in the 13th century, but most of it in the 15th century. In the course of time the church, which stood behind the solitary, stocky tower, fell almost completely into ruin. Its northern wall with two late-Romanesque windows, as well as the triumphal arch and parts of the choir, have remained standing. On the site of the one-time church scientific exploration and excavations are in progress.

The memorial which is sculptured in the wall of the **St. Nicholas Tower** at the street level is a replica of the one that was set up in the gate tower of the town of Bautzen (Upper Lausitz), in 1486. The **relief** is the lifelike image of **King Matthias.** The two wings of the memorial ornamented with the coats of arms of the provinces conquered by King Matthias and the coat of arms of the Hunyadis were restored by Kálmán *Lux* after a copperplate engraving originating from 1715.

South of the tower lie the ruins of the one-time **Jesuit College** building. The complex of buildings flanked the Matthias Church.

On the northern side of the square stands the building (No. 3) of a former inn, the **Vörös Sün** (Red Hedgehog). Medieval dwelling houses stood on its site. This was the first inn to open in the Castle area after the end of the Turkish occupation. It was already known as the Red Hedgehog as far back as 1696.

The **Fortuna Restaurant** with its **bar** and **espresso** on the west side of the square was opened in 1958, in genuine medieval premises. Its furnishings are exquisite and in harmony with the style. The Fortuna Restaurant is one of the most elegant of its kind in Budapest. The medieval vestiges, the entrance and the niches with seats, handsomely blend with the modern environment. In the neighbourhood stands a neo-Gothic building, the former Ministry of Finance. After 1945 it was completely reconstructed. Today it is a **hostel for the students of the Technical University.**

From Fortuna utca some little alleys lead in a western direction: Fortuna köz, Kard utca (Sword Street). Their atmosphere is characteristic of the Castle District. Országház utca (Parliament Street) runs parallel with Fortuna utca. In the house at **No. 2** the remains of a fine Gothic palace have been discovered. In the courtyard and on the ground floor Gothic arcades can be seen.

The house at **No. 18** recalls the 15th century. The oriel window over the entrance door has preserved its original form, with certain parts added in harmony with the style. Over the baroque doorway of the Gothic building at **No. 20** hangs the trade sign of a butcher master. This house of the 14th century has a fine moulding, rebuilt by the butcher master, Johannes Nickl, in 1711. In the doorway we find niches to sit in.

The house at **No. 22** shows an interesting mixture of medieval and baroque architecture. The valuable Renaissance ornaments on the lower part of the medieval baywindow date from the 16th century.

It is worth while contemplating these three houses. The buildings at Nos. 18, 20 and 22 truly reflect the street picture of the Middle Ages. This is the only part of the Castle Hill area where we can still see Gothic buildings standing side by side in their more or less original form. The siege and gunfire in 1686 wrought such devastation among the houses that only those situated outside gunfire range remained intact, and even there, in most cases only the lower walls. The cannonade came from Vérmező, Sun

Hill (Nap-hegy) and the Hill of Roses (Rózsadomb), that is from the west, south and north. Consequently the houses exposed to the east were comparatively sheltered from damage.

The building at **No. 9** is a restored medieval dwelling house. The **Bartók Béla Archives** of the Hungarian Academy of Sciences are kept here. Permanent exhibitions display material that have a bearing on the great Hungarian musician. In the house at No. 17 is the Régi Országház (Old Parliament) Restaurant with a fine garden and an interesting medieval wine cellar.

The houses at **Nos. 26, 28** and **30** are also worth mentioning. Parliament was once located here, from which the street obtained its name. After the ousting of the Turks the Orders of the Franciscans and the Poor Clares began to build their churches on this site when Joseph II suppressed the religious orders in 1782. Then the building of the Royal Supreme Court and Parliament was started here. The church was divided into storeys and the spire was removed. The hall of the Lower House of Parliament was in the wing facing Országház utca, in the northern wing, and the one looking onto the court went to the Upper House. The opposite side of the complex of buildings looks onto Úri utca (Lords' Street). Parliamentary sessions were held here in 1790, 1792 and 1807, and after the death of Joseph II the Council of Governors had its residence here. After 1791 it was also the headquarters of the commanders of Buda.

The westernmost street of Castle Hill is Úri utca. As a matter of fact, it is also the longest street on Castle Hill and leads as far as Dísz tér. In the Middle Ages the houses here reached on one side as far as the ramparts and leaned against them. In 1944-45 this part suffered most heavily, and many medieval monuments were discovered as a result.

In the doorway of the house at **No. 6** medieval niches with seats can be seen. A **marble tablet** tells us that **László Szalay,** an outstanding historian of the past century, was born here. On the headstone of the building at **No. 8** the coat of arms of the Széchenyi family catches the eye. Also the house at **No. 13** shows numerous details of medieval remains. As they had not been plastered over, they became apparent at first sight, and in the imagination it is easy to reconstruct the damaged house to its former shape.

The house at **No. 19** belonged at the time to a famous Italian general of King Sigismund, Filippo Scolari by name. According to tradition he built the arch spanning the street, because this architectural style was fashionable in Italy. The great political figure of the Reform Age and significant writer in the 19th century, József Eötvös, was born in this house.

At the corner of Úri utca and Szentháromság tér stands the **equestrian statue of András Hadik,** the legendary marshal of Empress Maria Theresa, who held Berlin to ransom. (The statue erected in 1937 is the work of György *Vastagh* Jr.) In this section we find only one two-storied building from the Middle Ages, which, despite the heavy destruction in the Castle District, remained fairly intact. This is the house at **No. 31.** Medieval window frames decorate its façade. Noteworthy are the windows on the upper storey which are divided into three parts and are connected with each other.

The building at **No. 32** shows evidence of an interesting architectural experiment. This house was almost completely destroyed in the Second World War, only the doorway remained intact. The architect left it untouched, and using it in his construction, he added a modern building to it. Such use of architectural elements of especially badly damaged houses in reconstruction can be observed at many places in the Castle District. The vaulted doorway, the niches with the seats originating from the time of King Matthias are all genuine structures. Medieval doorways of this kind may frequently be seen in Úri utca. They are easily recognisable as most of them have glass-framed entrance doors. The different varieties of niches are also of interest. Some have round, others pointed arches, still others have segment arches, or they end in an acute angle.

FROM SZENTHÁROMSÁG TÉR TO DÍSZ TÉR

Szentháromság tér (Trinity Square) with the streets converging upon it divides the residential quarter into two parts. In the centre stands a rich baroque **column to the Trinity.** It was erected by the citizens of the Castle area when the Turkish occupation had ended and an epidemic of the plague was raging (1710-1713).

On the eastern side of the square stands the historically

significant **Matthias Church.** In the Middle Ages it was known as the Church of the Blessed Virgin Mary.

According to ancient documents the original church was built here between 1255 and 1269. Hungarian kings, including Louis I the Great, Sigismund, and Matthias Corvinus in the first place, embellished and enlarged it. Many historic events are connected with this church. In 1424 Sigismund received the Greek emperor here, then they both took part in a procession. A solemn thanksgiving service was celebrated when, in 1444, King Wladislas I returned after a victorious campaign against the Turks. Both weddings of King Matthias took place in this church. Since several kings of Hungary were crowned here, it is called also Coronation Church.

When the Turks plundered Buda in 1526, they set fire to the church. In 1541 they reconstructed it and turned it into a mosque. The walls were white-washed and quotations from the Koran were inscribed on them. At the same time the furnishings were removed. After the recapture of Buda (1686), the church came into the possession of the Franciscans, and then the Jesuits. On both sides enormous buildings were erected, and the interior was decorated in the baroque style. In 1898 the remains of King Béla III (1173-1196) and his wife, Anne of Châtillon, were buried here. Between 1874 and 1896, to the designs of Frigyes Schulek, the church was freed of the surrounding buildings and restored to its medieval form.

The church has three naves and a row of chapels opens from the northern one. The sanctuary is enclosed by seven sides of a tredecilateral column. Looking at the church from the Trinity column, to the left we see the stocky Béla spire, and to the right the Matthias spire. The southern façade of the church is richly decorated, here we find the Mary portal. In the square, in front of the southern façade, stands the **equestrian bronze statue of King Stephen I**—or St. Stephen (1001-1038). He was the first king of Hungary. The statue is the work of Alajos Stróbl; the pedestal was designed by Frigyes Schulek (1906).

The **Fishermen's Bastion,** a splendid structure erected in the neo-Romanesque style by Frigyes Schulek in 1901-02, is behind the Matthias Church, on the site where in the Middle Ages the bastions of the fishermen's guild stood. The Fishermen's Bastion has never served any defence purposes. Its arches and columns of white stone on the eastern slopes of Castle Hill frame the view of the city and

Matthias Church

Fishermen's Bastion

ornament the system of stairs leading up from Víziváro-
(Water Town). A superb panorama opens before the viss
itor from the Fishermen's Bastion: the semicircular sky-
line of the hills and mountains of Buda, the silvery ribbon
of the Danube and the breathtaking picture of Pest with
its pulsating life. In the northern part of the Fishermen's
Bastion is the Lapidary of the Castle Museum (Vármúzeum
kőtára) where medieval relics of the area are displayed.
Below the Fishermen's Bastion winds Hunyadi János út,
leading up to Castle Hill. A **statue of János Hunyadi**
(the work of István *Tóth*, 1903) stands at a sharp bend.
János Hunyadi (1387-1456) was one of the most significant
figures in Hungarian history, a victorious military leader
in the wars tagains the Turks, who was famed throughout
Europe. In the period from 1446 to 1453 he was the regent
of Hungary.

The flight of stairs at the foot of the Fishermen's Bastion is named **Jesuit Stairs** after the Jesuits who lived here in the 18th century. A short distance away, in the east, we see ramparts, which, however, do not belong to the Fishermen's Bastion, they are ramparts built in the Middle Ages.

At the northern end of the Fishermen's Bastion, by the side of the choir of the old Dominican church, are the **statues of** two Dominican monks, **Julianus and Gerardus** (by Károly *Antal*, 1937). King Béla IV entrusted them with the task of travelling to the East and exploring the ancient homeland of the Magyars.

On the southern side of Szentháromság tér stands a single-storied building with a fine baroque façade. It is L-shaped, with a bow-window on each corner. This is **the one-time town hall** of Buda. Today it houses the **Castle Museum.** Its collection embraces the period beginning with the 13th century till the end of the Middle Age. A considerable part of the relics originating from the old Matthias Church, the Dominican church and the royal palace are preserved here.

A short street, Szentháromság utca, leads from this square to Tóth Árpád sétány. In the Middle Ages a food market existed here, and because of its many shops it was called "Boltosok utcája" (Shopmen's Street). In the house at **No. 7** is a well-known pastry-shop, the **Ruszwurm,** which became the property of the confectioner Vilmos Russwurm in 1890. A shop of this kind had existed in this place for several centuries. In the tastefully furnished premises souvenirs of the confectioner's trade are on display.

Turning from Szentháromság tér and Szentháromság utca to the south, we go into Úri utca, which we have already described, and into Tárnok utca. Just as in other streets of Castle Hill, we find in these streets several buildings with noteworthy relics, reminiscent of the Middle Ages. These are houses that have survived the past centuries and remained almost intact. In their present state they give a true picture of the form of medieval dwelling houses.

A good example is the house at **No. 14.** It was built in the 14th century and was extended to its present size in the 16th century. Its façade bears medieval lines. It has a protruding upper storey supported by a segment-arched barrel vault, which rests on six consoles. The semicircular windows have stone frames through which the goods were passed in the medieval shop that was here originally.

The whole façade is covered with murals dating from the 16th century. This was customary in medieval Buda and gave the streets a particularly oriental touch. The ground-floor premises have barrel vaults originating from the 14th to the 16th centuries. The doorway is built in a similar manner. These are the premises of the Tárnok Espresso. The narrow, short little lanes, like Balta köz, Anna utca, etc., in the neighbourhood of Tárnok utca have a veritable medieval Italian atmosphere.

The southern end of Tárnok utca runs into Dísz tér. This rather spacious square is the busiest place in the Castle District. In the centre, in the place of the former St. George Church, stands the **Honvéd Memorial** with the inscription: "May 21, 1849, For a Free Homeland". (It is the work of György *Zala*, dating from 1893.)

In 1944-45 nearly all the houses in this square were destroyed but since that time most of them have been rebuilt again. The house at **No. 3** was once the Batthyány Palace, built in 1744.

BASTION PROMENADES

Tóth Árpád sétány, named after the great poet of the 20th century, Árpád Tóth (1886-1928), begins in the north at Bécsikapu tér and runs in a southern direction as far as Dísz tér. Here the major part of the medieval ramparts still stand. From Dísz tér it is a short way to the **Fehérvár Round Bastion,** which is the biggest and strongest circular battlement of the Castle. It is located where Palota út joins the confines of the Castle District. The round bastion is 50 metres in diametre, and its walls are 4.5 metres thick. From the crenels it was possible to bombard not only the enemy's gun emplacements and the approaching enemy troops, but also the besiegers, trying to climb the western walls. Close to this bastion stands the **Fehérvár Gate.** Here Palota út ends.

The Fehérvár Gate obtained its name—like most castle gates—from the town that lay in the direction of the gate, or the place to which the road from the fort led. From this point the highroad led to Székesfehérvár. Its name has become historic because on May 21, 1849 the Hungarian Honvéds storming the Castle from this side took it from the Austrian forces in a single assault.

North of the Fehérvár Gate runs a 420-metre-long

straight rampart, the so-called Long Wall. At the middle
a covered stairway leads to the crossing of Szentháromság
utca and the Bastion Promenade. For a long time this was
the only way down from the western walls.

The Bastion Promenade (Bástyasétány) runs along the
walls on the inside. In the Middle Ages and during the
Turkish occupation buildings (dwelling houses) stood quite
close to the ramparts, at some places their walls were
even built into the ramparts.

North of the stairway at Szentháromság utca the walls are
interrupted by two projections. The one nearest was given
its name, **Sour-Soup Bastion**, by the Turks. The other
is the **Veli Bey Bastion**, which was built in the second
half of the 16th century. Within its semicircular line stands
an **equestrian statue** (by Lajos *Petri*, 1935).

At the northern end of the promenade, where a little alley
turns into Kapisztrán tér, another stairway leads down the
slopes of the hill into Sziklai Sándor út. From here we get
a splendid view of the **Esztergom Round Bastion** with
its powerful walls built of bricks of several colours. The
smaller dark-red bricks were made in the Middle Ages.
They were found when the bastions were reconstructed,
and then they were built into the wall. The Esztergom
bastion stands at the westernmost point of the fortification. A tablet in memory of the recapture of Buda in 1686
has been placed in the wall on the very spot where the
Christian armies first forced their way into the fort.

On the northern side of the Bastion Promenade which
leads to Bécsikapu tér, there are two other projections:
the **Tower of Siavus Pasha** (1648-1650) and the **Tower
of Murad Pasha** (1650-1653). This section of the bastions
is called the **Anjou Bastion**. A statue of **Abdurrahman
Pasha,** the Turkish defender of the fort of Buda, stands in
the middle. It was damaged in the Second World War.

To the north of Tóth Árpád sétány we can see the former
Ferdinand Barracks; today it shelters the **War History
Museum.** After the recapture of Buda from the Turks in
1686, two buildings stood here serving as barracks. The
present two-storied building in the neoclassic style was
erected in their place in 1847.

THE CASTLE

The area extending south of Dísz tér is called the Castle, although the palace itself occupies only half of this area. Temporarily it is closed to the public as architects and archaeologists are working on its reconstruction.

From Dísz tér two streets lead into the Castle. One of them, Szent György utca (St. George Street), still lies in ruins. The opening up and reconstruction of the street is now under way. The street running parallel with it is Színház utca (Theatre Street), named after the former Castle Theatre.

The Castle Theatre was built in 1787. László *Kelemen* and his ensemble gave their first performance in Hungarian here. In 1800 a concert was organised at this theatre with the participation of Beethoven. It was used till 1924, and now, after its restoration, it will be reopened again.

At the end of Szent György utca and Színház utca lies historic Szent György tér, which is flanked in the south by the buildings of the royal palace. In the Middle Ages this was Zsigmond tér (Sigismund Square), behind which was a deep moat and only a drawbridge connected the square with the palace. Under the reign of King Sigismund the main front of the "New Palace" faced this square, and the tournaments, known so well from books, ancient documents and poetic works, were held in this square. Executions also took place here, which the people of the court could watch from the windows of the palace.

No. 1-2 Dísz tér is the building of the former **Sándor Palace,** which was erected in 1806 on the site of three barracks dating from the Middle Ages. From 1867 onward this palace was the official residence of the prime minister in power. In 1944-45 the building was badly damaged. Its reconstruction is in progress.

At the southern end of the square begins the area of the former **royal residence.**

The construction of the palace was begun under King Béla IV in the middle of the 13th century. Till the Turkish occupation this was the residence of the Hungarian kings. The history of the palace can be divided into three periods.

The **Palace of King Sigismund and King Matthias.** The "New Palace" with its gigantic staterooms and courtyards, known all over Europe at the time, was built by Sigismund (Hungarian king and Holy Roman emperor) on the site of the palace of lesser importance, in the 15th century. The Broken Tower (Csonkatorony), which was used as a prison, was also erected at that time. During the Turkish occupation Hungarians languished in this prison. King Matthias added a few storeys to the east wing of the palace overlooking the Danube, and reconstructed several sections of the building. The famous Corviniana library with the valuable hand-written Corvina codices was located near the chapel. This period was the golden age of the palace, which was an intellectual and cultural centre of 15th-century Europe. Under the reign of Matthias the ornamental gardens, fountains and statues were especially famous. During the Turkish occupation the palace soon fell into ruins. Although the Turkish chroniclers spoke of Buda as the "Beautiful Red Apple", or the "Golden Apple of the Empire", they left the palace to its fate. The Turks used it as an ammunition store, and janissaries made it their quarters. In 1686 the palace was ruined by gunfire.

The **Palace of the Baroque Period.** After the recapture of Buda, the Baron Regal, a general of the Austrian emperor, started the restoration work of the palace in 1715, but then its fortress characteristics still played a predominant role. In 1749 the French architect Jean Nicolas *Jadot* began new construction by order of Maria Theresa. The building of the baroque palace was completed by Franz Anton *Hillebrandt* in 1770.

The **"Modern" Palace.** The building of the new representative palace was begun at the turn of the century. In 1890 the designs by Miklós *Ybl*, the best Hungarian architect of the time, were ready, and work itself started soon after. On the death of Miklós Ybl, in 1895, another famous architect, Alajos *Hauszmann*, was commissioned to continue the work. He left the west wing, the so-called Ybl wing, unchanged, but doubled the length of the wing facing the Danube. The cupola in the middle saved the 304-metre-long wing from the appearance of monotony. This part is called the Hauszmann wing. In 1944-45 the palace was badly damaged and, in addition to this, it also burnt out.

Restoration here, too, is in full swing, but it will still take many years to finish the job. The palace will be restored in its latest form, but care will be taken to render the unearthed medieval art monuments accessible to the public. After reconstruction the palace will be a centre of cultur-

The medieval Mace Tower

al life. The National Gallery, the National Széchényi Library, and various other museums will be given a new home in the palace.

At the southernmost points of the Castle the renovation of the old medieval bastions and ramparts has been more or less completed. The great southern **bastion** stands here. In the 14th century the wedge-shaped ramparts met at a gate tower, the former **Kelenföld Tower,** which connected the highroad from Tabán with the area of Castle Hill. King Matthias had the great southern bastion erected, being aware of how difficult this point was to defend. Behind the circular bastion runs a straight wall and at the western end of the southern wall stands the characteristically shaped **Mace Tower** (Buzogánytorony). During the reconstruction of the baroque palace these sections were walled in for the most part, and only after the siege of 1944-45 were these remains revealed and reconstructed according to records, descriptions and maps from the time of their origin.

2. VÍZIVÁROS

In the area between Castle Hill and the Danube little alleys climb up the mild slopes in zigzagging lines. Between the Suspension Bridge and the Margaret Bridge, however, long streets run from north to south along the narrow, flat strip by the bank of the Danube, from where squares of various sizes break the monotony of the streets like little windows to afford a glimpse of the Danube. In the morning blue haze settles on the roofs of the houses leaning so tight against one another, and from the midday hours on Castle Hill casts its shadow over them. In the evening the steps of passers-by ring hollowly, because life has already withdrawn into the courtyards behind ancient walls, where lilacs spread their lovely fragrance.

A real picture of Víziváros (Water Town) can be obtained from the Danube and the bridges. Along the river bank a green ribbon of chestnut trees and plane trees, like the stroke of a painter's brush, separates the silvery band of the river from the grey masses of houses, from slender church spires almost touching the crenels of the Fishermen's Bastion.

The past squeezed the life of the tradesmen, fishermen and the petty bourgeoisie of Víziváros, not only topographically but also socially, between the borders of a narrow band. In the west towered Castle Hill with its ministries and the royal palace, and on the Danube bank the sumptuous palaces of the aristocrats closed off the wider horizon from them. Within these confines time almost halted, and development and progress also came to a standstill. While the town on the plain of Pest began to grow at a dazzling pace, Víziváros continued its more or less secluded and sluggish life. The traces of this past are still clearly visible. The present has tried to penetrate these narrow streets of Víziváros, but only in recent years, with a few modern blocks of flats, or a new institution going up here and there.

The first records mentioning settlements in this area east of Castle Hill date from 1258. Mention was first made of the St. Peter Church of Víziváros at that time. Then the unassuming little settlement was not yet encircled by a stone wall. However, in accordance with custom of those times, but much later, in the 15th century, this part of the city, too, was surrounded by a wall.

The development of the Castle, this being the royal resi-

Panorama of the Water Town (Víziváros)

dence, entailed also a rapid expansion of Víziváros or, as it was called at the time, the Jewish town. Its population grew swiftly during the reign of Sigismund and Matthias. Under Turkish rule it assumed a somewhat oriental aspect, the line of medieval streets was interrupted by little winding and tortuous lanes and passages, the old churches were turned into mosques, and the quarter of tradesmen and fishermen was swamped with jugglers and beggars and other rabble. In 1566 Víziváros was devastated by fire, then in 1578 a terrible explosion occurred. In 1625 there was a fire again and in 1561 and 1641 earthquakes ravaged the district.

After the recapture of Buda the region between Castle Hill and the Danube was in ruins. Then Germans were settled here, mainly tradesmen and merchants. Within the medieval walls a baroque town began to rise and baroque monasteries and churches were built. Its character began to change substantially only in the 1870s. On the embankment of the Danube aristocrats had palaces built and at many places the little baroque houses had to give way to modern apartment buildings.

n the Second World War the old houses as well as the
new ones suffered serious damage. But thanks to recon-
truction efforts today many of the fine old buildings are
standing again in their original form and charm.

FROM MÁRTÍROK ÚTJA TO CSALOGÁNY UTCA

This area lies in the immediate neighbourhood of the former northern ramparts, and its ancient character as the
"settlement at the edge of the town" is still perceivable.
n a number of little back streets we find dwelling houses
still in good condition dating from the last century, and
even earlier; they are now protected historical monuments.
n Horváth utca, on the western side, a whole row of smaller houses in the neoclassic style stands almost intact.
Several houses (**Nos. 9, 23** and **24**) in Kacsa utca (Duck
Street) also show the characteristic architectural style used
at the beginning of the last century. In the house at
No. 26 is the Rózsafa (Rose Tree) Restaurant, a popular
spot for night entertainment. Those who appreciate fine
old houses should take a walk also through neighbouring
Kapás utca (Hoer Street), Fazekas utca (Potter Street),
Medve utca (Bear Street) and Vitéz utca (Warrior Street).
At the corner of Csalogány utca (Nightingale Street) and
Gyorskocsi utca, in the course of excavations the remnants of **St. Peter Church,** a medieval Gothic building
with three naves, were brought to light.
The only square worth mentioning in this part of the town
is Bem József tér. In its centre stands the **statue of Jó-
zef Bem,** the **Polish General of the Honvéds** of the
1848-49 War of Independence (by János Istók.) On the
river bank is the **landing pier** where boats leave northwards to Vác, Visegrád, Nagymaros, Esztergom and the
Danube Bend with its lovely countryside. At the corner
of Bem rakpart and Bem József tér stands the building
of the **Ministry for Foreign Affairs.**
From the south the oldest and busiest thoroughfare of
Víziváros, Fő utca (Main Street), leads into Bem József tér.
In former times a highroad ran along the river bank. It
was used also by the Romans. In the house at No. 90, at
the corner of Ganz utca, stands the Greek Catholic
Parish Church of Buda, which is also called the **Florian
Chapel.** It was built in the baroque style, to the designs of Máté Nepauer, between 1756 and 1760.

Again on the right side of the street, a few steps further in the house at No. 82-86, is an interesting monument dating from Turkish times: *Király Baths*. Its domed basin was built by Sokoli Mustafa Pasha in 1556. The 18th-century entrance building was designed in the baroque style. This oldest bath of the Hungarian capital was reconstructed in 1957-58, and an insignificant house, which hid the Turkish cupola from view, was removed. The bath obtains its medicinal water from the springs at Lukács Baths not far away.

FROM BATTHYÁNY UTCA TO CLARK ÁDÁM TÉR

The oldest part, and at the same time the centre of this quarter, lies here. The layout of its winding, narrow streets, which adapted themselves to the form of Castle Hill, still reminds us of medieval town planning. At many places the remains of the medieval wall were revealed when the restoration of the houses took place. After the Turkish wars this was where life began to flourish the soonest. The baroque houses and churches that can be seen in this quarter also show this.

The two most important thoroughfares of this quarter are Fő utca, which we have mentioned already, and Batthyány utca, leading down from Széna tér. At the crossing point of the two streets, at 41 Fő utca, stands the oldest church of Víziváros, the **St. Elizabeth Church.** This church was built on the site of an ornate Turkish mosque, between 1731 and 1737, by the Franciscans. The church, which is very modest on the outside, has a richly decorated interior, which dates from 1737 to 1757. The richly carved baroque benches are especially interesting. The skull of St. Flamidian, the staff of St. Elizabeth and, in a glass coffin, the relics of the martyr St. Fortunatus are preserved in the sacristy. Adjoining the church is the former **convent** (built from 1763 to 1777), which was used later as a hospital.

Resuming our walk along Fő utca, a few steps away we reach Batthyány tér. Formerly it was called Bomba tér (Bomb Square), because once an ammunition dump was kept here. In the square stand several old dwelling houses with exquisite forms, which today are protected ancient monuments. Here the entrances of the houses are below street level, which shows clearly to what extent the level of the inner city of Buda has been raised since the 18th century.

The two-storied house at **No. 3** was built in the Louis XVI style in 1793. The reliefs on the façade represent the four seasons. Its vaulted front doorway and the little courtyard inside present a romantic atmosphere. The house at **No. 4**, a one-storied rococo building, was erected in the first decade of the 18th century. It obtained its present form between 1755 and 1760. A triple flight of stairs leads up to the first floor. A vaulted landing crosses the inner courtyard. In the old times the White Cross Inn (Fehér Kereszt fogadó) was located in this building, where theatrical performances, gala balls and dances were held.

On Batthyány tér the most outstanding sight is the **St. Anne Parish Church.** Its beauty becomes especially apparent when seen from the Danube embankment. The main front has a breadth of 21 metres and the church is 55 metres high. The side front is 43 metres long. The church was built to Italian designs first by Kristóf *Hamon*, and afterwards by Máté *Nepauer*. Over the portal of the fine façade we see the allegorical figures of Faith, Hope and Charity. In the centre stands St. Anne with the child Mary (a work of Anton *Eberhard*), on the parapet are the statues of two angels paying homage to the symbol of Providence (also by Anton *Eberhard*).

The interior of the church gives a fascinating impression. Its eight-sided nave forms a single vaulted hall where everything vigorously stresses baroque mobility. The group of statues in the centre of the high altar is a fine example of Hungarian baroque plastic art. The composition glittering in red, grey and golden colours was done by the sculptor Karl *Bebo* between 1771 and 1773. The chancel with its rich decorative carvings and reliefs as well as the baptismal font made of red marble are worth seeing. The pictures of some of the saints were painted by Franz *Wagenschön*. In the choir a ceiling painting is by Gergely *Vogl* (The Trinity). The ceiling fresco of the nave dating from 1935 is the work of C. Pál *Molnár* and Béla *Kontuly*. This valuable baroque church was badly damaged during the Second World War. Its reconstruction was completed in 1958.

Not far off Széna tér (Hay Square) two streets, Iskola utca (School Street) and Donáti utca, branch off from Batthyány utca. On our walk through the former street we pass by a few monuments before we reach the house at No. 23, where Halászcsárda (Fishermen's Tavern) is located. Its

An old house in Fő utca

fish specialities are well known all over Budapest. Donáti
utca still runs as it did in the Middle Ages, and is flanked
by many monuments. From here, through Vám utca (Toll
Street)—past old houses—we reach Fő utca again, or
strictly speaking Szilágyi Dezső tér. (The square is named
after a liberal political figure of the 19th century who was
minister of justice, and promoter of the law of civil marriage.) Here stands the neo-Gothic Calvinist church,
built from 1893 to 1896. At the corner of the church is the
Pecz Samu Fountain, reminding us of the architect of
the church. A little further along Fő utca we come to Corvin tér. Most of the old houses here were built on medieval
foundations. The **Lajos Fountain** in the square is a
fine piece of sculpture by Barnabás *Holló* (1904). The
fountain represents a hunter at a spring. The northern
part of the square is occupied by the **Budai Vigadó.** It was

built in 1900, to the designs of Aladár *Árkay* and Mór *Kalina*. Today it is the **centre of the Folk Art Institute,** and the **Hungarian State Folk Ensemble** rehearses here. The southern end of Corvin tér is formed by the **Capuchin Church** (30-32 Fő utca).

In the house at 27 Fő utca is the Angler's Camp Inn (Horgásztanya), and in Halász utca (Fisherman Street), which runs to the Danube, is the Dunaparti Borozó (Tavern at the Danube Quay). In the house at No. 20 is the **Szép Ilonka** (Fair Helen) Espresso, one of Buda's most popular café-bars and next door is **Párizskert** (Paris Garden).

FROM CLARK ÁDÁM TÉR TO YBL MIKLÓS TÉR

Clark Ádám tér is named after the English engineer who built the Suspension Bridge. It is an important traffic junction of Buda. Motorcar and bus traffic enters the square from the Pest business and office quarter over the Suspension Bridge and crosses the Buda north–south traffic here. Hunyadi János út, a serpentine road, mounts the slopes of Castle Hill from this square. From Clark Ádám tér a **tunnel** runs under Castle Hill, continuing the straight line of the Suspension Bridge. Near the entrance of the tunnel stands a little statue with the inscription: **0 km.** This is the point of departure of the main highways converging on Budapest. Another ornament of this square is a **statue** showing a **workman** pointing ahead (a work by László *Molnár*).

At the corner of Fő utca and Clark Ádám tér is the **Lánchíd Café Espresso.** Further along this to the south we come to Várkert Bazár (Castle Bazaar). At the time (about 1875-1882) Miklós *Ybl* intended to provide an architectural piece to close the terraced gardens of the Castle on the Danube side. The serpentine stairway ends with a pavilion on either side. To the right and left, arcades were built at the foot of Castle Hill. Where the path begins to mount the slopes a one-storey-high **Gloriette** with four statues representing the four seasons (by Adolf *Huszár*) greets the visitor.

Part of the former Castle Gardens over the Bazaar is today a **cultural park for young people.** The oblong square in front of the gardens is Ybl Miklós tér. In its centre stands the bronze **statue of Ybl,** a work of Ede *Mayer*, erected in 1896.

3. FROM THE FOOT OF CASTLE HILL
TO KRISZTINAVÁROS

The main thoroughfare of Buda is the broad, seven-and-
a-half-kilometre-long Buda boulevard, which starts from
the Margaret Bridge and, describing a broad semicircle,
leads to the Petőfi Bridge. It is the organic continuation
of the Pest Great Boulevard, both regarding its shape and
character. Both these boulevards encircle Budapest like a
huge belt.

Speaking of the Buda boulevard, as a matter of fact, there
is not one, but two boulevards, because within the lines
of the outer circle there is also an inner circular road, which
however, does not follow the city walls so clearly as does
the Inner Boulevard of Pest. The inner boulevard of Buda
branches off from the outer one near the Southern Railway Terminal, at Magyar Jakobinusok tere. It surrounds
Castle Hill and the area at the foot of the hill, the so-called
Váralja, from the Margaret Bridge to the new bridge under
construction on the site of the former Elizabeth Bridge.

MÁRTÍROK ÚTJA, MOSZKVA TÉR

These are principal sections of the Buda boulevard. They
have excellent connections with all parts of the town. In
a few minutes by tram or bus one can reach the Inner City
of Pest, the Great Boulevard or the southern part of Buda.
The Buda hills, Óbuda and Margaret Island are also readily
accessible. The importance of this boulevard, as far as
tourism is concerned, is further increased by the fact that
the baths of northern Buda, the Lukács and the Császár
Baths, and also the Király Baths in Fő utca, are in its vicinity. In addition, the suburban electric trains to Római-
fürdő, Csillaghegy and Pünkösdfürdő start from here.

The history of this boulevard goes back far into the past.
Roman bronze coins from the period of Augustus Caesar
were discovered under a building. In the Middle Ages the
outer city walls were built along this thoroughfare, parts
of which can still be seen in Széna tér. When the city
walls were pulled down a highroad was built in their
place.

The Buda abutment of the Margaret Bridge opens up into
a spacious square. From its northern end the green cars
of the suburban railways depart for Aquincum, Római-fürdő,

Csillaghegy, Budakalász, Pomáz and Szentendre. Bus and tram lines coming from the south, passing along the Danube or from the inner parts of Buda, end here.

Here, at the beginning of this thoroughfare, first of all the Hill of Roses looms before us. This is an eloquent illustration of the old saying that each of the older bridges of the capital runs into a Buda hill. The Hill of Roses compels the thoroughfare to bend sharply to the south. On this short section we find a large number of espressos, pastryshops and inns. Among them the Gül Baba Restaurant is worth mentioning. It was named after a wise Turkish dervish, a great friend of roses, who lived here at the time of the Turkish occupation.

The building at 23 Mártírok útja, the **Buda church of the Franciscans,** is one of the most significant monuments of this neighbourhood. It was built to the designs of Máté *Nepauer* between 1753 and 1770. This church in baroque style was badly damaged in the Second World War. Its vaulting was restored in 1947.

Significant art treasures are preserved in this church, among them two pictures painted on wood, dating from the 15th century, the drinking cup of János Kapisztrán carved of wood, the wooden crucifix of György Cardinal Martinuzzi (archbishop and adviser to King John I, 1487-1540), and the manuscripts of Ignác Martinovics (leader of the Hungarian Jacobins). The former convent adjoining the church, a one-storied baroque building, is also a monument of art.

Beside the church two modern apartment houses were erected in 1959. At the next corner stood the so-called **Regent House,** in which the occupying German fascists stored up large quantities of ammunition in 1944. The cellar was hit by a shell which caused the ammunition to explode, blowing up the whole building. The people crowded together in the air-raid shelter within the house all died on the spot. This explosion was one of the most horrible episodes Budapest had to experience during the Second World War.

On the site of Regent House now stands a new six-storied apartment house, also built in 1959. The **Európa Restaurant** occupies its ground floor.

Mártírok útja then passes by Mechwart tér which was named after the outstanding Hungarian engineer and inventor András Mechwart (1834-1907). This square is a handsomely laid out park and it is the terminus of bus line

No. 11, which leads to the top of Rózsadomb. At No. 1 in this square rises the modern building of the **district council.**

The next block of flats, at 55 Mártírok útja, contains the biggest **cinema** of Buda, **Május 1.**

At the corner of Mártírok útja and Kis-Rókus utca begins the factory area of the **Ganz Electrical Works.** One of its buildings giving to Mártírok útja was at one time a military prison. After the Hungarian Republic of Councils of 1919 was crushed by the Horthy fascists many fighters of the Hungarian labour movement were imprisoned here, and a large number of them died martyrs during the Horthy era. The street was named Mártírok útja (Road of Martyrs) to commemorate them.

Not far from here, at the corner of Iparostanuló utca (Apprentice Street), parts of the **medieval city wall** can be seen. The remains of the wall dating from the 15th century were opened up and restored in 1934.

Now we have reached Széna tér, where the streets coming down Castle Hill end. The **Budavár Restaurant** as well as **Budavár Salon,** which stays open all night, are located here. At this end of Hattyú utca (Swan Street) old chestnut trees cast their shade over the Zöld Hordó (Green Barrel) Garden Restaurant which is very popular in this area.

Only a few steps separate us from Moszkva tér, which is one of the busiest squares of Buda. All bus and tramcar lines, as well as the main thoroughfares from northern Buda, converge on this square. It is also the starting point of the roads connecting Hűvösvölgy, Pasarét, Szabadsághegy, Sas-hegy, Zugliget and Farkasrét. From this square they lead to south Buda and over to Pest.

A huge red-brick building occupies the western side of the square. This is the building of the **Central Administration of Postal Services.** The top floor houses the **Museum of Postal Services,** where collections showing the development of telecommunications and the history of postal services are exhibited.

4. KRISZTINAVÁROS

Krisztina körút starting from Moszkva tér leads the visitor into a district which seems entirely different. The tall buildings that characterise Mártírok útja and Moszkva tér are absent here. On the left side is a spacious green field, Vérmező (Meadow of Blood). This park borders quite a good part of Krisztina körút, so that only on the right side of it are there any houses.

In this field of grass and shrubbery which spreads out at the foot of Castle Hill, splendid tournaments of knights were held in 1476, in honour of the brilliant wedding of King Matthias Corvinus and Beatrix of Aragon.

The present name, "Meadow of Blood", dates from 1795, when the field was the scene of mass executions. By order of the Hapsburg emperor the leaders of the Hungarian Jacobins, Ignác Martinovics, Jakab Sigray, Ferenc Szentmarjay, János Laczkovics and József Hajnóczy were beheaded here in that year. Two years later executions again took place in the meadow. On June, 3, 1797, two other companions of Martinovics, Sándor Szolarcsik and Pál Őz, were also put to death. The **memorial of the Jacobins** stands at the corner of Vérmező, where Krisztina körút and Attila út branch off. It is the work of Frigyes *Marton*. The entrance (departure platform) of the **Southern Railway Terminal** lies a few steps away from Magyar Jakobinusok tere. The tracks starting from this station were laid between 1859 and 1861. The station building was erected in 1873. However, it was almost completely destroyed in 1944. The greater part of it was reconstructed in 1949, and a new modern building was added in 1962. Trains depart from here for Lake Velence and Lake Balaton, as well as the southern and western parts of Transdanubia.

The building at 57 Krisztina körút houses the **Museum of Theatre History.** Somewhat farther on the boulevard passes through Krisztina tér, the geographical centre and main traffic junction of the district. In this square with a romantic atmosphere stands one of the most significant art monuments of the neighbourhood: the **Krisztinaváros Parish Church** built according to the designs of Kristóf *Hikisch* between 1795 and 1797.

The single-spired structure is built in the eclectic style. The middle of its façade juts out with a tympanum resting on the upper part. The two-storey spire of the church rises over the tympanum. The parapet of the fine portal rests on Doric columns. In both side sections of the façade there are niches with the statues of Kings St. Stephen and St. Ladislas (by Gyula *Szász*, 1884). In 1940 the church was reconstructed. The original choir, together with the

199

high altar, was moved backwards, and an arched transept-like protrusion was added to the church on each side.
The interior of the church is also interesting. On the sar-cophagus-shaped high altar stands the copy of a painting made in 1700, representing the "Bleeding Virgin Mary", whose original is in Rè, a village near Milan. Over the altar is a group of statues representing the Holy Trinity. The original altarpiece of the high altar which was painted by a contemporary artist, József F. *Falconer*, was destroyed during the siege of Budapest in 1944-45. Recently it has been replaced by the altarpiece of the former Castle Chapel. The statues of St. Joachim and St. Anne standing on the two sides of the altar are plaster casts, the work of the Pest sculptor Lipót *Salm*. The pulpit has special artistic value. The altarpieces and the ornaments of the side altars as well as the baptismal font of red marble from 1786 in the right-hand transept are quite remarkable. On the northwest wall of the building stands an exact replica of the statue of the Blessed Virgin Mary that stood here from the year 1702. Its original has been moved into the Castle Museum for preservation.
The popular **Déryné Pastry Shop,** a place of amusement with music and dancing, is located in this square (3 Krisztina tér). Alagút utca (Tunnel Street) leads into the square from the east. It is the continuation of the **Tunnel** which runs under Castle Hill. The Tunnel, which is 350 metres long, was designed by Dániel *Novák*, in 1837, and built by Adam *Clark*, in 1852. It was opened to traffic in 1857. The tunnel carries the traffic from the Inner City of Pest over the Suspension Bridge, straight here, into Krisz-tinaváros. It is a valuable shortcut both for motor vehicles and pedestrians.
To the left, behind Krisztina tér, situated somewhat lower than the boulevard, lies a pleasant and well-kept park, which was named **Horváth-kert** (Horváth Garden) after its one-time owner. In the first decade of the past century this garden of the Horváth House with its lemon and orange trees was one of the sights of Buda. At the time of the disastrous flood in 1838, the Institute for the Blind was moved here. On the side of this park, where Krisztina tér lies, was the building of the Buda summer theatre which stood here for many years, until it was pulled down in 1937. The **bust of** the great Austrian composer **Joseph Haydn** who spent many years at Fertőd, western Hungary, stands in the park (a work of András *Kocsis*).

ATTILA ÚT

The inner boulevard of Buda runs close to the foot of Castle Hill, starting behind the Horváth Garden. It continues its course in a southeastern direction, bearing the name Attila út.

Let us stop a few moments before the house at **No. 37,** which, although it is not a monument of art, is connected with two tragic events of the Second World War. On March 19, 1944, the day of the occupation of Hungary by the German fascists, Endre Bajcsy-Zsilinszky, the great patriot and noted political writer of the opposition, was dragged from his home and murdered because of his antifascist convictions. A few moths later, a fighter plane of the German Luftwaffe crashed on the roof of this house in an aerial battle with Soviet fighters. For many months the wreck of the plane could be seen hanging on the house top as a symbol of the defeat of fascism.

A few steps away from here the thoroughfare broadens into a square over which the western wing of the royal castle looms in its full majesty. This square is Dózsa György tér, named after the leader of the peasant uprising in 1514. The square lies on the site of the royal gardens of King Matthias. In the south of the square stands a **granite column** which once decorated the **garden of King Matthias** and was unearthed in nearby Váralja utca in 1925. The **statue of György Dózsa** was erected in 1961 (a work of István *Kiss*). Further on Attila út becomes still broader and leads through Szarvas tér (Stag Square). Here the house at No. 1, the so-called **Szarvasház,** built in Louis XVI style, is worth mentioning. Over the entrance a relief can be seen, which depicts a fleeing stag. The house was built at the beginning of the 18th century. The Szarvas Café was located here, and the square was named after its signboard. At the time of the great fire in 1810, which ravaged the Tabán district, the house burnt down, but was rebuilt the next year, and obtained its present fine architectural appearance. The vaulted doorway and the ground floor premises of the house are interesting sights. In 1962 the house was entirely reconstructed in its original form. It has been turned into a restaurant and a tavern called the Arany Szarvas (Golden Stag).

With its back facing Szarvas tér, in Attila út, is the old **Parish Church of Tabán** known also as St. Catherine

Church. On the site of this church, or close to it, stood a chapel named "Capella Virginia" during the reign of King Stephen I (1001-1038). The present-day church was erected by the Carinthian architect Christian *Obergruber* between 1728 and 1736. The spire and the main façade were completed according to the designs of Máté *Nepauer* between 1750 and 1753. A tympanum closes the façade of the baroque church, which is divided into three sections. The statues of St. Catharine, St. Gellért (Gerard) and St. Carlo Borromeo are seen in the middle of the tympanum. A fragment of the tympanum relief dating from the 12th century, the so-called "Christ of Tabán", was walled in under the organ choir at the time when the church was reconstructed. The original of this stone relief was later transferred to the Castle Museum, today a replica made of artificial stone replaces it. A Mohammedan mosque erected by Mustafa Pasha in the forties of the 16th century stood here during the Turkish occupation. It was transformed into a Christian chapel after the liberation of Buda.

THE SUBURBS

1. CITY PARK

The City Park (Városliget) is the largest and most popular
park of Budapest. Its area is approximately one square
kilometre. From the Inner City it can be reached best by
bus through Népköztársaság útja (People's Republic Avenue) or by the underground railway. As a matter of fact,
it is a natural park. The artificial pond, the Vajdahunyad
Castle on small Széchenyi Island, centuries-old trees and
well-kept promenades, children's playgrounds, flower
beds and numerous artistic monuments and statues make
the City Park a much frequented excursion point on the
Pest side.

Its history goes back to the Middle Ages. From 1298 to
1540, when the Diet met on the Rákosmező (Rákos Meadow), the lesser nobility was encamped here, thus expressing its isolation from the aristocracy residing in the Buda
Castle. In 1458, 40,000 of the lesser nobility proceeded
to Buda to proclaim Mátyás Hunyadi (Matthias Corvinus)
king of Hungary. The leader of the 1514 peasant uprising,
György Dózsa, camped here with his army. During the
Turkish occupation in the 16th and 17th centuries, almost
the whole region became a desert. By order of Empress
Maria Theresa it was planted with willows (1755-1757).
Its modern history begins, as a matter of fact, with this
period. In 1817 the region was turned into a park.

In 1896 the City Park was the site of the Millenary Exhibition (to commemorate the conquest of the land by the
Magyar tribes in 896).

The City Park also played a prominent role in the event-
ful decades of the Hungarian labour movement. The first
May Day demonstration and festivities in Budapest took
place here on May 1, 1890, with the participation of
great masses of workers. In 1917, at the news of the

Great October Socialist Revolution, the war-weary workers longing for peace assembled in the City Park and demanded an end to the war. In 1930 the greatest demonstration of the period between the two world wars took place here; the demonstrators demanded work and bread for the workers of Budapest. Since the liberation in 1945, the workers of Budapest have regularly celebrated May Day here every year.

Behind the Millenary Monument stands the building of the skating rink, by the shallow **City Park Pond.** It was erected to the designs of Imre *Francsek,* in the last decade of the 19th century. In front of the main entrance are two statues, the bronze **statue of St. Christopher** (by László *Hűvös*) and the "Archer" by Zsigmond *Kisfaludi Strobl.* In summer the pond is used for boating. In autumn the water is drained off and an artificial ice rink is made over an area of 4,800 sq. metres.

Bridges lead from all sides to the small island in the middle of the pond. One of the finest monuments of Budapest stands here: **Vajdahunyad Castle.** This group of buildings with crenellated ornaments was modelled after sections of 21 different monumental buildings. It was designed for the 1896 millenary exhibition by the architect Ignác *Alpár.* (The castle obtained its name from the Castle of Vajdahunyad in Transylvania, to which its most characteristic elements bear a very great likeness.) This is a splendid example of the art of Ignác Alpár, who was able to create harmony and unity out of the most dissimilar architectural styles. In the little park within the complex of buildings and along the promenade there are several noteworthy statues. The **statue of the architect Ignác Alpár** stands in front of the castle's entrance. In the courtyard of the castle is the **statue** (a work by Miklós *Ligeti*) **of the famous nameless chronicler "Anonymus",** who lived in the 12th century during the reign of King Béla III. Alajos *Stróbl* modelled the **statue of the** well-known economist **Sándor Károlyi** (1831-1906), the **stone figure of George Washington** was carved by Gyula *Bezerédi,* Ede *Margó* did the **statue of** the story-writer **Lajos Pósa,** János László *Beszédes* the **figure of a horseman,** and the **"Fountain of Youth"** is the work of the sculptor Géza *Horváth.*

The northern wing of the Vajdahunyad Castle houses the **Agricultural Museum** with permanent exhibitions in 21 rooms.

Not far away from the castle, at the terminus of the underground railway, stands the vast neo-baroque building of the **Széchenyi Medicinal and Open-Air Baths.** The three basins of the baths can accommodate 6,000 people. The Széchenyi Baths' spring erupts from a depth of 1,256 metres and yields 820,000 litres of medicinal water daily at a temperature of 76°C. The water contains sulphur, calcium and magnesium hydrocarbonate. It is one of the hottest springs in the whole of Europe. In the medicinal baths' establishment there are thermal and steam baths for men and women, hot air and steam chambers, individual thermal baths, and carbonate and salt baths. If the doctor prescribes it, patients can obtain mud packs and massages here. The water of the Széchenyi Baths has a powerful curative effect. It is indicated for the after-treatment of rheumatic troubles, articular disorders and injuries, and in case of chronic arthritis and nervous diseases. Drinking cures relieve gastric disorders and ailments of the respiratory tracts.

Beyond the Millenary Monument, along Állatkerti út, we find the well-known **Gundel Restaurant.** In the shade of ancient trees there is also a garden restaurant which accommodates 800 people. In winter the specialities of Hungarian cuisine are served in the luxuriously furnished inner premises.

Next to Gundel lie the **Zoo and Botanical Gardens of Budapest.** The main entrance with four huge stone elephants presents an oriental atmosphere. This area of about fourteen hectares is the home of some 3,500 animals from various parts of the world. Similarly to the Hamburg Hagenbeck Zoo, here, too, the aim is to show every animal in its original environment. The Zoo, over one hundred years old, is one of the best equipped in the whole of Europe with a wide range of animals. Next to the Zoo stands the **Municipal Grand Circus,** which is open all the year round giving varied performances with Hungarian and foreign stars.

Continuing our way, we reach the **Gaiety Park** (Vidám Park). Every year from early spring till late autumn some 2.5 to 3 million people, old and young, visit this amusement park, where they find merry-go-rounds, dodgems, a scenic railway, a Ferris wheel, the "Haunted Castle", side shows and all kinds of games where the youngsters can display their dexterity and patience.

In the middle of the City Park the **Budapest Internation-**

al Fair is organised in May every year on an area covering about 250,000 sq. metres. In recent years some 2,000 firms from 25 countries have taken part in the Fair to exhibit their goods and the products of their countries. The Fair which is usually open for eleven days attracts over one million visitors a year.

In the southeastern part of the City Park, at the crossing of Ajtósi Dürer sor (named after the famous painter Albrecht Dürer) and Népstadion út (People's Stadium Avenue) lies the **Model Garden of the Budapest Horticultural Enterprise.** This area covering about half a hectare is not only an ornament of the City Park, but also serves educational purposes. The visitor finds here herbs, plants grown for industrial purposes, weeds, vegetable plants, condiments, vineyard stocks, fruit trees, various kinds of water plants, flowers and plants growing in marshes and on rocks.

Opposite the model garden, on the other side of Népstadion út, stands the one-time building of the **Budapest Municipal Museum,** which was built in 1885 with rich majolica decorations. In the Second World War it was badly damaged, but was restored in 1961. Nearby stands a **statue** by Alajos *Stróbl* entitled the **"Reading Girl",** which was erected in 1929. A few steps further lies a **tombstone** made of red marble. It bears a single word in Latin: *"Fuit".* An eccentric Budapest lawyer, who left part of his fortune to the municipality, is buried here. He made his bequest on condition that he would be buried here nameless under the trees of the City Park. In compliance with his will, in 1809 a tombstone was placed on his grave.

The northeastern side of the City Park ends at Május 1. út. The building at No. 23 in this street flanked by villas and gardens is the little **Hermina Chapel,** built to the design of József *Hild* between 1843 and 1854. The church adjoining it was built in our century, and was restored a few years ago. The frescoes in the choir depict the life of St. Francis.

2. THE PEOPLE'S STADIUM AND ITS NEIGHBOURHOOD

South of the City Park are important sport establishments accessible from the Inner City through Thököly út, or from the City Park through Népstadion út.

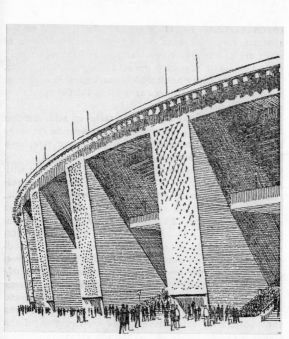

The People's Stadium

Leaving the crossing of Népstadion út and Thököly út behind, we pass by the house at 20 Népstadion út, where many statues can be seen in the garden. This is the **studio** of the famous sculptor Zsigmond *Kisfaludi Strobl*. Three houses further along (No. 14) we find the **Geological Institute**. The building was designed by Ödön *Lechner*, and was erected in 1898-99. Colourful Hungarian ceramics decorate the front of the building. A few steps from here the imposing reinforced concrete structure of the **People's Stadium** (Népstadion) comes into sight.

The building was erected between 1948 and 1953 after the designs of Károly *Dávid*. Sportsmen and fans alike helped in the construction of the building in their spare time. The monumental structure extends over an area of 22 hectares, and cost 150 million forints. The People's Stadium ranks as one of the most modern sports establishments in the world. The 30-metre-high, 15-metre-wide and 328-metre-long grandstands are supported by ornate concrete pylons. Elevators are at the disposal of the spectators at both ends of the pylons. The flights of stairs are of up-to-date construction, and through the 50 exits the public can leave the stadium in a few minutes. This huge structure holds 84,000 spectators. When sport events of major significance take place 100,000 spectators can be accommodated.

Full use has been made of modern technical achievements in the equipment of the stadium. Its telephone exchange disposes of 27 outside lines, and the house telephone system has 200 extensions. On the second floor of the main building there are sound-proof boxes for journalists with another twelve telephone lines. Radio running commentaries can be transmitted from 20 booths simultaneously. There are two electric scoreboards each with a clock five metres in diameter. The scoreboard installation is a Hungarian invention, which has been taken over by many stadiums in the world. All over the stadium a system of loudspeakers keeps the public informed of the results. Evening sports events have been held in the stadium under floodlights since 1959. Ten dressing rooms accommodate the competitors, each having its own bathing basin and shower room. Thirty-three buffets with 400 vendors serve the public with refreshments. The construction of the stands is not complete yet. When the semicircular stand will be built all round, its seating capacity will be increased by 25,000. The main entrance on the south side faces Ifjúság útja (Avenue of Youth), the two side entrances open on Verseny utca and Népstadion út. **Eight statues** representing the various sports flank Ifjúság útja.

In the immediate vicinity of the People's Stadium there are additional sport facilities. The **Little Stadium** (Kis Stadion) is the most recent of them. At the crossing of Istvánmezei út and Dózsa György út lies the **National Sport Hall** (Nemzeti Sportcsarnok). The building is surrounded by training grounds, one of these is the **"Ice Theatre"**, where the Budapest Ice Show, which is also famous abroad, holds its performances.

Northwest of the stadium, at the corner of Thököly út and Szabó József utca, lies the **Millenary Sport Ground** (Millenáris pálya) with a seating capacity of 20,000. Apart from cycling and motorcycling contests, it is used for other sports including skating contests and ice hockey matches.

3. ÓBUDA

Óbuda and its surroundings are the oldest parts of Budapest. Celts and Eraviscans founded a town at the northern
edge of present-day Óbuda some 2,000 years ago. Hardly
a historical period passed without leaving behind relics of
some kind to posterity, but owing to the difficult times
this part of the town experienced through the centuries,
almost no sights of greater importance have survived, for
this place of ancient culture was destroyed scores of
times.

Walking northwards from Margaret Bridge we reach Kolosy tér. This is the boundary of Óbuda, District 3 of Budapest. Here, at Bécsi út (Vienna Road), stands a **baroque
Parish Church.** It was erected between 1746 and 1759.
A number of baroque carvings and works of the goldsmith's craft can be seen in the interior of the church. The
road starting from here, Lajos utca (Louis Street), bears
the name of Louis the Great, a Hungarian king of the House
of Anjou. At the end of this street stands a **synagogue**
built in neoclassic style in 1820-21.

Near Nagyszombat utca lies the most significant historical
monument of this quarter, the former **Roman amphitheatre of the military town of Aquincum.** The remains of the walls date from the middle of the 2nd century
and show the characteristic ground plans of the Roman
circus: it had an oval arena, with stands widening as the
tiers ascended. Twenty-four buttresses support the outer
circular wall. Between them the public could enter the
stands through twenty smaller doorways. There were four
other entrances in the directions of the two main axes.
The whole amphitheatre could hold 13,000 spectators and
it covered an area 131.8 by 108.4 metres. The dimensions
of the arena itself were 89.6 by 66.1 metres.

To the west of the upper end of Lajos utca down to Korvin
Ottó utca we find a pleasant old part of the town with
small alleys and passages. At the corner of Nád utca (Reed
Street) and Dugovics Titusz tér stands the **Óbuda Parish
Church** built in 1744. [According to tradition Titusz Dugovics was a Hungarian knight who, during the siege of
Nándorfehérvár (today's Belgrade) in 1456, seized a Turkish warrior who was about to hoist the banner of victory, and plunged off the battlement with him to die a
hero's death.] The **Calvinist church** in Calvin köz was
built in 1785-86 on the site of the medieval royal palace,

whose stones were used for the construction of the church. Another building here is the **Goldberger Textile Works** of Óbuda, which was established in 1781. Its products are well known the world over.

Kiscelli utca connects this part of the town with the area to the west. The upper section of this road runs steeply up to the hilltop above Óbuda and ends at the **Castle of Kiscell,** which is a group of buildings dating from the 18th century. One side of the road is skirted by an old park surrounded by a stone wall. This is the ornamental garden of the castle. Today this castle houses the collection of **modern history of the Municipal Historical Museum.** Relics and documents relating to the history of the capital are kept here. Originally the building was the monastery of the Trinitarians, and was built by the Viennese architect *Entzenhoffer* between 1744 and 1748. The ornate baroque gate of the former Vienna war ministry was built into the wall facing the courtyard of the baroque building. The church that belonged to it—now in ruins—was also built by *Entzenhoffer* (in 1747 to 1760). South of the Museum, in Doberdó utca, stands the **Calvary Church** built in 1812-14.

According to the latest schedule of town planning the new centre of Óbuda will be shifted to the abutment of the Árpád Bridge. Korvin Ottó utca and Korvin Ottó tér are to form the nucleus of the new centre named after Ottó Korvin, a leading figure of the 1919 Hungarian Republic of Councils who died a martyr. The **Roman Camp Lapidary** connected with the history of the antique military town is housed at 63 Korvin Ottó utca. Among the carefully preserved exhibits a Roman heating system and the steps of a bath and the lead pipes serving as outlets from the bath are shown here. The museum contains a number of interesting finds from the Roman period: agricultural implements and other tools.

Korvin Ottó tér and Fő tér (Main Square) lie close to one another. Fő tér was the market-place of **Óbuda** in the 17th and 18th centuries. In the garden of the house at No. 1 stands the former **Zichy Castle,** the finest baroque building of Óbuda. It was built between 1746 and 1757 by the Buda architect Johann Heinrich *Jäger.* In front of the house stands the **statue of Gyula Krúdy,** an outstanding writer of the early 20th century. Another building worth seeing in Fő tér is the **former town hall of Óbuda** (No. 3). The one-storey building in Kórház utca (Hospital Street), which starts from Fő tér, still preserves to a great extent the architectural style of the 18th century. Among them, noteworthy is the house at **No. 18**, in Louis XVI style. In the cellar of the house at No. 3 in nearby Flórián tér a **Roman military bath** was discovered during recent excavations. The remains of the largest Roman military bath are preserved in two rooms below the ground, thus forming a little underground museum.

Szentendrei út leads to the northern part of Óbuda from Flórián tér and Fő tér. This road connects the capital with the excursion points at the Danube Bend. This road takes us also to **Aquincum** and **Római-fürdő** (Roman Baths). At the beginning of the road stands the **Máriakő Chapel**. In front of it a pillar of the one-time Roman aqueduct can be seen. There are several such pillars along this road. The aqueduct carried the water at the time from present-day Római-fürdő to the residential area of Aquincum. An indication of its length is that along this section stood some 500 pillars at a distance of three metres from each other. From Flórián tér opens Miklós utca, the site of the Óbuda **bus terminus.** From here buses run to Aquincum and to the holiday and bathing resort centres of Római-part (Roman Beach), and also to the nearby mountains.

Harrer Pál utca connects Flórián tér with Miklós tér. A most interesting sight is the **silk mill** located in the courtyard of the corner building at No. 46. This factory was built in 1785, and ranks among the industrial curiosities of the area. The oval, one-storey structure in the Louis XVI style was built by József *Tallherr* after the designs of *Mazzocato*, an Italian architect. Its main façade is divided by an arch-shaped flight of stairs.

The quarter situated west of Szentendrei út has two entirely different sights to offer. At the corner of Hunor utca and Raktár utca we find one of the oldest architectural monuments of Budapest: the foundation walls of an **old Christian chapel** dating from the 4th century. The trefoil-shaped ground plan of the chapel (Cella trichora) was discovered in 1930. In its neighbourhood the construction of a new housing estate was begun on Hévízi út in 1950. It is an **experimental housing estate** because the most up-to-date technological methods of housing construction are tested here.

In Óbuda there are many little inns, garden restaurants and pubs for those who like to spend their time in a homelike atmosphere.

4. AQUINCUM

Szentendrei út leads straight northwards to Aquincum. This place reminds us of the time of 2,000 years ago. Its ruins give eloquent evidence of the culture and civilisation of the Romans who ruled here at that time. Aquincum was the northeastern outpost of the Roman Empire, one of its strongholds of major importance; the Second Auxiliary Legion with no less than 8,000 men was stationed here. In its golden age the town had 60,000 inhabitants. This is an incredibly large number if we take into account that the whole area of present-day Budapest did not reach this figure until after 1810. Ancient Aquincum consisted of two parts: the fortified camp and the military colony of the area of present-day Óbuda, and the civilian town, which was situated some three kilometres to the north. This area has retained the name of Aquincum to the present day.

The area where the ruins of Aquincum lie clearly shows the ground-plan arrangement of part of the civilian town. Broad streets ran along the main axes of the town with rows of private houses and public buildings. The road which is lined today by sarcophagi is of modern construction. Underneath there are still unexcavated dwelling houses. The ruins that lie in the open show ample evidence of the building methods of the one-time Roman town, of the highly developed civilisation that existed in Aquincum from the 2nd century till the collapse of the province of Pannonia in 409. The streets here were paved by the Romans and along them are traces of large-scale representative public buildings made of stone and brick: a covered market hall, a sports hall, drainage canals, comfortable public and private baths.

Amidst the ruins on a grassy space stands the **Aquincum Museum.** The rich material it contains gives evidence of the tastes, education, architecture, world outlook and social structure of the one-time population. The most precious item in the collection is an old Roman organ. Its 52 pipes are arranged in four rows and have a range of two chromatic octaves. This most rare and antique instrument is popularly called a water organ, although it actually worked with bellows. The dedication tablet has also been preserved in good condition. From this we learn that the fire brigade of Aquincum got it as a present so that the men of the fire station might enjoy listening to it on festive occasions. The inscription on a sarcophagus unearthed here tells us that it contained the body of the first woman singer and organist who entertained the public by playing this instrument. The reconstructed organ, which can still be played, stands in a glass case in its original form.

The colonnade surrounding the building of the museum is very interesting with the tombstones from the Roman cemetery that had been opened up. Among the finds exhibited here there is also an altar stone in honour of the sun god Mithras, from the early 3rd century. (For further information, see page 269.)

North of the Aquincum Museum, beyond the present railway embankment, lie the **ruins of an amphitheatre** of the civilian town. It covers an area of 86.5 by 75.5 metres, and the arena itself is 53.4 by 45.5 metres. It is estimated that this amphitheatre must have seated six to seven thousand people. The platform with the seats round the arena is supposed to have had a height of two metres over which a 60-centimetre-high stone bar protected the spectators from wild animals. The names of the box owners are engraved on some of the stone blocks.

Remnants of the Roman times can also be found outside the ancient town, notably on the neighbouring slopes and on the Danube islands. Between 1951 and 1955 the ruins of the one-time **governor's palace** were uncovered on Hajógyári-sziget (Shipyard Island). The palace was built by Hadrian, the first proconsul of Aquincum and later Roman emperor, at the beginning of the 2nd century. It extended over an area of 120 metres by 95, and was furnished with all possible luxury, such as a central heating system, air heating and baths. As the excavations are still in progress, the ruins are not yet accessible to the public.

5. RÓMAI-FÜRDŐ AND RÓMAI-PART

Beyond Aquincum, from Szentendrei út down to the Danube, the area is dotted with villas, summer cottages, holiday centres and boat-houses.

In the immediate neighbourhood of Szentendrei út, amidst a picturesque wood, lies Római-fürdő (Roman Baths) with a pond of crystal clear water fed by fourteen springs. The name of this bathing spot indicates that the Romans already knew of these springs and used them. In the 15th century a hospital stood here and later the little brook formed by the springs served to drive a gunpowder mill. Early in the 16th century crusading knights had their quarters in the buildings erected round the pond. In the last century it was already used as a bathing resort, but its popularity really began to grow only a few decades ago. In order to meet the present-day requirements the bathing establishment is being completely rebuilt and modernised.

Adjoining the open-air bath is the **international camping-park** of the Municipal Tourist Office, which is at the disposal of tourists from May to September.

Római-part (Roman Beach) is a paradise for boating and swimming. This holiday resort begins at the Újpest Railway Bridge and extends upstream over a length of five kilometres. Some 400 villas, week-end houses and cottages cover this strip of land, 250 to 270 metres wide. Every Sunday morning in summer, when the weather is good, thousands of rowing craft and motorboats start out from here to various excursion points on the Danube.

Large-scale projects are in preparation to modernise this holiday resort, which so far has been developed at random without planning and has grown into a huge colony with comfortable boat-houses, hotels, restaurants. The river-bank will be regulated and streets and parks will be laid out, so that Római-part will be able to accommodate 100,000 to 120,000 visitors in the future.

6. RÓZSADOMB

Wandering along the tortuous little streets of the Hill of Roses (Rózsadomb) lined with trees and green lawns with fragrant flowers one might reflect on how suitable the names of these streets and squares are: almond, sorb, bilberry, rowan-berry, juniper, fig, tulip, lilac, bud, pansy, corn-flower.

From the geographical point of view the name of the Hill of Roses is not quite correct, because this area consists of several hills. Strictly speaking, however, only the south-eastern part, the hillside which descends steeply towards the Danube, is Rózsadomb; the hilly area beyond belongs to the southern foothills of the Hill of Three Boundaries, which are Szemlő-hegy, Ferenc-hegy and Rókus-hegy.

The inner part of the Hill of Roses can be reached from the Buda abutment of the Margaret Bridge through Margit utca (Margaret Street). Right at the beginning of this street (No. 15) we pass by the Margit Garden Restaurant where in the past writers and artists used to meet. Turning to the right at Mecset utca (Mosque Street), we come to an octagonal structure with a hemispherical dome, surrounded by a colonnaded building. This is the **tomb of Gül Baba** (Father of Roses), who was worshipped by the Mohammedans as a saint. He was a dervish who came to Buda with the troops of Sultan Soliman II. Originally his name was "Kel Baba", i.e. Bald-headed Father, and the byname Gül (rose) was given him later. Towards the end of his life he became the principal among the dervish monks and in this capacity he wore a rose-like emblem on his turban. The tomb was erected by the Pasha of Buda between 1543 and 1545. After the liberation of Buda in 1686, this building was turned into a Christian chapel for a short time, but was given back to the Mohammedans, this being their holy shrine. Even centuries afterwards pilgrims continue to visit his grave. (The key to visit the interesting tomb can be obtained from the caretaker of the house at 14 Mecset utca.)

The block of buildings at 5-7 Keleti Károly utca houses the **Central Office of Statistics,** and the house at 1 Kitaibel Pál utca, the **National Meteorological Institute.**

The bus climbs up the serpentine road through Rómer Flóris utca (named after the outstanding Hungarian archaeologist of the last century), Szemlőhegy utca and Vérhalom utca on the southeastern slopes of Rózsadomb, to Vérhalom tér (Blood Hill Square), on the hilltop.

The name of this hill recalls dreadful events in Hungarian history. During the reign of King Sigismund, in the first half of the 15th century, the bodies of the beheaded noblemen, István Kont of Hédervár and his companions, the leaders of a revolt in southern Hungary, were buried here. Half a century later the body of László Hunyadi, who was executed treacherously by order of King Ladislas V on March 16, 1457, was also buried on this hill. He was the son of János Hunyadi, regent of Hungary, who was famous for his victories over the Turks.

Passing through one of the streets leading northwards from this square, we reach Szemlő-hegy. During the siege of Buda in 1686, this was the "point of observation" of the northern wing of the German and Hungarian troops, hence its name (Observation Hill). On the summit of Ferenc-hegy there is a lookout tower, commanding a wonderful view of the Buda hills, the inner districts of Buda, especially of Szépvölgy, of the Óbuda hills, as well as of János Hill and Liberty Hill.

Over Pusztaszeri út and Barlang utca (Cave Street) we soon reach the **Szemlő-hegy Cave** (10 Barlang utca). This cave was discovered in 1930 while quarrying was in progress. It is 600 metres long, and consists of three chambers lying one on top of the other, the middle cavern being richest in dripstone. This is not the usual stalactite and stalagmite formation, but consists of aragonite, and its form suggests rose petals and cabbage heads. In the most beautiful part, in the "Bower of Roses", the aragonite formations lie more closely against one another than perhaps anywhere else in the world. These formations originate from the mineral substances of the thermal water which filled these caves some time long in the past.

Near the Szemlő-hegy Cave, at 65 Törökvész út, lies another cave, the **aragonite cave** of Ferenc-hegy. It was discovered at the time of the canalisation of this area, and was opened up in 1933.

The name Törökvész (Turkish Disaster) as well as those of Spáhi út (Spahi Street), Csatárka út (Warrior Street) and Bég utca (Bey Street) remind us of the 1686 siege of Buda. Forming a large crescent from Gellért Hill as far as Óbuda, the Hungarian and German troops encircled the Turks, who had entrenched themselves in the Castle under the command of Abdurrahman Pasha. Part of the troops which the sultan sent to relieve the besieged were destroyed on this spot by the besiegers.

The residential area of the Hill of Roses, which extends northwest of Gábor Áron utca and Pusztaszeri út, is less densely built in.

Ascending steep Szalonka utca, we reach the northernmost top of the Hill of Roses range: the 377-metre-high Lookout Hill (Látó-hegy or Gugger-hegy), which forms the northern boundary of this villa quarter. Over the pine-clad hilltop rises the **Árpád Lookout Tower**, erected in 1929. From here we get a splendid view of Budapest. Towards the south and west we see the range of the Buda hills, and in the north and northeast the big mass of the Hill of Three Boundaries. The view towards the east, especially in the evening hours, is almost beyond compare. The lights of the town are like garlands of pearls against black velvet, and the bridges illuminated by fluorescent lights span the Danube like sparkling bracelets.

Szépvölgyi út winds along the foot of the hill and takes us to the most extensive dripstone cave of Budapest, the **Pálvölgy Cave** (Pálvölgyi barlang). A permanent guide service and a **hostel** nearby serve the convenience of the tourists. Restaurants with excellent cooking (Erdei Lak, Fenyőgyöngye), have been built in the hills, at places where the visitor gets a superb view. They are popular places of entertainment for Hungarians and foreigners alike.

7. PASARÉT

The southern part of Outer Rózsadomb, extending from the Törökvész plateau and hillside down to Szilágyi Erzsébet fasor and Vöröshadsereg útja, bears the name Pasarét (Pasha's Meadow). The lovely residential area with its well-kept gardens is very much like the villa quarter of the Inner Rózsadomb. Its main thoroughfare is Pasaréti út. Walking uphill along Gábor Áron utca we cross Herman Ottó út, which is named after the outstanding Hungarian naturalist Ottó Herman (1836-1914). A big block of houses (No. 15) is the home of important scientific institutes, making it the centre of Hungarian agricultural science. Here we find the **Genetic Institute** of the Hungarian Academy of Sciences, the **Institute of Soil Research and Agrochemistry**, the **Research Institute for Viticulture**, the **Institute of Ornithology and Hydrobiology**, and the **Institute for the Sugar Industry**. A sports centre is also located in Pasarét, the **Vasas Sport Club** (11-13 Pasaréti út). The grounds here for athletics and tennis compare with the best in Budapest. At the end of Pasaréti út, in Pasaréti tér, stands a **church** built in modern style (designed by Gyula *Rimanóczy*).

8. THE RESIDENTIAL AREA OF HEGYALJA

On our way from Moszkva tér towards the Southern Railway Terminal to the left we leave Vérmező behind and to the right the quarter of Városmajor, as well as a few smaller streets, which lie at the foot of the hills. Among them is Ráth György utca, where the **Oncological Hospital** with a department for outpatients is the only building of importance. Then follows Nagyenyed utca. From here Istenhegyi út leads to Liberty Hill, Németvölgyi út touches the cemeteries of southern Buda, and Böszörményi út is the area's shopping centre. To the right of it lies Joliot-Curie tér. (It obtained its name from the great French scientist and advocate of world peace.) Most shops, restaurants and espressos of the area are located in Böszörményi út. Close by, at 9 Gaál utca, stands the **hotel of the Express Youth Travel Bureau.** The big building of red brick at No. 23-25 is the **Council House of District 12.** At the end of Böszörményi út begins Csörsz utca with the **Hungarian Optical Works.** The domed building to the right is the cultural centre which possesses a cinema, a theatre room, a ballroom, billiard rooms and lounges.

9. ZUGLIGET

The residential area which spreads out over the northern slopes of Liberty Hill also belongs to the district described above, but it has its own bus and tram line network connecting it with busy Szilágyi Erzsébet fasor and the Városmajor quarter.

Zugliget proper begins at the two northern foothills of Liberty Hill: Tündér-hegy (Fairy Hill) and Hunyad-orom (Hunyad Crest). Zugligeti út winds between them. In one of its side streets, Szilassy út, stands the old villa named "God's Eye", which is now the **Kossuth Children's Home.** In this building, surrounded by a lovely park covering four hectares, some 45 to 50 physically and mentally retarded children are cared for and educated. It was here that Lajos Kossuth was arrested on May 4, 1837. A detachment of 48 grenadiers marched up to the house to take him by force to the prison on Castle Hill, from where he was not released until 1840. A rather steep road leads from here to the best known spring on Liberty Hill, **Disznófő** (Boar's Head), which is also a very popular excursion place. In olden times many wild boar roamed the once dense forest in the region, hence the name. The spring, called **Mátyáscsorgó,** used to flow from the mouth of an iron boar's head. In the clearing above Disznófő stands a bronze **bust of Kossuth,** one-and-a-half times life-size. Unveiled in 1913, this was the first Kossuth statue in Budapest.

Parallel to Szilassy út, in a quiet and pleasant little vale, runs Csillagvölgyi út. Right at its beginning we come to a settlement called **Diogenesfalva.** In the last century when there were extensive vineyards in the Buda hills, one of the wine-growers was struck by the idea of decorating his house with a twelve-thousand-gallon barrel. This is how the Greek philosopher's name was linked with the name of the settlement. When the vineyards were destroyed by phylloxera, this huge barrel served for some time as a dwelling, but later on it was sold for timber. This is already the centre of Zugliget, one of Budapest's most popular excursion places. It was already much frequented 150 years ago. Later on a railway was constructed which led right to Zugliget. A long and winding street, Béla király útja, connects this area with the centre of Liberty Hill. From many points along this thoroughfare a fine view of Hűvösvölgy, Lipótmező and, in the background, the peaks of the Pilis and Dobogókő mountains can be seen. Right at the beginning of this street stood the one-time Pheasant Inn. Behind it there are several springs. **King Béla's Well** in front of the plot at No. 30/b was already used at the time of King Matthias Corvinus, and when the Turkish occupation was ended, its water was conveyed through a conduit to the Buda Castle. Not far away, where Csermely út ends, we come across another spring, which the Turks named **Kasim Pasha's Well**. With the construction of the Buda water supply system these springs lost much of their significance.

The most notable and also most abundant spring of the area is the **City Well Spring** (Városkút), which is located at the uppermost section of Béla király útja near the cogwheel railway. It is worth visiting the single-storey building that was erected there with its Romanesque gate pillars. In a frontal niche of the building a Romanesque sculptured stone monument was found, which now can be seen in the Municipal Historical Museum. A passage with a Gothic vaulted ceiling leads into the interior of the mountain. The well lies 170 metres higher than Castle Hill, and so the water that was conveyed there had sufficient pressure to feed the fountain standing in front of the Matthias Church. During Turkish rule this water-works system fell into ruin, and was only restored between 1717 and 1728. Coming to the end of Béla király útja, we have again reached the centre of Liberty Hill.

10. LIBERTY HILL AND SZÉCHENYI HILL

This hilly region of Budapest consists of two parts: the residential area with villas and gardens, and the open area of tourists and hikers. This latter area covers some 1,400 hectares and the town administration does not permit any of it to be parcelled out because the forests and green meadows are to supply the town with fresh air. The Buda hills are, in fact, the northeasternmost foothills of the Transdanubian Mountains. The low-lying valley of Hűvösvölgy (Cool Valley) and its immediate continuation divide the hilly countryside into two parts. One is the region north of the Margaret Bridge, which we have described earlier, and the other the area of Liberty Hill (Szabadság-hegy) János Hill and Linden Hill (Hárs-hegy).

Liberty Hill and its surroundings have been inhabited for several thousand years. In the vicinity of the City Well Spring bone implements and pieces of pottery were found that go back to the neolithic period. Celts and later Romans settled here. On the slopes leading towards Farkasrét (Wolves' Meadow) implements and articles of personal use dating from the bronze age were unearthed.

Hungarian historic sources mention the mountain for the first time in the 12th century. During the reign of Kings Géza II and Béla III the clearing of the vast woodland was begun, and vineyards were planted in its place. In the 18th century the hillside was populated mainly by German and Serbian settlers. In the 18th and 19th centuries the sunny slopes were the scene of colourful vintage celebrations, but towards the end of the last century the flourishing vineyards were destroyed by phylloxera.

Before the liberation the mountain was called Sváb-hegy (Swabian Hill), named after the German troops that camped here during the 1686 siege of Buda. It obtained its present name on July 4, 1945.

The upper part of Liberty Hill reaches 477 metres at Normafa (Norma Tree). A bus line leads to Liberty Hill, but most visitors prefer to take the cogwheel railway, which is the traditional and most popular means of communication, starting at Szilágyi Erzsébet fasor.

The **cogwheel railway** is one of the oldest public conveyances of Budapest. Its track was built 90 years ago. It was opened to traffic on July 24, 1874, as the third mountain railway in the world. At that time a steam locomotive was used to push the carriages uphill, but in 1929 the line was electrified. At first the track of the cogwheel railway ended at Liberty Hill and in 1890 the line was extended to Széchenyi Hill. Before 1910 it was considered only a holiday and tourist railway, and winter operation started only when the villa quarter came into existence on the summit of Liberty Hill. A 14 HP electric engine drives the trains up and downhill at a speed of 12 kilometres an hour. With the help of a special mechanism it is possible to feed back into the power network during descent one-third of the power consumed on the uphill ride. The track is 3,733 metres long. The difference in level between the terminuses is 315 metres.

As soon as the train has left the lower terminus at Városmajor, a splendid view of the northern Buda hills begins to unfold. To the right we pass by the buildings of the János Hospital and the Kútvölgyi út Hospital, and as the train ascends the panorama widens every minute. One after the other, first the western slopes of the Hill of Roses (Rózsadomb), Lookout Hill (Látó-hegy) and the Hill of Three Boundaries (Hármashatár-hegy) appear before our eyes, then the green peak of János Hill and the southern hillside of Linden Hill. To the left, we see the villas of Martinovics Hill, and the northern hillsides of God's Hill (Isten-hegy) and Orgonásdűlő sink lower and lower.

The sixth stop from the town is the most important station of the trip: the Liberty Hill station. Here we find the shopping and traffic centre of the area, from where buses also leave for the interior of the hilly region.

In the little park near the station building stands the **statue of** the writer **József Eötvös**, erected in 1890, and at the corner of Eötvös út and Normafa út is the **statue of Mór Jókai** which was unveiled in 1906 (the former is by Alajos *Stróbl* and the latter by Gyula *Jankovich*). A few steps from the cogwheel railway station, in the middle of a large park, rises the large building of the State Tuberculosis Sanatorium.

The construction of the residential area of Liberty Hill on a regular scale began about a hundred years ago. The first houses built on the summit were intended for holiday purposes, and most of them were transformed from presshouses and former lodgings of vine dressers.

The main thoroughfare of the old colony is Költő utca (Poet Street). Considering its many sharp turns one can readily see that it was originally a field path leading through

221

the vineyards. The first part of the street with its single-storey houses gives the impression of bygone times, and one might think they belong to Óbuda. On the plot at No. 19-21 stands the former **villa of** the great Hungarian novelist **Mór Jókai,** now an apartment house. Only the **bronze statue** before the house and the **commemorative tablet** on the wall reminds us of the former owner. Below the Jókai villa, at one of the bends of Költő utca, is the house of the one-time actor of the National Theatre, Károly Benza, which attracts attention with its spiral chimney.

The centre of the former wine-growing region is Diana utca. At the intersection of Diana utca and Költő utca stands a two-storied school building, with a sundial on its façade. (This school also preserves many keepsakes of Mór Jókai.) The house at No. 25 is the famous **Clock Villa.** From the arcades of the neoclassic building one can get a fine view of Buda. During the siege of Buda in 1849, General Arthur Görgey had his headquarters here, and from this point he and his staff observed the outcome of the siege as well as the decisive assault on May 21. The villa obtained its name from the clock located in the tympanum of the building. Diana utca continues its tortuous course down to Orbán tér, the centre of the quarter extending to the eastern hillside.

The third street worth mentioning in the residential area of Liberty Hill is Eötvös út. József Eötvös acquired a plot for his villa here in 1846. Not far from here (now 14 Karthausi utca) he had a Swiss châlet erected, where he wrote many of his works. After his death the family sold the property. The buildings were pulled down to make room for the **State Tuberculosis Sanatorium.**

From the Liberty Hill station Evetke út leads up to the **Széchenyi Hill lookout tower,** which was built according to designs by Miklós *Ybl* in 1898. The old stone column next to it was erected already in 1860, when the hill was named after István Széchenyi. In a pine-grove stands the bronze **bust of István Széchenyi** on a stone pedestal (by Alajos *Stróbl*, 1891). The bust was unveiled on the 100th anniversary of Széchenyi's birth. The bronze bust weighing 130 kilogrammes was once stolen and found in Vienna later, in 1901.

The cogwheel railway ends on the summit of Széchenyi Hill (427 metres) and it is here that the **Pioneer Railway** starts its winding track. Thus we have reached the bor-

der of the "green belt" and this is where the extensive
forests of Buda begin. Near the station building of the
cogwheel railway rises the **Vörös Csillag** (Red Star)
Hotel, one of the best situated resort hotels of Budapest. In its park is a **Soviet war memorial.** Beyond the
park we can see a tall oblong building, the **Television
Transmitter.** Its tower is 60 metres high, telecasting to
a distance of some 80 to 100 kilometres. The first TV broad-
casting took place on February 20, 1954. The construction of the modern transmitter was completed in January
1958.

11. NORMAFA, JÁNOS HILL

The best way to get acquainted with the hills, valleys and
forestland in the west of Buda is to start at the Széchenyi
Hill terminus of the **Pioneer Railway**. The Pioneer Railway is one of the most popular institutions of the capital.
This railway was a gift to the children from the government of the People's Republic, but the grownups also enjoy
it very much. The winding track of the narrow-gauge railway with a length of 12 kilometres connects Széchenyi
Hill with Hűvösvölgy along the slopes of the Buda hills.
The first stretch, three kilometres long, was opened on
July 31, 1948, the second section on July 7, 1949, and the
third and last section early in the period of the First
Five-Year Plan (1950).

The staff of the Pioneer Railway consists of Young Pioneers, members of a youth organisation (8 to 14 years of
age). The Young Pioneers must first undergo a three-
month course of training. They put on the handsome uniform of railwaymen after they have passed the examina-
tion of the state school for traffic regulations with excellent result.

At first sight the Pioneer Railway appears to be a play-
thing, but it has to perform important tasks: it is a means
of education for children, and offers those who intend to
go into the railway service a possibility of acquainting
themselves with its rudiments already from childhood on.
In addition, this railway handles the greatest tourist traffic in the capital. The track of the Pioneer Railway passes
over two viaducts and through a tunnel, and riding the
train the visitor is delighted by the otherwise hidden
beauties of the Buda hills.

The first stop after the Széchenyi Hill terminus is **Nor-**

mafa (Norma Tree). This spot offers perhaps the most splendid view of the vicinity. From here we can enjoy the sight of the dense forest of Budakeszi on the one side, and the beautiful wide panorama towards Zugliget on the other. Above the valley our eyes rest for a moment on the white villas of Hunyad-orom and Tündér-hegy. To the north the dark green conical peak of János Hill throws its shadow over the countryside, in the northeast the bluish outlines of the Hill of Three Boundaries come into sight, and down below spreads the Pest flatland.

We may search in vain for the Normafa itself. The old beach tree, under the shade of which King Matthias is said to have rested, perished in 1927, after being struck by lightning. Everything was done to save the remains of the famous tree from total decay. The broken trunk was put into the artesian basin of Margaret Island, in the hope of preserving it with calcareous water. Unfortunately, this did not work, and the trunk fell to pieces.

The old tree and the surroundings obtained the name Normafa towards the end of the last century. At that time opera singers and actors often came for a walk to this huge tree to enjoy the splendid view. Once they improvised an opera performance and one of them sang the great aria from Bellini's Norma, hence the name of this spot.

The surroundings of Normafa are also very popular in winter. The steep slope provides a considerable test for skiers. Here we find a tourists' hostel, a station for tourists and skiers, and two ski-jumps. The big one was rebuilt in 1955, and in 1959 it was covered with a layer of plastic material so that skiers can train here even in summer.

The **Normafa Resort and Restaurant** accommodate hikers and skiers and serve excellent meals.

After the Normafa stop the Pioneer Railway describes a large arc towards the south, passing by the Astronomical Observatory. The next stop is **Úttörőváros** (Pioneer's Town), a children's summer camp, built in 1948 and furnished with every modern comfort. The camp is equipped with a medical centre and an up-to-date cultural house. The eight sub-camps can accommodate about a thousand pioneers at a time.

Extending over an area of about a hundred hectares at an altitude of 450 metres, the camp is provided with a swimming pool, an open-air stage, and a sport stadium.

In adjoining Konkoly-Thege út stand two research institutes of importance. One is the **Astronomical Institute** of the Hungarian Academy of Sciences (No. 13-17). The first astronomical institute in this country was founded by the Hungarian astronomer Miklós Konkoly-Thege in 1871 at his own expense. He bequeathed his institute with all its equipment to the state in 1900. Originally it was set up in Ógyalla (now Stará Dala, Czechoslovakia), but was transferred to its present place in 1919. An observatory was built after the First World War, and in 1945 an institute for solar physics was added. The other important institute is the **Central Institute for Physics Research,** which was established in 1950. Its experimental atomic reactor built with Soviet help was put into service in the autumn of 1959. To the east from here is Csillebérc, a resort colony.

The next stop of the Pioneer Railway is called "Előre" (Forward), after the salute of the Young Pioneers. From here a road leads to a pleasant excursion site of the Buda mountain region, **Makkosmária.** This little spot hidden in the valley is a place of pilgrimages. Apart from its **church,** it has a tourists' shelter, a forester's lodge, and a few cottages. From this clearing surrounded by oak trees, roads and tourist's trails lead to Normafa, Hűvösvölgy, János Hill and Farkasrét.

János Hill has its own station on the line of the Pioneer Railway. This highest hill in the Buda range (529 metres) has been a favourite excursion point of the Budapest people for over a hundred years. Its name is said to have come from a magistrate of Buda and fort commander who lived in the 13th century.

The **lookout tower** on top of János Hill, which can be reached by bus, was built to the designs of the architect Frigyes *Schulek* (the builder of the Fishermen's Bastion) between 1908 and 1910. The 23.5-metre-tall structure in the neo-Romanesque style consists of four circular terraces standing on top of one another. The uppermost terrace, to which a hundred steps lead, offers a view within a distance of 70 to 80 kilometres. The panorama is quite unique. On bright days one can see as far as the peaks of the High Tatra Mountains, some 215 kilometres away. At the foot of the lookout tower is an inn, from where excursionists can enjoy a view of the capital while dining in comfort.

Two kilometres away is the following station of the Pioneer Railway at **Ságvári liget** (Ságvári Grove), where tourists find a station restaurant with a shady terrace and a fine view. From the next stop, **Linden Hill,** there is an easy walk to the top of this hill. Near the peak we can see the remnants of an old tourist home. Right below the peak is the entrance of the **Báthory Cave,** named after the Paulite monk László Báthory who lived here as a hermit from 1437 to 1459. From the entrance narrow steps lead about three metres down into a large hall, and from the back of it a passage communicates with the interior of the hill. After a few steps the passage broadens somewhat and branches off into several side passages and caverns. Following the death of its lodger the cave was forgotten to be rediscovered in 1830. As it was thought to be dangerous it was sealed up. In 1870 it was opened again but in order to prevent accidents, an iron railing was built round the entrance in 1910.

After the Linden Hill stop the little railway turns towards the west, and we approach the so-called **Petneházy Meadow,** which covers about 25 hectares. (It was named after the hero Dávid Petneházy, who was one of the first to reach the ramparts of the fort in the siege of Buda, on September 2, 1686.) Then the train runs through a 198-metre-long **tunnel,** and soon we arrive at the end of our journey, the Hűvösvölgy terminus.

12. FARKASRÉT

Farkasrét (Wolves' Meadow) and Farkasvölgy (Wolves' Valley) spread over the southern slopes of Liberty Hill and Széchenyi Hill. Probably they obtained their name from the great number of wolves that were formerly found here. The most characteristic point for one's orientation is **Ördögorom** (Devil's Peak). On its southern slopes are abandoned quarries. The rocky walls clearly show the deposits of thermal springs. Below the rocks, at the beginning of Edvi Illés út, lies **Ördögorom Csárda,** the most popular outdoor restaurant of the region.

South of it, on the top of Frank Hill, stands a favourably situated **tourists' hostel.** From here we can get a splendid view of southern Buda, down to Csepel Island.

13. LÁGYMÁNYOS, KELENFÖLD

South of Gellért Hill extends a district of Budapest that has grown fastest of all. In the northern part, on the slopes of Gellért Hill and Eagle Hill (Sas-hegy), lovely villas with fragrant gardens tempt the stroller. The southern part with dozens of factories, however, is the third largest industrial centre of the capital. Lágymányos is significant also as an agricultural area. On the slopes of Bird Hill (Madár-hegy), the orchards of Sasad and Budaörs grow excellent fruit, especially peaches, pears and apples.

This district is also a centre of higher education. The University of the Building Industry, the Technical University and, along Villányi út, the College of Agricultural Science occupy extensive areas.

There are still large open areas in Lágymányos. A few years hence, however, the buildings of the Budapest International Fair will stand here. For the time being the fairs are still organised in the exhibition halls of the City Park.

The most important sight in this district is the **new housing estate of Lágymányos.** This building site is bordered by four streets, and seven-to-nine-storied houses with some 4,500 apartments are being built here.

The middle of this district is Kelenföld, a characteristic working-class area. South of the railway embankment there is a large housing estate covering an area of about 150 hectares. Mention should be made here of **Kelenföld Railway Station,** too.

14. ALBERTFALVA, SASAD

Wedged in between the Danube and Kelenföld in the southernmost tip of the district lies Albertfalva, which was an independent community until 1950. The area has an interesting past: it was situated on the eastern border of the Roman province of Pannonia. The chain of watchtowers, which ran from north to south along the Danube, disappeared in Buda without leaving any traces. Only here, at the southern end of the town, did the monuments of the Roman period appear again. On the plain of Albertfalva archaeologists have uncovered the remains of a **Roman camp** and also a **colony** dating from the 1st and 2nd centuries. In 1957, when the southern Buda factory grounds were expanding, the western gate of the Roman camp which was formerly flanked by towers, was unearthed Remnants of the towers and the 125-metre-wide stone wall are still clearly visible.

At the foot of Eagle Hill (Sas-hegy) and Farkasrét lies the quarter named Sasad. Its sunny slopes grow delicious fruit. Especially the peaches here are famous. For peaches the name Sasad is as good a trade-mark as Tokaj or Badacsony is for wine.

The most characteristic sight of the landscape is double-peaked Eagle Hill with its barren rocks. The slopes, especially in the east and south, show interesting dolomite formations. Because of its rare flora and fauna, the hill was declared a nature reserve in 1958.

Formerly the hill was named King's Hill (Király-hegy) after the royal and noble hunters who often came to hunt in this area from the Buda Castle. Later the hill became the property of the Franciscans of Buda, and then it was named Priest's Hill, Monk Hill, also God's Hill. According to certain historical sources its present-day name goes back to the time when Buda was recaptured from the Turks. Tradition has it that in September 1686, on the occasion of a parade to commemorate the victory over the Turks, eagles flew from here to Castle Hill.

At the southwestern end of the district, on the fields of Örsöd, lies the second airfield of Budapest, **Budaörs Airport.** Since the building of the modern airport at Ferihegy, Budaörs has been of no importance for air transport.

THE ENVIRONS OF BUDAPEST

1. THE OUTER DISTRICTS OF THE CAPITAL

On the outskirts of Budapest we find industrial towns, housing estates, agricultural areas, garden cities, and resort centres side by side. Incorporated in the capital on the Pest side lies

ÚJPEST

Váci út, which is considered one of the most important thoroughfares of the capital, connects Újpest with the inner districts of Budapest. Újpest is the most developed outlying district of the rebuilt and embellished capital. Formerly it was only an industrial town. Today it is becoming more and more a cultural centre. New housing estates are under construction, health and medical institutions and sport establishments have been laid out here. Újpest is one of the centres of Hungarian industry, and is noted for its furniture, leather, textile, shoe, radio valve and electric bulb factories. An important plant here is the **Chinoin Pharmaceutical Factory,** which is one of the most modern pharmaceutical works in Europe. In the **United Incandescent Lamp Factory** the well-known Tungsram bulbs as well as television picture tubes are manufactured.

The **winter port** of Újpest accommodates the Danube steamers and boats when the cold season sets in.

In the east Újpest borders on

RÁKOSPALOTA

A small village just a few decades ago, Rákospalota is becoming urbanized with its family houses, cottages, and gardens.

When Greater Budapest was formed

A housing estate in Thälmann utca

PESTÚJHELY

also became part of the capital. Today, together with Rákospalota, it is District 15 of Budapest.

District 16 is made up of CINKOTA, MÁTYÁSFÖLD, SASHALOM, RÁKOSSZENTMIHÁLY and ÁRPÁDFÖLD. These communities are mainly agricultural areas which supply the capital with vegetables and fruit. The history of Cinkota goes back a thousand years. In the Hungarian War of Independence of 1848-49 a battle was fought in its proximity, which ended with the victory of the Hungarian Honvéd army. Mátyásföld is a summer holiday resort of the capital. Noteworthy here is the **Ikarus Chassis and Vehicle Factory,** where the manufacture of the world-famous Hungarian buses was started in 1949. Earlier Sashalom formed a part of Cinkota. It is inhabited mainly by

workers and civil service and office employees. Rákosszentmihály has a similar character.

The largest district of the capital is District 17, which is
named

RÁKOS

after several communities that have the word Rákos in
their name. Rákoscsaba is one of them. Formerly it was
a desert of sand. Today this place, as well as Rákosliget,
its neighbour, consists mainly of cottages. Rákoskeresztúr
was formerly an independent community. South of it lies
Rákoshegy, a one-time health resort. This part of the
district is developing rapidly, and the number of cottages
is growing steadily. In the south of this district lies **Ferihegy Airport,** one of the most modern in Europe. An
express highway and a bus line connect the airport with
the capital. Restaurants, lounges, a post office, shops,
and a banking office are located in the modern building
of the airport. One wing of the building has been turned
into a transit hotel to accommodate foreign travellers
passing through Budapest. The hotel has 38 rooms with
bathrooms.

District 18 was formed of two communities,

PESTLŐRINC and PESTIMRE

Pestlőrinc is a garden city, Pestimre is mainly an agricultural community. Significant industrial plants are located in Pestlőrinc, such as the **Lőrinc Spinning Mill** and
the **Lőrinc Rolling Mill.** There is also a meteorological
observatory.

District 19 of the capital is the industrial suburb of

KISPEST

This district borders on Pestlőrinc, Pesterzsébet, Kőbánya
and Ferencváros. It is nearly a hundred years old. Today
it has large industrial plants, such as the **Red Star Tractor
Factory,** the **Red October Men's Clothing Factory**
and the **Meat Processing Enterprise of Kispest.**

District 20 comprises two communities of the Pest out-

skirts, PESTERZSÉBET, an industrial suburb, and SOROK-
SÁR, an agricultural suburb. The district boasts of a significant manufacturing industry. Here we should mention
the **Atra Factory** (making spare parts for motorcars and
tractors), a **knitwear works,** and the **Sortex Textile
Mill.** There are also a number of aquatic sport establishments here. A special point of interest in Pesterzsébet is
the Local History Museum.

District 21 of the capital lies on Csepel Island. The industrial city of

CSEPEL

was an independent community until 1950. Twenty years
ago Csepel consisted mainly of poor cottages. Today,
blocks of healthy flats with every comfort have largely
replaced them. The modern public buildings and beautifully laid out walks will soon eclipse old Csepel. An **elec-
tricexpress train** connects this district with the capital.
The **Csepel Iron and Steel Works,** the workshops and
assembly plants of the greatest Hungarian industrial enterprise, are situated in the western part of the district.
In addition to the Iron and Steel Works, a **paper mill,**
an **oil refinery** and a **cloth factory** are located on the
island, which we have already described more fully. (See
page 155.)

District 3 of Budapest lies on the Buda side and comprises
Óbuda, Aquincum (see pages 209, 212), Csillaghegy and
Békásmegyer. Near Római-part and Római-fürdő are the
open-air baths of

CSILLAGHEGY

This is a very popular outing place of the Budapest population. Springs supply the pools with thousands of litres
of fresh water per minute.

BÉKÁSMEGYER

is the northernmost area of Buda. It has been part of the
capital since 1950 and is rural in character. The **open-air
baths of Pünkösdfürdő** lie near the river bank. It is
very popular with excursionists. The southernmost part
of District 11 is formed of the recently incorporated
community of

ALBERTFALVA

The best-known industrial plants here are the **First Hungarian Agricultural Machine Factory** (EMAG), the **Chemical Works of Albertfalva**, the **Enamel Wire Factory**, the **Yarn Factory**, and the **Ventilator Works**.

The southernmost administrative unit of Budapest is District 22, which consists of several communities. The first of them is

BUDAFOK

The Romans called this place Promontorium. Budafok is world famous for its wine cellars. A very interesting place to see is the **Wine Museum,** where the visitor can taste many varieties of wine.

NAGYTÉTÉNY

was the site of the Roman military camp of **Campona** in the 2nd century. The ruins and the **Castle Museum of Nagytétény** are worth seeing. The road leads to Nagytétény past the largest **pig-fattening farm** of Hungary. In

BUDATÉTÉNY

the foundation walls of the old **church** of the medieval community of Cset (uncovered some twenty years ago) and the **Research Institute of the Horticultural Enterprise** are interesting sights.

2. THE MORE REMOTE COMMUNITIES AROUND THE CAPITAL

Among the towns not too remote from Budapest, we would first recommend excursionists to visit

GÖDÖLLŐ

This community on the Pest side can be reached easily, and in a short time, by train or the suburban electric railway. The fine building of the **University of Agricultural Science** is located near the railway station. In a pine wood along the railway line lies the so-called "poultry town" of the **Research Institute for the Breeding of Small Animals**. This establishment supplies the whole country with breeding stock and brood eggs.

A valuable monument is the **Grassalkovich Castle** with its four watch towers from the 18th century. The building is surrounded by a large park and a domed palm house.

BÖRZSÖNY

A relatively high mountain range at a short distance from the capital, it is within easy reach by train from the Western Railway Terminal. The train runs northwards on the Budapest—Szob main line along the left bank of the Danube. Across the river, on Szentendre Island, lies

HORÁNY

a bathing resort, frequented by hosts of people every summer. Our train will then stop at Dunakeszi-Alag, Felsőgöd and Sződliget. Felsőgöd is a very delightful place for bathing. Surány, on the opposite side, is also very popular with water sports enthusiasts. Many aquatic sport establishments can be found in this region.

VÁC

is a typical town of Hungarian baroque architecture. Its finest monument is the **cathedral,** a work of the Viennese architect *Canevale*. Another sight there is the 20-metre-high **Stone Gate,** the only triumphal arch in Hungary. It was erected by Bishop Migazzi to commemorate the visit of Queen Maria Theresa in 1764. A popular outing place is the **Town Park** with its many ornamental plants. An ethnographic speciality of Vác is **Rácváros** (Serbian Town). Its old inns still prepare dishes of Danube fish in

the traditional manner of past centuries. North of the
town we can see **Naszály**, 652 metres high, a much frequented mountain with many caves on its slopes. It is
also worth while visiting the famous **botanical gardens**
of Vácrátót.

The next station after Vác is

NÓGRÁDVERŐCE

This is a summer resort lying on the elevated river bank
opposite the northern tip of Szentendre Island. Here is
the **Migazzi Castle.** Then the popular holiday resorts of
the Börzsöny Mountains follow. Kismaros lies where the
narrow course of the Danube widens out before Visegrád.

NAGYMAROS

is well known for its **beach** on the Danube, its good wine
and its vineyard and fruit cultures. In its vicinity there are
many excursion places. Nagymaros lies in the Danube
Bend. Its splendid landscape is one of the beauty spots of
Hungary.

On the opposite side of the river lies Visegrád. A little
further upstream, still on the left bank, lies **Zebegény,**
whose beauty is enhanced by **Hegyes-tető** (Pointed
Peak) and **Szentmihály-hegy** (St. Michael Hill).

The right bank in the Danube Bend is within easy reach
of Budapest by boat, train or long-distance bus. We may
also go by the suburban electric railway as far as Szentendre, and take a bus from there.

By this latter route, it is worth one's while to pay a visit
to Szentendre Island and the town of Szentendre.

Crescent-shaped Szentendre Island begins below Visegrád
and ends above Budapest. There are four villages on the
island: Kisoroszi, Tótfalu, Pócsmegyer and Szigetmonos-
tor. The Pokolcsárda Inn located at the Vác ferry crossing
is a popular excursion place.

SZENTENDRE

This is a romantic township, which has preserved its old
look. Its picturesque zigzagging streets are pressed in

between the Danube and the nearby mountains. Small squares, narrow winding alleys, passages and stairways are found all over the town. In Marx tér there are several old monuments. The finest of them is the baroque **Town Hall.** The **Serbian episcopal church,** over 500 years old, is ornamented with square stones inside and outside. The icons on the walls are rare sights. The romantic atmosphere of the town has always attracted many famous painters, among them Károly Ferenczy, the great Hungarian master of the Nagybánya School. A **colony of artists** is still active here. Today the studios of a number of Hungarian artists stand in the middle of a large park. After Szentendre follows

LEÁNYFALU

In the summer months thousands of visitors come to bathe here in the Danube. This was where Zsigmond Móricz, an outstanding Hungarian writer, spent the last years of his life. Today his house is a **museum.** On the top of **Vöröskő** (Red Rock) towering 523 metres above the village stands a **Liberation Monument.** The road leads along the Danube to

VISEGRÁD

The visitor is not only under the spell of the beauty of its countryside, the history of the place is also fascinating. The name Visegrád was already known at the time of the first kings of Hungary. King Andrew I founded a monastery for Greek monks here. King Solomon was held in captivity here by order of King St. Ladislas in 1082. Under King Charles Robert, Visegrád became a royal residence. He gave the order to build a sumptuous palace. The famous congress of Visegrád was held here in 1335. King Matthias had various new elements added to the palace, which stood at the foot of the mountain. Soon the number of palaces belonging to magnates increased all around it. In 1529 the palace fell into the hands of the Turks and was finally liberated from Turkish rule in 1684. In 1702 the fortifications were blown up, and the remnants of the palace of Charles Robert and Matthias fell into ruin. Only parts of the upper citadel, the Solomon Tower, and parts of the walls have remained standing. In 1940 excavations were started, and the **palace chapel** from the 14th century and parts of the palace itself were opened up. By now a great part of the palace's ruins have been brought to light, and many thousands of visitors come here to admire its restored halls, courtyards and foundation walls.

The original **palace** consisted of two large wings. In one of them were the apartments of King Matthias, and in the other those of his Italian-born queen, Beatrix. The so-called "red fountain" now stands in its original place, in the arcaded courtyard. In the centre of this fountain there was a little figure of Hercules astride a seven-headed hydra. This figure is now kept in the neighbouring museum. Entering the site of the excavations, first we step into the **central courtyard** of King Matthias, which was formerly surrounded by Gothic arcades. Over the restored arcades there was an open **pergola**, at level with the top of the red marble fountain, the work of the great master of Renaissance art, Giovanni *Dalmata*. Among the **terraces** of the castle so far three have been opened up.

Another item of interest in Visegrád is the **Solomon Tower,** which was originally five stories high. At the base of this dungeon we can still see a number of Turkish cannon balls, relics of sieges long past. From the Solomon Tower a defensive wall runs to the **citadel,** which was erected by King Béla IV after the Mongol invasion.

Visegrád and its surroundings are a starting point of pleasant excursions to many lovely spots.

Near the landing pier a sign with a map of the surrounding countryside gives information about excursion places, paths and road marks. This is also the starting point to **Nagyvillám,** a plateau which commands a fine view of the Danube Bend, and where an up-to-date hostel is at the disposal of the tourists; to **Lepence Valley,** which is a paradise for anglers; to **Matthias Peak, Magda Spring, Malom-hegy** (Mill Hill) and **Apátkút Valley.**

DÖMÖS

was a favourite residence of the kings of the House of Árpád in the 11th and 12th centuries. The provostship of Dömös was founded in 1107 by Prince Álmos, who, after being made blind, lived in hiding here until his death.

The last township on the right river bank of the Danube Bend is

ESZTERGOM

This town, some fifty kilometres away from Budapest, can be reached easily by train, which runs through a most varied countryside.

Under the kings of the House of Árpád, Esztergom was the royal residence. The town is rich in historic monuments. In Széchenyi tér, the main square, is the arcaded house of the Kuruc general Vak Bottyán. Today it is the **Town Hall.** Fine old houses stand in the square all around it. The wife of King Béla III had the first public baths in Hungary built at the site of the present-day **open-air bath** of Esztergom.

The **Christian Museum** in the Primatial Palace contains world-famous treasures of art (Hungarian art treasures of the 14th and 15th centuries, masterpieces of Italian, Dutch and Flemish artists, stained glass pictures, wood carvings, statues, ceramics). The **Balassi Bálint Museum** in the library of the chapter-house of the Primatial Palace contains valuable historical relics relating to the town of Esztergom. (Bálint Balassi, 1554-1594, was the greatest Hungarian poet of his time. He died in battle when the Turks besieged the town.)

The **Esztergom Castle Hill** offers a superb view of the Danube and of the plainland and the mountains on the other side of the river. On the hill we can see the remains of the royal palace of the late Middle Ages that was unearthed and reconstructed a few years ago: the chapel, the throne room, halls and apartments. Another sight worth seeing is the reconstructed model of a basilica dating from the period of King Béla III, and casemates from the Turkish times, with a lapidary. On the hill stands the **Archiepiscopal Cathedral of Esztergom, the Basilica,** the largest church in Hungary. On the occasion of its consecration in 1856, Ferenc Liszt composed his famous Esztergom Mass. In the left-side aisle is the **Bakócz Chapel,** and the **crypt** of the Basilica where several Renaissance sepulchres can be seen.

South of Budapest, on the right bank of the Danube, lies the garden-city of

ÉRD

This region is famous for fruit growing. In the village of

ZSÁMBÉK

we can find a **church** which, though in ruins, is an impressive sight. It was built in the 13th century and belonged to the Premonstratensian order. During the Turkish occupation Zsámbék was the seat of a pasha. Its fort was destroyed, and today a castle stands in its place. If the visitor is keen on making excursions, he should certainly see the **Pilis Mountains.** From the window of the train that leaves Budapest's Western Railway Terminal for Esztergom, the beautiful landscape of this region opens up before the eye. Shortly after Üröm, in the distance are the peaks of **Nagykevély,** 535 metres, and **Kiskevély,** 483 metres. The Kevély saddle between the two mountains is a popular outing place. These are the outposts of the Pilis Mountains, the highest of which are **Pilistető,** 757 metres, and **Dobogókő,** 700 metres.

DOBOGÓKŐ

can easily be reached from Budapest by motorcar or by bus in about an hour and a half. The view from the mountain top is wonderful. To the north, towards Malom-völgy (Mill Valley) at Dömös, the mountain ends with a steep rocky wall. Forests, clearings, the houses of Dömös and Visegrád, and the wonderful panorama of the Danube Bend can be observed from the top. In bright weather even the peaks of the High Tatra are visible. Not so very long ago there were only a couple of houses at Dobogókő, but today **tourists' hostels** and **resort homes** can be found close to one another. In winter the slopes of Dobogókő are much frequented by skiers.

PART III

PRACTICAL INFORMATION

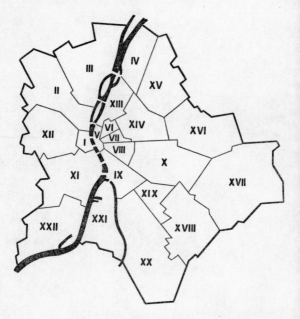

Map of Budapest districts

In part III of our book addresses in Budapest are given in the Hungarian way. E.g. V. Váci utca 4. The Roman number denotes the district, while the number following the street name is the house number.

HOW TO GET TO BUDAPEST

Budapest is the centre of the Hungarian railway system. Most of the main railway lines start from here, connecting the regions west and east of the Danube. Eight of the eleven railway lines converging on Budapest have express train service, seven of them with international non-stop trains, and two lines are electric powered (from Budapest's Eastern Railway Terminal to Hegyeshalom and to Miskolc). An increasing number of Diesel engines and motor trains are in use on the express lines. Three railway terminals serve international passenger traffic (Western, Eastern and Southern Terminals).

The Budapest suburban electric railways (BHÉV) handle a considerable part of the suburban traffic. There are four main lines with their terminals within the Budapest area. For excursionists the route to Szentendre is of special interest. Its terminus is located at the Buda abutment of the Margaret Bridge.

Budapest is also the centre of the Hungarian highway network and at the same time the main crossing point over the Danube. This applies not only to inland roads, but also to international communication lines. Among the European roads recognised by the U.N., Highway E5 (London—Brussels—Vienna — Budapest—Belgrade—Istanbul) crosses the Danube here.

Seven of the eight first-class main roads start out from Budapest:

1. Budapest—Hegyeshalom—(Vienna), coinciding with Highway E5;
2. Budapest—Nógrádszakál—(Košice);
3. Budapest—Miskolc—Tornyosnémeti—(Košice);
4. Budapest—Debrecen—Záhony (Soviet Union);
5. Budapest—Szeged—(Belgrade), coinciding with Highway E5;

6. Budapest—Pécs—Barcs;
7. Budapest—Lake Balaton—Letenye—(Zagreb).

Five second-class roads also start out from Budapest (Nos. 11, 26, 31, 51 and 80). Especially Road No. 11 leading past the Danube Bend is of importance for international tourism.

There is rapid and efficient bus service on the long-distance roads. Long-distance buses start out from the Central Bus Terminal, at Engels Square, Budapest. Among these, the coaches going to the Mátra Mountains, for instance, are of great importance. Towards Lake Balaton there are no bus routes. This traffic is handled exclusively by the railways.

The distances by road between Budapest and some European cities (in kilometres): Amsterdam 1,476, Belgrade 442, Berlin 900, Bern 1,117, Brussels 1,417, Bucharest 854, Copenhagen 1,344, London 1,796, Moscow 1,943, Oslo 1,964, Paris 1,513, Prague 536, Rome 1,395, Sofia 865, Stockholm 1,999, Vienna 276, Warsaw 902.

Budapest also plays an important role in water navigation. Its significance is constantly increasing through the National Free Port at Csepel, which is the terminus of sea-going ships on the Danube. The Danube is navigable for ships up to 1,200 tons. Passenger and goods traffic is handled on the Danube and its branches (the Szentendre branch and the backwaters of the Soroksár branch). The terminuses for passenger traffic are at Vigadó tér (upstream) and at Belgrád rakpart (downstream).

The importance of air transport in Budapest is increasing steadily. The Ferihegy Airport has been completely reconstructed recently. Its main runway is 3.1 kilometres long. The airport has been furnished with the necessary equipment for instrument landings (ILS and radar), so that safe landings can be made under all weather conditions and in the dark. A hotel has been built at the airfield for transit passengers. On an average, 15 to 20 planes take off from Budapest daily, and most of the great cities of Europe can be reached directly, or by changing planes only once. There are direct flights to cities in Africa and Asia. America can be reached by a single change. Budapest is an air-stop between the Soviet Union and the rest of Europe. Air traffic between the socialist countries north and south of Hungary passes exclusively through Budapest.

TRAVEL TO BUDAPEST

By railway

From	Route	km
Amsterdam	Cologne—Frankfurt a/M—Linz— Vienna	1,513
Ankara	Istanbul—Sofia—Belgrade	2,024
Antwerp	Brussels—Cologne—Frankfurt a/M— Nuremberg—Vienna	1,524
Arad	Lökösháza—Szolnok	254
Athens	Skoplje—Niš—Belgrade	1,565
Barcelona	Narbonne—Lyon—Geneva—Bern— Vienna	2,288
Basel	Zurich—Vienna	1,222
Belgrade	Subotica—Kelebia	365
Berlin	Dresden—Prague—Bratislava	997
Bern	Zurich—Vienna	1,262
Bologna	Venice—Udine—Vienna	1,053
Bordeaux	Clermont-Ferrand—Lyon—Geneva— Zurich—Vienna	2,232
Bratislava	Galanta—Szob	217
Brussels	Luxembourg—Basel—Zurich—Vienna or Cologne—Frankfurt a/M—Vienna	1,488
Bucharest	Arad—Lökösháza—Szolnok	875
Cluj	Oradea—Biharkeresztes—Püspök-ladány—Szolnok	401
Cologne	Frankfurt a/M—Nuremberg—Vienna	1,254
Copenhagen	Malmö—Trelleborg—Sassnitz— Berlin—Prague—Bratislava	1,452
Dresden	Prague—Bratislava	824
Florence	Bologna—Venice—Udine—Vienna	1,150
Frankfurt a/M	Nuremberg—Vienna	1,029
Geneva	Bern—Zurich—Vienna	1,420
Genoa	Milan—Venice—Udine—Vienna	1,314
Graz	Vienna—Hegyeshalom—Győr	474
The Hague	Brussels—Cologne—Frankfurt a/M— Vienna, or	1,654
	Cologne—Frankfurt a/M—Vienna	1,532
Hamburg	Würzburg—Passau—Linz—Vienna	1,437
Helsinki	Stockholm—Berlin—Prague—Brati-slava	2,405
Innsbruck	Salzburg—Vienna—Hegyeshalom	849
Istanbul	Edirne—Sofia—Belgrade or through	

245

From	Route	km
	Bucharest	1,446
Kiev	Lvov—Záhony—Nyíregyháza—	
	Debrecen	1,239
Klagenfurt	Bruck—Vienna	595
Košice	Hidasnémeti—Miskolc	274
Leipzig	Dresden—Prague—Bratislava	928
Leningrad	Moscow—Kiev—Lvov—Záhony	2,762
Linz	Vienna—Hegyeshalom—Győr	475
Lisbon	Hendaye—Lyon—Geneva—Zurich—	
	Vienna	3,596
Ljubljana	Graz—Vienna	696
London	Ostende—Brussels—Cologne—Frank-	
	furt a/M—Nuremberg—Vienna	1,846
	or Paris—Strasbourg—Munich—	
	Vienna	2,145
Luxembourg	Basel—Vienna	1,584
Madrid	Bordeaux—Lyon—Geneva—Bern—	
	Zurich—Vienna	2,957
Marseille	Ventimiglia—Genoa—Milan—Venice—	
	Udine—Vienna	1,754
Milan	Venice—Udine—Vienna	1,161
Moscow	Lvov—Záhony—Nyíregyháza—	
	Debrecen	2,111
Munich	Salzburg—Linz—Vienna	747
Naples	Rome—Florence—Venice—Vienna	1,680
Nuremberg	Passau—Linz—Vienna	798
Odessa	Zhmerinka—Lvov—Záhony	1,353
Oradea Mare	Biharkeresztes—Püspökladány—	
	Szolnok	252
Oslo	Göteborg—Malmö—Berlin—Prague—	
	Bratislava	2,053
Paris	Belfort—Basel—Zurich—Vienna	1,748
	or Strasbourg—Karlsruhe—Munich—	
	Vienna	1,680
Prague	Bratislava—Szob	614
Rome	Florence—Bologna—Venice—	
	Udine—Vienna	1,466
Rotterdam	Cologne—Frankfurt a/M—Vienna	1,528
Salzburg	Vienna—Hegyeshalom—Győr	593
Sofia	Niš—Belgrade—Kelebia	780
Stockholm	Malmö—Berlin—Prague—Bratislava	1,996
Strasbourg	Basel—Zurich—Vienna	1,362
	or Stuttgart—Munich—Vienna	1,172

From	Route	km
Stuttgart	Munich—Salzburg—Vienna	987
Trieste	Graz—Vienna	839
Turin	Milan—Venice—Udine—Vienna	1,314
Venice	Udine—Bruck—Vienna	892
Vienna	Hegyeshalom—Győr	276
Warsaw	Bohumin—Bratislava—Szob	902
Zurich	Buchs—Innsbruck—Salzburg—Vienna	1,134

Baltic-Orient Express: Berlin—Dresden—Prague—Budapest (WesternTerminal)—Bucharest;
Wiener Walzer: Basel—Zurich—Innsbruck—Salzburg—Vienna—Budapest (Eastern Terminal)—Bucharest;
Pannonia Express: Berlin—Dresden—Prague—Budapest (Eastern Terminal)—Belgrade—Sofia.
In addition to the great international express trains there are the following international fast motor trains:
Hungaria Express: Berlin—Prague—Budapest (Western Terminal);
Budapest—Vienna Express: Vienna—Budapest (Eastern Terminal), with direct connection to the Orient Express (Paris—Munich—Vienna).
There are also through carriages from Budapest (Eastern Terminal) to Moscow via Kiev, from Budapest (Eastern Terminal) to Warsaw via Katowice, and from Budapest (Southern Terminal) to Rijeka (Fiume). In the winter months, however, this latter train runs only as far as Zagreb. There are through carriages to the Tatra (Poprad) as well, attached to the *Borsod Express* running to Miskolc. In the peak season other trains are added to those already mentioned.

By plane

From	Flight time	From	Flight time
Amsterdam	2 h. 30 m.	Brussels	2 h. 30 m.
Athens	2 h. 00 m.	Bucharest	2 h. 20 m.
Bagdad	6 h. 50 m.	Cairo	5 h. 45 m.
Beirut	7 h. 10 m.	Cologne	3 h. 00 m.
Belgrade	1 h. 10 m.	Copenhagen	4 h. 55 m.
Berlin	2 h. 40 m.	Damascus	7 h. 50 m.

From	Flight time	From	Flight time
Dusseldorf	2 h. 20 m.	Prague	1 h. 40 m.
Frankfurt a/M	1 h. 50 m.	Rome	3 h. 50 m.
Istanbul	3 h. 05 m.	Sofia	2 h. 20 m.
Kiev	4 h. 20 m.	Stockholm	7 h. 10 m.
London	4 h. 20 m.	Tirana	2 h. 45 m.
Lvov	1 h. 35 m.	Vienna	50 m.
Moscow	2 h. 15 m.	Warsaw	2 h. 20 m.
Paris	3 h. 30 m.	Zurich	3 h. 00 m.

BUDAPEST—CENTRE OF AIR TRANSPORT

Four foreign airline companies have permanent representations in Budapest:
Aeroflot (Soviet Air Transport Company)
V. Váci utca 4
ČSA (Czechoslovak Airlines)
V. Vörösmarty tér 2
KLM (Royal Dutch Airlines)
V. Vörösmarty tér 2
Sabena (Belgian Airlines)
V. Váci utca 5
The Hungarian capital is easily accessible from all parts of the world by the scheduled flights of these airline companies and MALÉV (Hungarian Air Transport Company). MALÉV maintains direct flights with the following large cities of Europe:

Amsterdam	Copenhagen	Lvov	Sofia
Belgrade	Frankfurt a/M	Moscow	Stockholm
Berlin	Helsinki	Paris	Tirana
Brussels	Kiev	Prague	Vienna
Bucharest	London	Rome	Warsaw
			Zurich

TABLE TO COMPARE LOCAL TIMES

(In relation to Greenwich Mean Time)

Amsterdam	+1	Brussels	+1
Athens	+2	Bucharest	+2
Bagdad	+3	Budapest	+1
Belgrade	+1	Cairo	+3**
Berlin	+1	Cologne	+1

Copenhagen	+1	Prague	+1
Damascus	+3**	Rome	+1
Frankfurt a/M	+1	Sofia	+2
Helsinki	+2	Stockholm	+1
Kiev	+3	Tirana	+1
London	+1	Vienna	+1
Lvov	+3	Warsaw	+2*
Moscow	+3	Zurich	+1
Paris	+1		

* From Oct. 1 +1
** From Oct. 1 +2

CURRENCY AND CUSTOMS

The Hungarian currency unit is the forint (Ft) which consists of 100 fillérs. Banknotes are issued in the following denominations: 100, 50, 20, 10 forints; coins: 5, 2, 1 forints, 50, 20, 10, 5, and 2 fillérs.

Foreign currencies are exchanged by the Hungarian National Bank, the Hungarian Foreign Trade Bank, the IBUSZ Touring, Travelling, Transport and Purchase Co. Ltd. offices, and at border stations.

Travellers crossing the Hungarian frontier may bring in and take out without special permit all articles of personal use and articles required in practising their profession. In the same manner articles produced by the domestic industry, of folk art, goldsmith's work up to the value of 4,000 forint can be taken out duty free. Duty is charged on other articles brought in and not serving personal use, according to the rate established in the Traveller Tariff. When leaving the country travellers may take out without special permit Hungarian money up to the value of 50 forints in coins.

Upon entry into Hungary the customs issue an Import Value Certificate for the currency (cash, cheques), gold and gold objects, platinum and platinum objects, gems and pearls brought in, and thus the valuables mentioned may be taken out again within a period of three months. After more than three months the above-mentioned valuables may be taken out only with a special permit issued by the Hungarian National Bank. In matters concerning currency, customs, passports and visas your hotel as well as the IBUSZ and other tourist agencies can supply full information.

249

SOJOURN IN BUDAPEST

BUDAPEST PUBLIC TRANSPORT

The means of communication of the capital are: trams, buses, trolleybuses and taxis. In addition, the underground railway running under Népköztársaság útja (People's Republic Avenue) from Vörösmarty tér to Széchenyi fürdő in the City Park, the electric cogwheel railway from Városmajor to Széchenyi Hill, in the outer districts the suburban electric railways, on the Danube water buses and ferryboats are at the disposal of the public. The Pioneer Railway runs in one of the most picturesque regions of the Buda hills. Microbuses with guides take the visitors along Margaret Island. Taxi stands can be found all over the town, but a cab may be ordered by phone by dialling 222-222.

At busy traffic junctions of the town there are so-called "double stops". At these places trams and buses stop and line up behind each other, but the cars at the back do not stop again. A single letter M on the sign-post indicates a single stop, MM is the sign of a double stop.

On the bus, tram and underground lines there are two types of tickets: through tickets (vonaljegy) and transfer tickets (átszállójegy).

The most important tram, bus and trolleybus lines are:

TRAMS

Line
No.

2 Petőfi-híd (Petőfi Bridge)—Pest Danube Embankment—
Margit-híd (Margaret Bridge)

4 Albertfalva—Nagykörút (Great Boulevard)—Lukács
fürdő (Lukács Baths)

6 Móricz Zsigmond körtér—Nagykörút (Great Boulevard)—Moszkva tér

250

9 Móricz Zsigmond körtér—Margit-híd budai hídfő (Margaret Bridge Buda abutment)

11 Óbuda forgalmi telep—Margit-híd budai hídfő (Margaret Bridge Buda abutment)

15 Margit-híd pesti hídfő (Margaret Bridge Pest abutment)—Váci út (Újpest)

18 Kelenföldi pályaudvar (Kelenföld Railway Station)—Óbuda—Margit kórház (Margaret Hospital)

23 Közvágóhíd (Slaughterhouse)—Keleti pályaudvar (Eastern Railway Terminal)

25 Nagyvárad tér—Baross tér—Állatkert (Zoo)

44 Zugló—Rákóczi út—Felszabadulás tér (Liberation Square)

45 Keleti pályaudvar (Eastern Railway Terminal)—Felszabadulás tér (Liberation Square)

47 Budafok—Kiskörút (Inner Boulevard)—Marx tér

49 Kelenföldi pályaudvar (Kelenföld Railway Station)—Kiskörút (Inner Boulevard)—Marx tér

53 Kispest—Üllői út—Marx tér

56 Hűvösvölgy—Moszkva tér

58 Zugliget—Moszkva tér

59 Farkasrét—Moszkva tér

60 Csörsz utca—Madách Imre tér

61 Moszkva tér—Móricz Zsigmond körtér

63 Nagyvárad tér—János kórház (Hospital)

66 Óbuda—Nagykörút (Great Boulevard)—Goldmann György tér

67 Rákospalota—Rákóczi út—Felszabadulás tér (Liberation Square)

68 Kerepesi út (Housing Estate)—Felszabadulás tér (Liberation Square)

TROLLEYBUSES

No.   Line

70 Erzsébet királyné út (Queen Elizabeth Avenue)—Kossuth Lajos tér

71 Marx tér—MÁV Kórház (Railwaymen's Hospital)

72 Marx tér—Thököly út

73 Marx tér—Keleti pályaudvar (Eastern Railway Terminal, Arrival platform)

74 Orczy tér—Felszabadulás tér (Liberation Square)

76 Keleti pályaudvar (Eastern Railway Terminal)—Margit-híd pesti hídfő (Margaret Bridge Pest abutment)

251

77 Orczy tér—Calvin tér
78 Baross tér—Kossuth Lajos tér
79 Baross tér—Váci út

BUSES

No.   Line

1 Hősök tere (Heroes' Square)—Kelenföldi pályaudvar (Kelenföld Railway Station)
2 József nádor tér—Orbán tér, Szabadság-hegy (Liberty Hill)
4 Váci út—Lékai János tér
5 Városliget (City Park), Dózsa György út—Pasaréti tér
6 Nagyvárad tér—Óbuda
7 Kelenföldi pályaudvar (Kelenföld Railway Station)—Zugló
7/c Kosztolányi Dezső tér—Zugló
8 Madách Imre tér—Irhásárok
8/a Madách Imre tér—Sasadi út
9 Vörösmarty tér—Pataki István tér (Kőbánya)
11 Mechwart tér—Rózsadomb (Hill of Roses), Nagybányai út
12 Roundabout traffic through the Pest and Buda Boulevards
15 Boráros tér—Váci út
16 József nádor tér—Budai Vár (Castle Hill)—Moszkva tér
21 Moszkva tér—Szabadság-hegy (Liberty Hill), Cogwheel Railway Station
26 Vígszínház (Comedy Theatre)—Grand Hotel Margitsziget (Margaret Island)
27 Móricz Zsigmond körtér—Gellérthegy (Gellért Hill), Citadella
28 Moszkva tér—Zugligeti út
39 Dániel út—Aszódi út Housing Estate
45 Kosztolányi Dezső tér—Kamaraerdő
49 Moszkva tér—Rókus-hegy (roundabout traffic)
53 Móricz Zsigmond körtér—Farkasrét
56 József nádor tér—Hűvösvölgy
60 Madách Imre tér—Óbuda Railway Station
90 Szabadság-hegy (Liberty Hill)—Csillebérc
91 Vígszínház (Comedy Theatre)—Rózsadomb (Hill of Roses), Pusztaszeri körönd
93 Nagyvárad tér—Ferihegy Airport

121 Blaha Lujza tér—Jánoshegyi kilátó (János Hill Lookout) (only Sundays and holidays)
134 Calvin tér—Római-part (Roman Beach) (only in summer)
156 József nádor tér—Hűvösvölgy
193 Vörösmarty tér—Ferihegy Airport

WATER BUSES

Places of call: Gellért tér, Petőfi tér, Bem József tér, Lower Margaret Island, Grand Hotel Margaret Island, Szabadság strandfürdő (Liberty Baths), Árpád út in Újpest.

MOTORCAR SERVICE STATIONS AND REPAIR SHOPS:

Enterprise No. 2
XIII. Révész utca 1-5. Tel: 200-810
(Robur, Mercedes)
Enterprise No. 4, Shop No. 1
XIII. Lehel utca 25. Tel: 200-825
(Skoda 440, 445, Octavia, Felicia, Tatra 603)
Enterprise No. 4, Shop No. 2
XIII. Dózsa György út 61. Tel: 202-270
(Nysa, Pobeda, Warszawa, Volga)
Enterprise No. 7, Shop No. 1
XIII. Dévai utca 17. Tel: 203-143
(Moskvitch, Simca, Renault, Fiat, Zastava 600)
Enterprise No. 7, Shop No. 2
XI. Bicskei utca 3-7. Tel: 250-772
(Skoda 1101, 1102, 1200, Renault, Fiat, Zastava 600)
Enterprise No. 7, Shop No. 5
VIII. József utca 21. Tel: 143-427
(Wartburg, Trabant)
Auras Service
XIII. Szabolcs utca 34. Tel: 200-825
(Service only)
Car Emergency Service
XIII. Szegedi út 22. Tel: 202-953

FILLING STATIONS

Abbreviations: B - Petrol, Gasoline; G - Diesel fuel; K - Mixture; S - Super petrol

		Open
Kerepesi út 89	B.G.	6 a.m. to 10 p.m.
Southern Railway Terminal	B.G.K.	day and night
Eastern Railway Terminal (Departure platform)	B.K.	day and night
Dimitrov tér	B.S.K.	day and night
Kispest, Határ út	B.G.	6 a.m. to 10 p.m.
Gellért tér	B.	6 a.m. to 10 p.m.
Árpád fejedelem útja 103	B.G.	6 a.m. to 10 p.m.
Csepel, Kossuth Lajos utca 76	B.G.K.	6 a.m. to 2 p.m.
Váci út 208	B.	6 a.m. to 10 p.m.
Szilágyi Erzsébet fasor	B.S.	6 a.m. to 10 p.m.
Liszt Ferenc tér	B.S.	6 a.m. to 10 p.m.
Western Railway Terminal (Arrival platform)	B.G.	6 a.m. to 10 p.m.

MORE IMPORTANT POST OFFICES

- I. Fő utca 4
- V. Bajcsy Zsilinszky út 16
- V. Deák Ferenc utca 16-18
- V. Dorottya utca 9
- V. Engels tér, MÁVAUT Central Bus Terminal
- V. Kossuth Lajos tér 13
- V. Szabadság tér 10
- V. Városház utca 18
- VI. Lenin körút 105
- VI. Western Railway Terminal
- VI. Filatelia, Népköztársaság útja 53
- VI. Gorkij fasor 1
- VII. Verseny utca 1
- VII. Eastern Railway Terminal
- VIII. József körút 8
- XI. Kelenföld Railway Station
- XI. Vásárhelyi Pál utca 4
- XII. Southern Railway Terminal
- XII. Alkotás utca 83
- XII. Böszörményi út 19/a
- XVIII. Ferihegy Airport

TELEPHONE NUMBERS
OF TRANSPORT ENTERPRISES

Budapest telephone numbers consist of six figures. The local public telephones operate with special coins to be inserted in the slot. (Such tokens can be bought in post offices and tobacco shops.)

Eastern Railway Terminal	429-150
Western Railway Terminal	125-426
Southern Railway Terminal	158-282
Kelenföld Railway Station	259-652
Electric Suburban Railway, Kerepesi út	131-741
MÁVAUT Central Bus Terminal	182-828
Boat Landing Stage, Vigadó tér	354-907
Taxi Enterprise	222-222
MALÉV Air Transport Company	180-744
Automobile Club	127-720

FOREIGN DIPLOMATIC REPRESENTATIONS
IN BUDAPEST

Albania (Embassy)
VI. Munkácsy Mihály utca 6. Tel: 229-278
Austria (Legation)
VI. Benczúr utca 16. Tel: 229-467
Argentina (Legation)
XI. Balogh Tihamér utca 5. Tel: 150-031
Belgium (Embassy)
I. Donáti utca 34. Tel: 158-828
Brazil (Legation)
XI. Gellért tér, Hotel Gellért. Tel: 466-100
Bulgaria (Embassy)
VI. Népköztársaság útja 115. Tel: 220-836
China, People's Republic of (Embassy)
VI. Benczúr utca 17. Tel: 224-872
Cuba (Embassy)
II. Harangvirág utca 3. Tel: 365-536
Czechoslovakia (Embassy)
XIV. Népstadion út 22. Tel: 297-800
Denmark (Legation)
II. Herman Ottó út 8. Tel: 152-066
Finland (Embassy)
XII. Székács utca 29. Tel: 351-355

France (Embassy)
VI. Lendvay utca 27. Tel: 127-260
German Democratic Republic (Embassy)
VI. Benczúr utca 26. Tel: 225-258
Ghana (Embassy)
II. Árvácska utca 11. Tel: 353-378
Greece (Embassy)
VI. Szegfű utca 3. Tel: 228-004
India (Embassy)
II. Búzavirág utca 14. Tel: 153-243
Indonesia (Embassy)
II. Orló utca 7. Tel: 355-305
Israel (Legation)
VII. Gorkij fasor 37. Tel: 425-393
Italy (Embassy)
XIV. Népstadion út 95. Tel: 225-077
Japan (Embassy)
II. Rómer Flóris utca 53. Tel: 150-043
Korea, Democratic People's Republic of (Embassy)
VI. Benczúr utca 31. Tel: 425-154
Mongolia (Embassy)
I. Bérc utca 23. Tel: 469-551
Netherlands (Legation)
XII. Mátyás király út 32. Tel: 166-414
Norway (Legation)
I. Fő utca 21. Tel: 158-051
Poland (Embassy)
VI. Gorkij fasor 16. Tel: 228-437
Rumania (Embassy)
XIV. Thököly út 72. Tel: 246-944, 227-689
Soviet Union (Embassy)
VI. Bajza utca 35. Tel: 124-749
Sweden (Embassy)
XIV. Ajtósi Dürer sor 27/a. Tel: 229-880
Switzerland (Embassy)
XIV. Népstadion út 107. Tel: 229-491
Turkey (Legation)
VI. Benczúr utca 15. Tel: 354-162
United Arab Republic (Embassy)
I. Bérc utca 16. Tel: 258-144
United Kingdom (Embassy)
V. Harmincad utca 6. Tel: 182-880
United States (Legation)
V. Szabadság tér 12. Tel: 124-375
Vietnam, Democratic Republic of (Embassy)

VI. Benczúr utca 18. Tel: 429-922
Yugoslavia (Embassy)
VI. Dózsa György út 92/b. Tel: 420-566
Danube Commission
VI. Benczúr utca 25. Tel: 228-085

TOURIST AGENCIES

The Municipal Tourist Office (FIH) provides for the suitable advertisement of everything that concerns tourism. It arranges hotel accommodations, sightseeing tours, the publication of prospectuses, the reservation of tickets to theatres and sport events, etc.

IBUSZ, which has fourteen agencies in Budapest, plays an important role in handling tourism in the capital. Both the head office and the branch offices are at the disposal of the guests from abroad and help them with travelling and accommodation problems. Among the important functions of these offices we mention the sale of railway tickets, the organisation of individual and conducted tours, currency exchange, etc.

The Express Travel Bureau for Young People organises trips abroad and in Hungary, as well as vacation trips for young people.

1. Secretariat of the National Council of Tourism
VIII. Múzeum utca 11. Tel: 343-532

2. Municipal Tourist Office (FIH)
V. Roosevelt tér 5. Tel: 380-581 and 180-609

Tourists' Hostel in the Citadel, camping at Római-part and booking of rooms: Tel: 381-106; advance booking of tickets to theatres, sport events, concerts, etc.: Tel: 181-109; bus sightseeing tours, guide and interpreter service: Tel: 182-161.

3. IBUSZ General Management, Head Office
V. Felszabadulás tér 5. Tel: 180-860

Booking of sleeping-car tickets for domestic and international railway lines and other inland tickets, banking service.

4. IBUSZ International Air Traffic and Maritime Navigation Agency
V. Vörösmarty tér 5. Tel: 187-544

5. IBUSZ Vacation and Paying Guest Service
V. Vörösmarty tér 5. Tel: 187-484

6. IBUSZ Hotel Reservations

V. Apáczai Csere János utca 4. Duna Hotel;
XIII. Grand Hotel, Margaret Island

7. IBUSZ Autobus Tours

V. József Attila utca 18. Tel: 380-507
Advance booking of bus tickets. Information service for tours. Registration.

8. IBUSZ Branch Offices

Information on travel, booking offices, currency exchange:
Eastern Railway Terminal. Tel: 426-990
Western Railway Terminal. Tel: 112-627

   II. Mártírok útja 67. Tel: 350-782

   IV. (Újpest) Bajcsy Zsilinszky út 13. Tel: 293-475

   VI. November 7. tér. Tel: 420-583. Tickets issued for inland traffic only.

   VII. Lenin körút 6. Tel: 227-467. Tickets issued for inland and international traffic; tickets to theatres, concerts and sport events.

   X. Kőrösi Csoma Sándor út 3. Tel: 148-834. Tickets issued for inland traffic only.

   XI. Bartók Béla út 9. Tel: 269-432

   XIII. Bulcsú utca 19. Tel: 206-546. Passport and visa section.

   XIX. Vöröshadsereg útja 151. Tel: 146-476

   XXI. Rákóczi Ferenc út 87. Tel: 144-418

9. Express Travel Bureau for Young People
(City Office)

V. Szabadság tér 18. Tel: 317-777
Inland and international travel for young people, board and lodging for youth visiting Hungary, camping and vacation service, railway and theatre tickets.

10. Managing Committee of Lake Balaton

VIII. Múzeum utca 11. Tel: 134-000

11. Budapest International Fair Managing Office

XIV. Városliget. Tel: 225-478

12. Office of the Hungarian Agricultural Exhibition and Fair

X. Alberti-Irsai út 10. Tel: 330-970

HOTELS

Astoria
V. Kossuth Lajos utca 19. Tel: 183-854
Béke
VI. Lenin körút 97. Tel: 123-530

Citadella
I. Gellérthegy. Tel: 267-848
(Cheap accommodation for tourists with shared bedrooms)
Continental
VII. Dohány utca 42-44. Tel: 221-257
Duna
V. Apáczai Csere János utca 4. Tel: 189-260
Erzsébet
V. Károlyi utca 13-15. Tel: 187-305
Hotel of the Express Travel Bureau
XII. Gaál utca 9. Tel: 158-891
(Cheap accommodation for students)
Gellért
XI. Gellért tér. Tel: 466-100
Grand Hotel Margitsziget
XIII. Margaret Island. Tel: 111-100
Ifjúság
II. Zivatar utca 1-3. Tel: 154-260
Metropol
VII. Rákóczi út 56. Tel: 421-174
Nemzeti
VIII. József körút 4. Tel: 334-748
Opera
VI. Révay utca 24. Tel: 123-339
Palace
VIII. Rákóczi út 43. Tel: 136-000
Park
VIII. Baross tér 10. Tel: 131-420
Royal
VII. Lenin körút 49. Tel: 229-800, 421-120
Szabadság
VII. Rákóczi út 90. Tel: 229-050
Vörös Csillag
XII. Rege út 21. Tel: 166-404
Normafa
XII. Eötvös út 52-56. (Tourists' hotel)
Transit Hotel
Ferihegy Airport. Tel: 336-379

TOURISTS' HOSTELS

There are eight tourists' hostels in the Buda hills. Three of them are only resting places without night accommodation, in the others beds can be obtained. All of them are under the management of the Enterprise for the Administration of Tourists' Hostels (VI. Lenin körút 55. Tel: 224-412). It is advisable to consult the Budapest office about the booking of rooms or beds.

Tourists' hostels: Csúcs-hegy, Frank-hegy, Makkosmária, Nagyszénás, Pálvölgy and Zsíros-hegy.

CAMPING

The Municipal Tourist Office maintains a transit tourists' hostel in the Citadel, on Gellért Hill, and a tent camp at Római-part on the Danube. Advance booking: V. Roosevelt tér 5. Tel: 381-106.

PAYING GUEST SERVICE

There are 400 beds in all at the disposal of paying guests in private houses in Budapest. Advance booking of rooms at the Municipal Tourist Office, V. Roosevelt tér 5. Tel: 381-106.

CATERING ESTABLISHMENTS

CAFÉS AND RESTAURANTS

District I
Fortuna
Hess András tér 4
Márványmenyasszony
Márvány utca 6
Pest-Buda
Fortuna utca 3
Várkert Kioszk
Ybl Miklós tér 9
Vendéglő a
   Régi Országházhoz
Országház utca 17

District II
Budagyöngye
Vöröshadsereg útja 16
Európa
Mártírok útja 43
Gül Baba
Mártírok útja 2
Rózsadomb
Keleti Károly utca 9
Trombitás
Moszkva tér 4

District III
Barlang
Szépvölgyi út
Hármashatárhegyi
étterem
Hármashatár-hegy

District IV
Árpád
Árpád út 66

District V
Apostolok
Kígyó utca 4-6
Astoria
Kossuth Lajos utca 19
Belvárosi
Szabadsajtó út 5
Berlin
Szent István körút 13
Duna
Apáczai Csere János utca 4
Erzsébet
Károlyi utca 13-15
Kárpátia
Károlyi utca 4-8
Kék Duna
Floating restaurant at the
   Pest abutment of the
   Suspension Bridge
Mátyás Pince
Március 15. tér 7
Országház
Kossuth Lajos tér 13-15
Pilvax
Városház utca 10
Százéves étterem
Pesti Barnabás utca 2

District VI
Abbázia
Népköztársaság útja 49
Béke
Lenin körút 97

Budapest
Nagymező utca 17
Kékes
November 7. tér 3
Opera
Népköztársaság útja 44
Savoy
Népköztársaság útja 48

District VII
Emke
Lenin körút 1
Hungária
Lenin körút 9-11
Moszkva
Gorkij fasor 36/b
Royal
Lenin körút 49

District VIII
Baross
József körút 45
Deák
József körút 55-57
Múzeum
Múzeum körút 12
Nemzeti
József körút 4
Pannonia
József körút 37
Palace
Rákóczi út 43

District XI
Borostyán
Bartók Béla út 48
Búsuló Juhász
Kelenhegyi út 58
Gellért
Kelenhegyi út 4
Kis Rabló
Zenta utca 3
Park
Kosztolányi Dezső tér

District XII
Fogas
Hollós út 2
Jánoshegyi
Jánoshegyi kilátó
Kis Royal
Márvány utca 19
Vörös Csillag
Rege út 21
District XIII
Casino
Margaret Island
Club
Szent István körút 16
Grand Hotel
Margaret Island
Sabaria
Marx tér 4

District XIV
Gundel
Állatkerti út 2
Ezerjó
Állatkerti út 3
Tóterasz
City Park
Vidámpark vendéglő
Május 1. út 75

SNACK BARS

Budai Mackó
I. Széna tér 7
Mézes Mackó
V. Kígyó utca 4-6
Napoletana
V. Váci utca 16

Anna (Édes Mackó)
V. Váci utca 7
Gresham Mackó
V. Roosevelt tér 5
Budapest Mackó
VI. Nagymező utca 17

Emke
VII. Akácfa utca 1
Baross Mackó
VIII. József körút 45
Mackó Bistro
VIII. Rákóczi út 9
Budai Bistro
XII. Kiss János altábornagy utca 38
Casino
XIII. Margaret Island
Ferihegyi Mackó
XVIII. Ferihegy Airport

PASTRY SHOPS

Déryné
I. Krisztina tér 3
Ruszwurm
I. Szentháromság tér 7
Bambi
II. Frankel Leó út 2-4
Mecsek
II. Mártírok útja 73
Rózsadomb
II. Keleti Károly utca 9
Anna
V. Váci utca 7
Bonbon
V. Szent István körút 29
Gresham
V. Roosevelt tér 5
Jégbüfé
V. Petőfi Sándor utca 2
Vörösmarty
V. Vörösmarty tér 7
Béke
VI. Lenin körút 97
Különlegességi
VI. Népköztársaság útja 70
Művész
VI. Népköztársaság útja 29
Párizsi
VI. Népköztársaság útja 37

Rózsa
VI. Népköztársaság útja 76
Mosoly
VI. Lenin körút 61
Erkel
VIII. Rákóczi út 49
Casino
XIII. Margaret Island

COFFEE SHOPS
(ESPRESSOS)

Bécsikapu
I. Táncsics Mihály utca 26
Lánchíd
I. Fő utca 2
Párizskert
I. Fő utca 20
Várkert
I. Ybl Miklós tér 9
Fortuna
I. Hess András tér 4
Ágnes
II. Mártírok útja 46
Budagyöngye
II. Vöröshadsereg útja 16
Európa
II. Mártírok útja 43-45
Fény
II. Mártírok útja 4
Gyergyó
II. Pasaréti út 72
Mecsek
II. Mártírok útja 73
Pasaréti
II. Pasaréti út 129
Astoria
V. Kossuth Lajos utca 9
Duna
V. Apáczai Csere János
   utca 4
Aero
V. Dorottya utca 1
Anna
V. Váci utca 7

Dunakorzó
V. Vigadó tér 3
Gourmand
V. Semmelweis utca 2
Kedves
V. Váci utca 19
Luxor
V. Szent István körút 5
Nárcisz
V. Váci utca 32
Pique Dame
V. Petőfi tér 3
Pilvax
V. Városház utca 10
Városkapu
V. Kecskeméti utca 17
Abbázia
VI. Népköztársaság útja 49
Budapest
VI. Nagymező utca 17
Fészek
VI. Népköztársaság útja 81
Lido
VI. Népköztársaság útja 11
Művész
VI. Népköztársaság útja 29
Negro
VI. Népköztársaság útja 19
Párizsi
VI. Népköztársaság útja 37
Trojka
VI. Népköztársaság útja 28
Marika
VIII. Rákóczi út 15
Nemzeti
VIII. József körút 4
Palace
VIII. Rákóczi út 43
Rózsa
VIII. József körút 31
Park
XI. Kosztolányi Dezső tér
Vörös Csillag
XII. Rege út 21

Kis Royal
XII. Márvány utca 19
Casino
XIII. Margaret Island

LITTLE RESTAURANTS

Halászcsárda
I. Iskola utca 29
Horgásztanya
I. Fő utca 27
Hársfa
II. Vöröshadsereg útja 132
Kis Lugas
II. Szilágyi Erzsébet fasor 15
Paksi Halászcsárda
II. Mártírok útja 14
Veronika
II. Vöröshadsereg útja 34
Erdei Lak
III. Szépvölgyi út 149
Evezős Sörkert
III. Nánási út 97
Hableány
III. Római-part 2.
Halászkert
III. Emőd utca 11
Híd (Kéhli)
III. Mókus utca 22
Komp Csárda
III. Kossuth üdülőpart
Óbudai Halászkert
(Sípos)
III. Lajos utca 46
Óbudai Népkert
III. Vörösvári út 131
Sport
III. Békásmegyer
Martos Flóra út 99
Árpád söröző
IV. Árpád út 84
Kakukk
IV. Nádor utca 31

Apostolok Söröző
V. Kígyó utca 4-6
Csendes
V. Múzeum körút 13
János Pince
V. Károlyi utca 13-15
Béke Borozó
VI. Lenin körút 97
Erdélyi Sörkert
VI. Népköztársaság útja 80
Kéményseprő
VI. Dózsa György út 106
Kispipa
VII. Akácfa utca 38
Borharapó Halvendéglő
VIII. Bláthy Ottó utca 13
Magyar Csárda
VIII. József körút 75
Csiky
IX. Angyal utca 37
Matróz
IX. Vámház alsó rakpart
Aranykerék
X. Kőbányai út 59/a
Csajkovszkij Söröző
X. Kápolna tér 4
Vidám Kert
X. Gergely utca 33
Panoráma
XI. Balatoni út 151
Víg Hajós
XI. Budaörsi út 7
Aranyflaskó
XII. Németvölgyi út 96
Árnyas
XII. Diósárok 16
Búfelejtő
XII. Németvölgyi út 136
Ördögorom
XII. Edvi Illés út
Kisbojtár
XIII. Dagály utca 17
Csalogató
XIV. Amerikai út 64
Flekken Tanya

XIX. Vöröshadsereg
   útja 150
Gödör
XIX. Vöröshadsereg
   útja 153

GARDEN RESTAURANTS

Citadella
I. Citadel
Bécsikapu
I. Táncsics Mihály utca 26
Márványmenyasszony
I. Márvány utca 6
Párizskert
I. Fő utca 20
Várkert Kioszk
I. Ybl Miklós tér 9
Vendéglő a
   Régi Országházhoz
I. Országház utca 17
Hűvösvölgyi Népkert
II. Vöröshadsereg útja 207
Trombitás
II. Moszkva tér 4
Fenyőgyöngye
III. Szépvölgyi út 155
Óbudai Halászkert
III. Kossuth üdülőpart
Duna
V. Apáczai Csere János
   utca 4
Dunagyöngye Sörkert
V. Apáczai Csere János
   utca 4
Erdélyi Sörkert
VI. Népköztársaság útja 80
Moszkva
VII. Gorkij fasor 35/b
Aranyflaskó
XII. Németvölgyi út 96
Fogas
XII. Hollós út 2

Kis Royal
XII. Márvány utca 19
Grand Hotel
XIII. Margaret Island
Gundel
XIV. Állatkerti út 2
Vidám Park
XIV. Május 1. út 75

NIGHT CLUBS WITH MUSIC AND DANCING

Bécsikapu
I. Táncsics Mihály utca 26
Szép Ilonka
I. Fő utca 20
Várkert Kioszk
I. Ybl Miklós tér 9
Budagyöngye
II. Vöröshadsereg útja 16
Rózsafa
II. Kacsa utca 26
Fenyőgyöngye
III. Szépvölgyi út 155
Kis Flórián
III. Tavasz utca 19
Vadászkunyhó
III. Kolosy tér 4
Belvárosi Grill
V. Szabadsajtó út 5
Duna
V. Apáczai Csere János
   utca 4
Dunakert
V. Apáczai Csere János
   utca 4
Jereván
V. Semmelweis utca 3
Kék Duna
Floating restaurant at the
   Pest abutment of the Sus-
   pension Bridge
Pilvax
V. Városház utca 10

265

Pipacs
V. Aranykéz utca 5
Városkapu
V. Kecskeméti utca 17
Savoy
VI. Népköztársaság útja 48
Budapest Táncpalota
VI. Nagymező utca 17
Trojka
VI. Népköztársaság útja 28
Hungária
VII. Lenin körút 9-11
Kulacs
VII. Osvát utca 11
Lúdláb
VII. Lenin körút 39

Moszkva
VII. Gorkij fasor 35/b
Pannonia
VIII. József körút 37
Szimfónia
IX. Üllői út 65-67
Búsuló Juhász
XI. Kelenhegyi út 58
Gellért Hullámterasz
XI. Kelenhegyi út 4
Kis Rabló
XI. Zenta utca 3
Grand Hotel
XIII. Margaret Island

PLACES OF AMUSEMENT

THEATRES

Állami Operaház
(State Opera House)
VI. Népköztársaság útja 22
Erkel Színház
(Erkel Theatre)
VIII. Köztársaság tér
Nemzeti Színház
(National Theatre)
VI. Nagymező utca 22-24
Katona József Színház
V. Petőfi Sándor utca 6
Vígszínház
(Comedy Theatre)
XIII. Szent István körút 14
József Attila Színház
XIII. Váci út 63
Madách Színház
VII. Lenin körút 31
**Madách Színház
  Kamaraszínháza**
VII. Madách tér 6
Thália Színház
VI. Paulay Ede utca 35

**Fővárosi Operett-
  színház**
(Municipal Operetta
  Theatre)
VI. Nagymező utca 17
Tarka Színpad
(Revue Stage)
VII. Dohány utca 42-44
Déryné Színház
VII. Éva utca 19
Irodalmi Színpad
(Literary Stage)
VI. Nagymező utca 11
Vidám Színpad
VI. Révay utca 18
Állami Bábszínház
(State Puppet Theatre)
VI. Népköztársaság útja 69
Kamara Varieté
VI. Lenin körút 106.
Kis Színpad
VI. Jókai tér 10
Egyetemi Színpad
V. Pesti Barnabás utca 1

Bartók Béla Terem
(Bartók Béla Hall)
V. Váci utca 9
Ódry Színpad
VIII. Vas utca 2/c
Állami Déryné Színház
VIII. Kulich Gyula tér 6
Jégszínház
(Ice Show)
XIV. Istvánmezei út,
    Sports Hall

CULTURAL CENTRES

József Attila Művelődési Ház
III. Dugovics Titusz tér 2
Ságvári Endre Művelődési Otthon
IV. Árpád út 66
MEDOSZ Móricz Zsigmond Kultúrotthon
VI. Jókai utca 2-4
Pedagógus Szakszervezet Budapesti Kultúrotthona
(Cultural Centre of the Teachers' Union)
VI. Gorkij fasor 10
Postások Központi Kultúrotthona
(Cultural Centre of Post Office Employees)
VI. Benczúr utca 27
Rózsa Ferenc Kultúrotthon
VI. Dózsa György út 84/a
Egressy Gábor Kultúrotthon
VII. Dohány utca 22-24
Jókai Kultúrotthon
VII. Akácfa utca 32

Szakszervezeti Művelődési Ház
(Cultural Centre of the Trade Unions)
XI. Fehérvári út 47-51
MOM Művelődési Otthon
(Cultural Centre of the Hungarian Optical Works)
XII. Csörsz utca 18
József Attila Kultúrház és Úttörőház
XIII. József Attila tér 4
Fémmunkások Kultúrotthona
(Cultural Centre of the Metalworkers)
XIII. Frangepán utca 16

LEADING CINEMAS

Alfa
VIII. Kun Béla tér 6
Bartók
XI. Bartók Béla út 64
Bástya
VII. Lenin körút 8
Budai Híradó
(Newsreel Cinema)
II. Mártírok útja 5/b
Corvin
VIII. Kisfaludy köz
Duna
XIII. Fürst Sándor utca 7
Filmmúzeum
VII. Tanács körút 3
Gorkij
VII. Akácfa utca 4
Híradó
(Newsreel Cinema)
VII. Lenin körút 13
Kossuth
XIII. Váci út 14

267

Május 1.
II. Mártírok útja 55
Művész
VI. Lenin körút 88
Puskin
V. Kossuth Lajos utca 19
Szikra
VI. Lenin körút 120
Toldi
V. Bajcsy Zsilinszky út 36
Uránia
VIII. Rákóczi út 21
Vörös Csillag
VII. Lenin körút 45
Vörösmarty
VIII. Üllői út 4

**Bartók Béla Open-air
Stage**
XI. Kosztolányi Dezső tér
**Városmajor Open-air
Stage**
XII. Városmajor

CONCERT HALLS

**Liszt Ferenc Academy
of Music**
VI. Liszt Ferenc tér 8
Bartók Béla Hall
V. Váci utca 9
Kamaraterem
V. Semmelweis utca 1-3

OPEN-AIR THEATRES
AND CONCERT
STAGES

Károlyi Kert
V. Károlyi utca 16
**Kulich Gyula Open-air
Stage**
VIII. Kulich Gyula tér
**Csajkovszkij Open-air
Stage**
X. Martinovics tér

OTHER ATTRACTIONS

Zoological Gardens
XIV. Állatkerti út 6
**Botanical Gardens
of the University**
VIII. Illés utca 25
Municipal Grand Circus
XIV. Állatkerti út 7
Vidám Park
(Amusement Park)
XIV. City Park

Every afternoon and evening in the summer months pleasure boats go on a two-hour cruise upstream from the landing pier at Vigadó tér.

NATIONAL ART COLLECTIONS

The museums and libraries of Budapest offer very rich and valuable material to the visitor. Here we give a short survey of the most important art collections.

MUSEUMS

Aquincum Museum

(III. Szentendrei út 193)

Its collection contains finds of the excavations in and around Aquincum.

Central room. Relics of religious worship and similar objects are displayed in glass cases.

Room 2. Stone monuments are ranged along the wall, and in the middle of the other side stands a barrel in almost perfect condition. Next to it and in

Room 3. Objects of various crafts and trades are exhibited, and in the centre of the room stand the remains of statues and a votive altar stone.

Room 4. In two cabinets the original bronze parts and a reconstruction of the famous Roman organ of Aquincum can be seen. The stone monuments exhibited here represent gods of antiquity.

Room 5. It contains relics of ancient art, objects of religious worship and funeral ceremonies as well as the finds of the latest excavations.

Large-size stone monuments stand in front of the entrance and in the colonnades of the museum.

Excavation area. The ruins around the museum from the central part of the remains of the civilian town of the Roman period.

Bajor Gizi Memorial Museum

(XII. Stromfeld Aurél utca 16)

This is a collective exhibition in memory of three great Hungarian actresses: Mari Jászai (1850-1926), Emilia Márkus (1862-1949) and Gizi Bajor (1893-1951).

Philatelic Museum

(VII. Dob utca 75-81)

This collection contains Hungarian and foreign postage stamps from the earliest issues to the most recent, comprising over 130,000 specimens. The Hungarian material is complete. Among the Hungarian rarities we can find there the whole set in seven different colours of the first Hungarian lithographed stamp issued in 1871, as well as specialities of perforation and misprinted stamps.

The museum also has a philatelic library and stamp-examining equipment.

269

Budapest Municipal Museum—Modern History Department

(III. Kiscelli utca 108)

This collection preserves relics and documents relating to the history of the capital, beginning with the period following liberation from Turkish rule to the present day.

Corridor on the upper floor: Etchings, contemporary descriptions, commemorative medals, weapons dating from the Turkish occupation and the period after the recapture of Buda.

Room 1. Documents on international reaction to the recapture of Buda.

Room 2. Relics of 18th-century guilds.

Room 3. A few relics of the 18th-century art of Buda.

Room 4. Documents and souvenirs of Pest and Buda from the early 19th century.

Other sections of the corridor show views of Pest and Buda from the early 19th century, and contain documents and pictures portraying the early development of communications, commerce and industry in the capital.

Statues and relics from the 18th and 19th centuries are exhibited in the rooms of the ground floor.

Castle Museum

(I. Szentháromság tér 2)

Ground floor. The Budapest area from prehistoric times to the Magyar conquest of the land.

Room 1. Prehistoric finds originating from the area of Budapest.

Room 2. From 1000 B.C. to the period of the Roman conquest.

Room 3. Relics from the Roman period.

Room 4. Most of the objects exhibited here come from the excavations of the palace of the Roman proconsul, which was discovered on present-day Shipyard Island in Óbuda.

Room 5. Finds from the Aquincum area dating from the 2nd to the 4th centuries.

Room 6. A map showing the Aquincum villa colony and finds originating from there.

Upstairs. Buda in the Middle Ages.

Room 1. Relics of the early Middle Ages.

Room 2. Relics from the period of King Sigismund.

Room 3. Relics from the period of King Matthias.

Room 4. Relics of the Renaissance period.

Room 5. Renaissance remnants originating from the Nyék hunting-seat.

Room 6. Material from the 13th and 15th centuries relating to the town population of the Castle District.

Room 7. Relics of the Turkish period.

Room 8. Seventeenth-century furniture.

The lapidary of the museum is in the northern tower of the Fishermen's Bastion.

War History Museum
(I. Kapisztrán tér 2-4)

Documents on Hungarian military history and a collection of arms and military equipment from the period before 1700, as well as from recent times.

Industrial Arts Museum
(IX. Üllői út 33-37)

Exhibition of artistic copper and bronze works. European goldsmith's works. The first cabinet holds the finest piece of the collection, the Matthias flask. Other items are Italian, Persian and Moorish majolicas and ceramics, stove tiles, stone and tin-glazed vessels, faience, Meissen and Vienna porcelain, and Hungarian pottery.

The museum has a collection of glass objects, and one of textiles, rugs and carpets. The major part of the furniture collection is exhibited in the Nagytétény Castle Museum.

Fine Arts Museum
(XIV. Dózsa György út 41)

Ground floor, to the right of the entrance. Egyptian collection. Greco-Roman collection.

Room 1. Greek art from 3,000 to 480 B.C.

Room 2. Greek art from the 5th and 4th centuries B.C.

Room 3. Hellenistic art in Greece and Italy.

Room 4. Roman art.

Renaissance hall on the ground floor. Collection of modern foreign sculpture.

Room 1. Works of German, Austrian, Scandinavian and Italian masters.

Room 2. French and Belgian sculpture.

Room 3. Pavel Trubetskoy: "Sitting Woman", M. Rosso: "Woman's Head", Rodin: "Nereides", E. Rombaux: "The Daughters of Satan", I. Meštrovic: "Maternal Care", G. Minne: "Young Man with Shell".

First floor, right wing. Old Gallery. Italian and Flemish painting.

Room 1. Tuscany, 13th and 14th centuries.

Room 2. Tuscany, 14th and 15th centuries.

Room 3. Central Italy, 15th and 16th centuries.

Room 4. North Italy, 14th and 15th centuries.

Room 5. North Italy, 16th century.

Room 6. North Italy, 15th and 16th centuries.

Room 7. Italy, 16th and 17th centuries.

Room 8. Italy, 17th and 18th centuries.

Room 9. Flemish painting, 16th and 17th centuries.

Rooms 10-11. Flemish painting, 17th century.

First floor, left wing. Old Gallery.

The two central rooms contain Flemish masterpieces of the 17th century.

In the adjoining four rooms German and Austrian painting from the 15th to 18th centuries can be seen.

The next room contains English paintings from the 17th to 19th centuries.

In the last two rooms and in the Italian cabinets the material of the modern foreign gallery is shown.

Staircase from first to second floor. Collection of old foreign sculpture, Italian decorative wood carvings.

Second floor. Collection of old foreign sculpture. Works of the Italian and Nordic Schools from the 13th to 18th centuries in 13 cabinets and two rooms.

The graphic collection comprising nearly 100,000 drawings and etchings is shown in temporary exhibitions.

Roman Camp Lapidary

(III. Korvin Ottó utca 63)

Excavated ruins of one building belonging to the Roman military camp. The ruins indicate that several houses built on top of each other were destroyed and later rebuilt. In the garden in front of the museum sarcophagi and various sepulchres can be seen.

Underground Museum

(V. Március 15. tér)

Relics of the Roman camp built in the 2nd and 3rd centuries. A significant document is a stone fragment with inscriptions giving an account of the fortifications extending between Aquincum and Intercisa.

Museum of Eastern Asiatic Arts
(VI. Népköztársaság útja 103)
The collection of the museum was founded by Ferenc Hopp who gathered valuable objects of art in East Asia. They are preserved in his villa, which he bequeathed to the state. The first exhibition of the collection comprising several thousand items took place in 1923. The museum organises various exhibitions from year to year, as the villa is not large enough to show the whole material at one time.
The former Ráth György Museum (VI. Gorkij fasor 12) also belongs to this museum. Its premises house the permanent Chinese exhibition and thus it is now called Chinese Museum.

Hungarian National Gallery
(V. Kossuth Lajos tér 12)
This Gallery contains the largest collection of 19th and 20th-century Hungarian works of fine art. Paintings from the 19th century are exhibited on the first floor, those from the 20th century on the second floor. Sculptures are displayed on the ground floor and in the corridors of the upper storey.
The graphic collection of the Gallery, comprising some 15,000 valuable drawings and etchings, is shown in temporary exhibitions.

Botanical Collection of the Natural Sciences Department of the Hungarian National Museum
(XIV. City Park, Széchenyi Island)
The most characteristic plant communities of Hungary, plant physiology, cultivated plants, soil research. Mushroom collection.

Hungarian National Museum
Museum of History
(VIII. Múzeum körút 14-16)
Entrance hall on the ground floor. Stone monuments of the Roman period from various regions of the country.
Upstairs. History of the Hungarian people from the period of the conquest of the country until 1848.
Room 1. Relics from the time of the conquest of the country and the early centuries subsequent to it.
Room 2. Relics of the 13th and 14th centuries.
Room 3. First half of the 15th century, relics of the Anjou period.

Room 4. The period of King Matthias.

Room 5. The period after the death of King Matthias.

Room 6. Relics related to landlords and town life from the 17th century.

Room 7. Relics of the Turkish wars and the wars of independence under Thököly and Rákóczi.

Corridors. Relics dating from the 18th and the early 19th centuries.

The other collections of the museum are not permanently exhibited. The archeological collection comprises relics from the paleolithic period to the conquest of the land. The collection of coins and medals is very rich.

The historical picture gallery also belongs to this Museum.

Agricultural Museum

(XIV. City Park, Széchenyi Island)

Twenty-one rooms are filled with the material of permanent exhibitions.

In room after room the section on animal husbandry follows the development of livestock keeping from one epoch to another beginning with prehistoric animals to domestication, pastoral life to modern cattle breeding, dairy farms, foraging, poultry farming, etc.

The exhibition of machine and implement models shows the historic development of mechanisation in plant cultivation.

The exhibition on viticulture displays about 500 original items, showing past and present winegrowing, and the implements and working processes employed.

The section on forestry comprises the history of forests, forest botany, and deals with the problems of forest culture and protection of forests.

The hunting exhibition is located in the Hall of Knights on the first floor, and the exhibition pertaining to fishing in one of the halls of the Gothic wing.

Nagytétény Castle Museum

(XXII. Kastélymúzeum utca 9)

Exhibition of furniture from the collection of the Museum of Industrial Arts.

Room 1. Gothic furnishing from the 14th and 15th centuries.

Room 2. Italian Renaissance.

Room 3 South German and Swiss furniture.

Room 4. Dutch furniture from the 17th century.

274

Room 5. Hungarian furniture of the 17th and 18th centuries.
Upstairs. Room 1. Rococo and Transylvanian furniture.
Room 2. Biedermeyer furniture from the early 19th century.
Room 3. The reception room of a bourgeois apartment in the first half of the 19th century.
Room 4. Works of the famous Pest cabinetmaker, Ferenc Steindl, from the 1840s.
The furniture exhibition is supplemented with a collection of carpets, chandeliers, paintings and various textiles.

Roman Camp, Nagytétény

In Roman times this place was called Campona, one of the fortified camps of the *Limes* along the Danube. The walls that have been partly unearthed can be seen in present-day Piac tér.

Ethnographic Museum

(VIII. Könyves Kálmán körút 40)
The Hungarian material embraces nearly all aspects of material culture, primitive farming and plant gathering, agriculture, livestock keeping, fishing, peasant building, room and kitchen furniture, communications, folk costumes and the arts and crafts over the ages.
The Oceanian and Australian material is the richest among the international exhibits, then follow the European, Asian, African and finally the American and Indonesian collections. A Hungarian folk-music collection is also kept here.

Petőfi Literary Museum

(V. Károlyi utca 16)
Periodical exhibitions of documents on Hungarian literary history.

Postal Services Museum

(I. Krisztina körút 6-8)
This is a permanent exhibition of the material covering the history of the Hungarian postal service.

LIBRARIES

Library of the Eötvös Loránd University
(V. Károlyi utca 10)
The library contains, first of all, literature on the various
sciences taught at the University, especially the social and
natural sciences. The periodicals section comprising 90,000
volumes subscribes to 402 Hungarian and 1,209 foreign
periodical and other publications.
The archives of manuscripts (42,000 items) preserves 175
codices with eleven from King Matthias's famous Corviniana Library and eight Hungarian-language documents
dating from the first two decades of the 16th century.
The section of rarities preserves etchings dating from the
period before book-printing.

Municipal Szabó Ervin Library
(VIII. Szabó Ervin tér 1)
The collection of this library serves the needs of the
largest sections of the population. The central building
houses 380,000 volumes.
Over half a million volumes are distributed among the 44
branch libraries.

Library of the Hungarian Academy of Sciences
(V. Roosevelt tér 9)
Its main purpose is to supply scientific research workers
with the necessary Hungarian and foreign books, periodicals, bibliographies, to maintain relations with scientific
institutions and libraries abroad, and to organise the exchange of publications. It possesses about half a million
books, 1,100 incunabula and 6,200 old Hungarian prints,
as well as 13,612 volumes of manuscripts, 230,416 manuscripts of small size, 15,291 manuscripts with oriental
themes, and 1,079 works on microfilm.

Library of the Technical University
(XI. Budafoki út 4-6)
This library possesses over 300,000 volumes, 63,000 period-
icals, and 470,000 small publications.

Parliament Library
(V. Kossuth Lajos tér, Parliament Building)
This is the richest library in the country with regard to
works on politics and political law.

National Technical Library
(VIII. Múzeum utca 17)

It comprises over 180,000 books and patent archives with nearly 5 million patents. With its rich documentation and bibliographies this library has become a centre of technical and scientific life in Hungary.

National Széchényi Library
(VIII. Múzeum körút 14-16)

Its material of over four million volumes makes it a really national library. It is at the same time the largest scientific library in Hungary. The collection consisting of books, manuscripts, rarities, periodicals, maps, newspapers, posters, musical scores, etc., is invaluable. The earliest literary relics of the Hungarian language from the "Funeral Oration" (end of the 12th century) to the Corvinian codices of the epoch of King Matthias, from the first Hungarian incunabula to the first Hungarian printed publication are deposited here.

SPORT ESTABLISHMENTS

People's Stadium
Covering an area of 22 hectares it was opened on August 20, 1953. The costs of construction amounted to 150 million forints. The structure is buttressed by 18 huge ornamented reinforced concrete pylons. The grandstand is 30 metres high, 50 metres wide and 328 metres long. There are 50 entrances. Originally the stadium holds 84,000 spectators. When sport events of major significance take place 100,000 spectators can be accommodated.

The stadium is equipped with the most up-to-date technical facilities. The telephone exchange handles 27 main lines and 200 extensions. On the second floor of the main building there is a lounge for newspapermen, and twelve sound-proof telephone booths for their use. Radio broadcasts of sports events can be made from 20 radio cabins simultaneously. The scoreboards and the clock, five metres in diametre, are illuminated by 14,000 incandescent bulbs. They are of Hungarian construction. Similar scoreboards are used in a number of sport stadiums abroad. The stadium's system of loudspeakers, which is internationally famous, keeps the public informed of the results. In the evening contests can be held under floodlights.

Ten separate dressing rooms are at the disposal of the competitors, each of them provided with a little basin or a shower room. Thirty-three buffets with 400 vendors serve the spectators with refreshments.

The grandstand is under reconstruction. After this is completed there will be seats for 25,000 more spectators. Later on, in the main building a twelve-storied hotel will be erected.

The main entrance of the stadium opens on Ifjúság útja. In addition to this, there are two side entrances. The way to the main entrance is decorated by eight statues on either side.

National Sports Hall

This sport establishment is situated in Istvánmezei út close to the corner of Dózsa György út. National and international indoor contests (table-tennis, basket-ball, volley-ball, wrestling, boxing, gymnastics, fencing, etc.) take place here. The building, which can hold 2,200 spectators, was erected in 1942. Outdoor training grounds are maintained round the building and one covered training building is used now for the Ice Show.

Millenary Sport Ground

It lies northwest of the People's Stadium, at the crossing of Thököly út and Szabó József utca. It has a seating capacity of 20,000. Apart from cycling and motorcycling races, figure skating and ice-hockey matches have regularly taken place on artificial ice since 1955.

Little Stadium

This is located between the People's Stadium and the Millenary Sport Ground. It was opened in 1960, and can hold 13,000 people. In addition to sport events, concerts are sometimes held here.

FTC Sport Ground
(IX. Üllői út 129)

This sport ground is closely connected with the history of significant Hungarian sports events, especially with the history of soccer. Construction of this field was started in 1910. The grandstand, which was planned originally for 10,000 to 12,000 spectators, was enlarged later to accommodate 25,000. Reconstruction and modernisation of this traditional sports centre is under way.

MTK Football Ground

This sports establishment lies at the intersection of Salgó-tarjáni út and Hungária körút. It ranks among the largest and oldest in Budapest.

National Riding Hall

It is in the neighbourhood of the Eastern Railway Terminal, at 9 Kerepesi út. Formerly called the Tattersall it is an important centre of Hungarian riding sport.

Next to the National Riding Hall, at 11 Kerepesi út, lies the **trotting race course.** In the same street, at No. 57, is the **gallop race course.**

A sport establishment in Buda worth noting is that of the Vasas Sport Club, at 11-13 Pasaréti út. There are athletics fields, cinder tracks, tennis courts, and a large hall for various sports.

Other sport establishments in Buda include the

BEAC Sport Ground

(XI. Mező utca 4) and the

Artifical Ice Rink

(XI. Budafoki út 189).

Sports centres on the Pest side are:

Stadium of the Újpest Dózsa Sport Club

IV. Megyeri út 13

Vasas Sport Ground

XIII. Fáy utca, corner of Béke utca

Honvéd Sport Ground

XIII. Dózsa György út 53

Young Pioneers' Stadium

XIII. Margaret Island

Dózsa Tennis Stadium

XIII. Margaret Island

Artificial Skating Rink

XIV. City Park

Kispest Sport Ground of the Budapest Honvéd Sport Club
XIX. Temető utca 2

Csepel Sport Ground
XXI. Béke tér 1

*

Any foreign visitor who intends to go hunting or angling in Hungary can apply for a hunting or a fishing licence at the following addresses:

National Association of Hunters
VI. Népköztársaság útja 86. Tel: 123-626

Hungarian Co-operative Enterprise for the Marketing of Game (MAVAD)
V. Honvéd utca 16. Tel: 122-668

National Association of Anglers
V. Galamb utca 3. Tel: 182-124

BUDAPEST AS A SPA

Budapest is both a health and holiday resort. There are 123 warm springs which yield a total of more than 40 million litres of warm and 30 million litres of lukewarm water.

Extensive bathing establishments have been built in the vicinity of the thermal springs in Budapest. The temperature of the springs varies a great deal. Among the artesian springs, Well No. 2 in the Széchenyi baths is the hottest (76°C). Then, among the natural springs, the St. Stephen's spring in the Császár Baths ranks first with a temperature of 62°C (at present 50°C). The water of these hot springs must be cooled down for bathing.

An essential substance found in the Budapest thermal springs is sulphur, which is important in the vital functions of the human body. Another noteworthy pecularity of the thermal water is its radioactivity.

Mud baths contribute significantly to the effectiveness of water cures. There is a warm open-air mud pound in the Lukács Baths.

The water of the Budapest thermal springs can also be used for drinking cures.

The abundance and varied temperatures of the waters of the thermal springs of Budapest make them suitable not only for medicinal uses but also for supplying flats in nearby districts, swimming pools, open-air baths, etc.

MEDICINAL BATHS, SWIMMING POOLS, OPEN-AIR BATHS

District I
Imre Medicinal Baths
Hadnagy utca 10
Thermal steam baths, hot-air and steam chambers, thermal tub baths.
Rudas Medicinal Baths
Döbrentei tér 9
Thermal steam baths for men only, hot-air and steam chambers, radioactive tub baths, drinking fountains, indoor swimming pool.

District II
Császár Baths
Frankel Leó út 31-33
Thermal steam bath, hot-air and steam chambers, mud cures for men and women, Turkish tub baths.
Császár Swimming Pool
Árpád fejedelem útja 8
Király Medicinal Bath
Fő utca 84
Lukács Medicinal Baths
Frankel Leó út 25-29
Thermal tub bath, aerated water and salt baths, mud cures for men and women, Turkish steam and tub baths, drinking cures, swimming pool.

District III
Árpád Open-air Swimming Pool
Csillaghegy, Pusztakúti út 3
Pünkösdfürdő
Békásmegyer, Vöröshadsereg útja 272

281

District IV
Újpest Baths
Berzeviczy Gergely utca 4
Steam baths, hot-air and steam chambers, tub and salt baths, mud cures.
Vasas Izzó Sport Swimming Pool
Váci út 77

District XI
Gellért Medicinal Baths
Kelenhegyi út 4
Thermal steam baths for men and women with hot-air and steam chambers, baths for intestinal ailments, mud cures, massage, traction baths, wave baths and bubble baths, rheumatic treatment.

District XIII
Szabadság Open-air Baths (Dagályfürdő)
Népfürdő utca 5
National Sport Swimming Pool
Margaret Island
Palatinus Open-air Bath
Margaret Island

District XIV
Széchenyi Medicinal Baths
XIV. City Park, Állatkerti út 11
Swimming Pool
Szőnyi út

DRINKING FOUNTAINS

Lukács Medicinal Spring
In the park of the Lukács Baths
Széchenyi Baths Medicinal Spring
XIV. City Park, Állatkerti út 11

WHERE TO GO SHOPPING

A great number of fashionable stores and attractively decorated shop windows invite the visitor to drop in and make his purchases. The richest shops with the widest range of goods are in the Inner City, especially in Kossuth

Lajos utca, Váci utca and Petőfi Sándor utca. The largest
Budapest department stores are:

Otthon Áruház (home furnishings), VII. Rákóczi út 74-76

Corvin Áruház, VIII. Blaha Lujza tér 1-2

Úttörő Áruház, V. Kossuth Lajos utca 9

Extra Áruház (department store for extra sizes), VII.
Rákóczi út 4-6

Szabadság Áruház, IX. Calvin tér 7

Luxus Áruház, V. Vörösmarty tér 3

Lottó Áruház, VII. Rákóczi út 36

Csillag Áruház, VII. Rákóczi út 20-22.

In the following shops objects of Hungarian folk art can
be obtained, such as carpets, curtain materials, embroi-
dery, laces, ceramics and wood carvings:

V. Kossuth Lajos utca 2

V. Váci utca 14

VII. Rákóczi út 32

VII. Lenin körút 5

XI. Bartók Béla út 50

XIII. Szent István körút 26.

There is a special gift shop at 2 Vörösmarty tér. Items of
fine worksmanship are sold in the shop of arts and crafts
(Iparművészeti Bolt), at 14 Kossuth Lajos utca.

LIST OF THE MOST IMPORTANT SIGHTS, IN BUDAPEST

ARCHITECTURAL MONUMENTS

FROM THE PERIOD PRECEDING THE MAGYAR CONQUEST OF THE LAND

I. Tabán Park. Part of the wall of a Roman watch tower.

III. Area of ruins in Aquincum.

III. Flórián tér 3. Roman military bath.

III. Korvin Ottó utca 63. Remnants of a Roman colony and baths.

III. Nagyszombat utca. Roman military amphitheatre.

III. Raktár utca. Old Christian chapel: Cella trichora.

III. Római út. Roman aqueduct.

III. Szentendrei út. Remnants of pillars of a Roman aqueduct.

III. Szentendrei út. Máriakő Chapel. Remnants of pillars of a Roman aqueduct.

III. Szentendrei út. Foundation walls of the civilian amphitheatre at the northern border of the Roman town.

III. Óbudai utca. Roman building with a semicircular ground plan.

III. Vörösvári út 44. Fragments of the Roman aqueduct.

V. Március 15. tér. Remnants of a watch tower of the Roman camp on the Pest side.

V. Március 15. tér. Foundation walls of another corner tower of the Roman camp, seen south of the choir wall of the Inner City Parish Church.

V. Március 15. tér. Wall of a building of the Roman camp, in the basement of the Inner City Parish Church.

XI. Albertfalva. Foundation walls of a Roman building and a dwelling house near Budafoki út.

XXII. Nagytétény. Walls and a gate structure of the Roman camp, beside the baroque castle.

XXII. Nagytétény. Roman heating system in the cellar of a school building.

ROMANESQUE ARCHITECTURE

I. Hess András tér. Ruins of an old Dominican church.
II. Pesthidegkút. Ruins of a church.
II. Vöröshadsereg útja 48. Foundation walls of the church of the old village of Nyék.
III. Calvin köz. Foundation walls of a building in the basement and the courtyard of the Calvinist church.
V. Március 15. tér. Wall remains within the southern tower of the Inner City Parish Church.
XI. Kamaraerdő. Ruins of a monastery and a church near the Balaton highway.
XIII. Remains of the church of the Premonstratensian Order.

GOTHIC ARCHITECTURE

I. Castle. Medieval ramparts of the Fortress of Buda, built for the protection of the residential area.
I. Szent György tér. Ruins of the former royal castle and fortress.
I. Kapisztrán tér. Tower of the one-time Garrison Church.
I. Országház utca 26. A niche with seat in the doorway.
I. Szentháromság tér. Matthias Church.
I. Úri utca 6. Four medieval niches with seats in the doorway.
I. Úri utca 32. Eight niches with seats in the doorway.
I. Úri utca 64-66. A large medieval hall with octagonal pillars on the ground floor of the building.
I. Bugát utca. The foundation walls of the St. Lazarus Church.
I. Fishermen's Bastion. Church walls east of the triumphal arch of the Dominican church.
I. Lánchíd utca 23. Section of the medieval ramparts.
I. Tabán Park. Ruins of a medieval building.
II. Budakeszi út 93. Remains of the Budaszentlőrinc Pauline monastery and church.
II. Budakeszi út 95. Foundation walls of a tall quadrangular tower.
II. Mártírok útja 66. Section of the medieval ramparts of Víziváros.
II. Vöröshadsereg útja 48. Foundation walls of the church of the old village of Nyék.
V. Királyi Pál utca 13/b. Section of the medieval city wall of Pest with crenellation.

V. Calvin tér 1 and 5. Part of the Pest city wall.

V. Ferenczy István utca 26. Part of the Pest city wall.

V. Gerlóczy utca 6. Section of the city wall.

V. Magyar utca 2, 26, 28, 30, 36, 42. Fragments of the city wall.

V. Múzeum körút 7. Part of the city wall.

V. Semmelweis utca 11, 21, 23. Fragments of the city wall.

V. Március 15. Inner City Parish Church.

VI. Bajza utca 41. Mulberry Garden.

XII. At the beginning of Béla király út. City Well Spring.

XII. Béla király út 30. King Béla's Fountain.

XIII. Margaret Island. Ruins of the Dominican convent and church.

XIII. Margaret Island. Front wall with Gothic windows and parts of the spire of the Franciscan church.

RENAISSANCE ARCHITECTURE

I. Szent György tér. Renaissance fragments between the ruins of the former royal castle and the fortress.

I. Castle area. Fragment of the medieval ramparts of Buda.

II. Glück Frigyes utca. Walls of the medieval game-reserve of King Matthias in Nyék.

II. Vöröshadsereg útja 48. Wall remains of the Nyék hunting seat.

V. Március 15. tér. Pastophoria of a Pest town magistrate and of Provost Endre Nagyrévi in the side chapels of the Inner City Parish Church.

TURKISH ARCHITECTURE

I. Gellért rakpart. Eight-pillared cupola of the Rudas Baths with original vaults and five bathing pools.

I. Hadnagy utca 8-10. The cupola of the St. Imre Baths.

II. Fő utca 82-86. Cupola of the Király Baths.

II. Frankel Leó út 31. Cupola of the Császár Baths.

II. Mecset utca 14. Tomb of Gül Baba.

V. Március 15. tér. Remains of a Turkish *mihrab* (praying niche) in the sanctuary of the Inner City Parish Church.

BAROQUE ARCHITECTURE

I. Hess András tér 3. The "Red Hedgehog" house.

I. Szent György tér. Southern wing of the former royal castle.

I. Szentháromság tér. Holy Trinity Column.

I. Szentháromság utca 2. Old Buda town hall with remnants from the Middle Ages.

I. Tárnok utca 5. One-storey house, late baroque style.

I. Úri utca 24. One-storey dwelling house with medieval remnants.

I. Úri utca 48-50. One-storey dwelling house with medieval remnants.

I. Attila utca 40. Tabán Parish Church.

I. Batthyány tér 7. St. Anne Church.

I. Corvin tér 3. One-storey dwelling house with arcaded courtyard.

I. Döbrentei tér 9. Two-storey building of a former inn in the courtyard.

I. Fő utca 43. Roman Catholic church.

I. Fő utca 90. Greek Catholic church.

I. Krisztina tér. Krisztinaváros Parish Church.

II. Bécsi út, corner of Szépvölgyi út. Single-spired Roman Catholic church of the parish of Újlak.

II. Mártírok útja 23. Twin-spired Franciscan church.

II. Pesthidegkút. Roman Catholic church.

II. Zsigmond tér. Holy Trinity statue.

III. Farkastorki út. St. Donatus chapel.

III. Kiscelli utca 108. Building of an old Trinitarian monastery.

III. Óbudai utca. Single-spired Roman Catholic church of Óbuda.

V. Károlyi utca. Franciscan church.

V. Március 15. tér. Baroque reconstruction and the façade of the Inner City Parish Church.

V. Eötvös Loránd utca 7. Central Seminary. University Church.

V. Szerb utca 4. Greek Orthodox Serbian Church.

V. Városház utca 9-11. Building of the Budapest City Council.

VI. Bajza utca 41. Old Budapest calvary.

VIII. Rákóczi út 31. St. Roch Chapel.

X. Kápolna tér. Greek Catholic chapel.

XI. Törökbálinti út, corner Nagyszeben utca. Holy Trinity column.

XXII. Nagytétény. Csóhári Pál utca. Statue of St. John of Nepomuk.

XXII. Nagytétény, Rózsa Ferenc tér. Florian statue.

XXII. Nagytétény. Holy Trinity column.

LOUIS XVI ARCHITECTURE

I. Bécsikapu tér 5. One-storey corner house.

I. Bécsikapu tér 6. One-storey dwelling house.

I. Bécsikapu tér 7. One-storey dwelling house.

I. Kapisztrán tér. Entrance hall in front of the medieval tower of the one-time Garrison Church.

I. Színház utca 1-3. Former Castle Theatre.

I. Batthyány tér 17. One-storey rococo dwelling house.

I. Szarvas tér 17. One-storey apartment house, corner building.

II. Harrer Pál utca 44-46. One-storey factory building with oval ground plan.

V. Petőfi tér. Greek Orthodox church.

V. Szerb utca 4. Garden gate and corner structure.

VI. Nagymező utca 1. Terézváros Parish Church.

NEOCLASSIC ARCHITECTURE

I. Fortuna utca 6. One-storey dwelling house with sculptures over the doorway.

I. Kapisztrán tér 2-4. Façade of the War History Museum.

I. Szent György tér 1-2. One-storey palace in the early classicist style.

I. Clark Ádám tér. Eastern entrance portal of the Tunnel.

I. Suspension Bridge.

II. Fő utca 82-86. Király Baths.

II. Frankel Leó út 31. Császár Baths.

II. Frankel Leó út 32. One-storey bathing establishment.

II. Frankel Leó út 54. Single-spired chapel with portico.

II. Iparostanuló utca 2. Old Buda shooting range.

III. Lajos utca 163. Synagogue of Óbuda.

V. Apáczai Csere János utca 7. Three-story apartment house.

V. Akadémia utca 1. Four-storey corner house.

V. Arany János utca 15. Three-storey apartment house.

V. Deák Ferenc tér 4-5. Lutheran church.

V. Károlyi utca 16. Former Károlyi Palace.

V. Március 15 tér. Inner City Parish Church.
V. Szent István tér. St. Stephen's Basilica.
V. Váci utca 9. Three-storey hotel building.
V. Városház utca 7. Building of the County Council.
VI. Nagymező utca. Interior of the Terézváros Parish Church.
VIII. Múzeum körút 14-16. Two-storey building of the National Museum.
IX. Calvin tér. Calvinist church.
IX. Üllői út 49-51. Three-storey one-time barracks building.
X. Népliget. Fountain with Fisherwoman.
XII. Zugliget. Disznófő (Boar's Head). Well house.

ROMANTIC ARCHITECTURE

I. Fő utca 30-32. Former Capuchin church and monastery.
V. Károlyi utca. Stone spire of the Franciscan church.
V. József nádor tér 5-7. Four-storey apartment house.
V. Vigadó tér 2. "Vigadó" (former concert hall).
VI. Lenin körút 109-111. Western Railway Terminal building.
VII. Dohány utca 2-8. Synagogue.
VIII. Rákóczi út 3-5 Four storey hotel building.
X. Harmat utca, Gitár utca 1. Field-guard's tower.
XIV. Május 1. út 23. Hermina Chapel.

ECLECTIC ARCHITECTURE

I. Fishermen's Bastion.
I. Ybl Miklós tér 11. Várkert Kioszk.
V. Deák Ferenc utca 16. Seven-storey office building.
V. Guszev utca 5. Four-storey office building.
V. Kossuth Lajos tér. Parliament building.
V. Kossuth Lajos tér 11. Ministry of Agriculture.
V. Kossuth Lajos tér 12. National Gallery.
V. Roosevelt tér 9. Building of the Hungarian Academy of Sciences.
V. Liberty Bridge.
VI. Népköztársaság útja 22. State Opera House.
VI. Népköztársaság útja 69. Old Art Gallery.
VII. Gorkij fasor 17. Lutheran church.
VIII. Múzeum körút 4. Two-storey university building.

VII. Múzeum körút 6-8. Two-storey university building.
VIII. Szabó Ervin tér 1. Szabó Ervin Library.
IX. Bakáts tér. Ferencváros Roman Catholic Parish Church.
IX. Dimitrov tér 7-8. University of Economic Sciences.
IX. Üllői út 33-35. Museum of Industrial Arts.
X. Szent László tér. Kőbánya Parish Church.
XIV. Hősök tere. Art Gallery.

STATUES AND MONUMENTS

Ady, Endre, poet (1877-1919)
XIV. City Park, Artists' Promenade. By Géza Csorba, 1952.

Ady, Endre
VI. Jókai tér. By Géza Csorba, 1961.

Alpár, Ignác, architect (1855-1928)
XIV. City Park, By Ede Telcs, 1931.

Anonymus, medieval chronicler
XIV. City Park, Széchenyi Island, opposite the entrance of the Agricultural Museum. By Miklós Ligeti, 1903.

Arany János, poet (1817-1882)
VIII. Museum Gardens. By Alajos Stróbl, 1892.

Arany, János
XIII. Margaret Island. By Alajos Stróbl. Damaged during the war, recarved in 1953.

Archer
XIV. City Park. In front of the hall of the Artificial Skating Rink. By Zsigmond Kisfaludi Strobl. Bronze statue on limestone pedestal. This figure was cast in four copies. The first was erected in 1925 on Margaret Island, but later it was removed. The second was set up in its present place in 1929, the third is in Stockholm, and the fourth in Santa Barbara, Calif., U.S.A.

Balassi, Bálint, poet (1554-1594)
VI. Körönd. By Pál Pátzay, 1959.

Baross, Gábor, promoter of the Hungarian railway system (1848-1892)
VII. Baross tér. By Antal Széchy.

Batthyány Memorial Tablet
V. Károlyi utca, Károlyi Palace. Batthyány, prime minister at the time of the War of Independence, was dragged away from here on January 8, 1849, by the henchmen of Haynau and imprisoned. Later he was executed. A perpetual light at the corner of Báthori utca and Rosenberg házaspár utca marks the place of his execution.

Beethoven
XII. Városmajor Park. By János Horvay.

Bem, József, Polish general of the Honvéds at the time of the 1848-49 War of Independence (1794-1850).
II. Bem József tér. By János Istók, 1934.

Berzsenyi, Dániel, poet (1776-1836)
VIII. Museum Gardens. By Miklós Vay, 1860.

Bolyai, János, mathematician (1802-1860)
XIV. City Park, Artists' Promenade. By Viktor Vass.

Crayfish Catcher
XIII. Margaret Island. By Miklós Ligeti. After the damage caused by the war it was repaired and set up in the rock garden in 1956.

Csengery, Antal, historian (1822-1880)
VII. Almássy tér. By János Csiszár.

Csokonai Vitéz, Mihály, poet (1773-1805)
XIV. City Park. Artists' Promenade. By Dezső Erdei, 1953.

Fountain of the Danaides
V. Sütő utca. By Ferenc Sidló, design by Dénes György.

Deák, Ferenc, political figure (1803-1876)
V. Roosevelt tér. By Adolf Huszár, pedestal by Albert Schickedanz, 1887.

Déryné Széppataki, Róza, actress (1793-1872)
XIV. City Park, Artists' Promenade. By Erzsébet V. Schaár.

Dimitrov, Georgi
V. Dimitrov tér. The work of the Bulgarian sculptor Jordan Kratchmarov, 1954.

Dózsa, György, leader of the Hungarian peasant uprising of 1514.
I. Dózsa tér, below the former royal castle. By István Kiss, 1961.

Eötvös, József, writer (1813-1874)
V. Eötvös tér. By Adolf Huszár, to the designs of Miklós Ybl, 1879.

Eötvös, József
XII. Eötvös Park. By Alajos Stróbl, 1890.

Eötvös, Loránd, physicist (1848-1919)
XIV. City Park, Artists' Promenade. By György Ősz Nemes, 1952.

Erkel, Ferenc, composer (1810-1893)
XIV. City Park, Artists' Promenade. By Sándor Boldogfai Farkas, 1953.

Erkel, Ferenc, memorial tablet
IX. Corner of Erkel utca and Üllői út, on the wall of the house where the founder of Hungarian national opera and composer of the National Anthem lived and worked.

Garibaldi, Giuseppe, Italian champion of freedom (1807-1882)
VIII. Museum Gardens. By Lívia Kuzmik, 1932.

Gárdonyi, Géza, novelist (1863-1922)
XI. Bartók Béla út, corner of Bercsényi utca. By János Horvay, 1932.

Hadik, András, marshal of the hussars (1710-1790)
I. Castle Hill, at the intersection of Úri utca and Szentháromság utca. By György Vastagh, jr., 1937.

Herman, Ottó, naturalist (1835-1914)
VIII. Museum Gardens. By János Horvay, 1930.

Holy Trinity Statue
I. Szentháromság tér. By Fülöp Ungleich, 1713. It was raised by the citizens of Buda after the epidemic of the plague that raged in Buda early in the 18th century. Since its erection it has been restored several times.

Honvéd Memorial
I. Dísz tér. By György Zala, 1893. The monument was set up in memory of the Honvéds who died for their country during the recapture of the Fortress of Buda from the Hapsburg forces on May 21, 1849.

Hungarian Academy of Sciences, foundation scene. Bronze relief on the wall of the Hungarian Academy of Sciences, in Akadémia utca. By Barnabás Holló, 1893.

Hunyadi, János, victorious general in the Turkish wars, first regent of Hungary (d. 1456).
I. Hunyadi János út, in front of the Fishermen's Bastion. By István Tóth, 1903.

Pope Innocent XI
I. Hess András tér. By József Damkó, 1936. The memorial was raised in memory of the recapture of Buda under the papacy of Innocent XI.

Jedlik, Ányos, physicist (1800-1895)
XIV. City Park, Artists' Promenade. By János Csiszár, 1952.

Jókai, Mór, novelist (1825-1904)
VI. Jókai tér. By Alajos Stróbl, 1921.

Jókai, Mór
XII. Liberty Hill, at the intersection of Normafa út and Eötvös út. By Gyula Jankovich, 1906.

Joliot-Curie, Frédéric (1900-1958)
XII. Joliot-Curie tér. By László Marton, 1960.

József, Attila, poet (1905-1937)
XIII. József Attila tér. By András Beck, 1952.

József, Palatine of Hungary (1776-1847)
V. József nádor tér. By Johann Halbig, 1869.

Julianus and Gerardus, Dominican friars
I. Fishermen's Bastion. By Károly Antal, 1937. The statue was raised in memory of the two Dominican monks who had explored the original homeland of the Magyars in the 13th century.

Kammermayer, Károly, first mayor of Budapest (1829-1897)
V. Kammermayer Károly tér. Made of aluminium, pedestal of limestone, by Béla Szabados, 1942.

Kapisztrán (Capistrano), János, Franciscan monk
I. Kapisztrán tér. By József Damkó, pedestal by Ernő Foerk. The statue was erected in 1922, on the 460th anniversary of the death of the evangelist and leader of János Hunyadi's army.

Katona, József, writer (1791-1830)
XIV. City Park, Artists' Promenade. By Lajos Petri, 1952.

Kazinczy, Ferenc, writer, poet and neologist (1759-1831)
VIII. Museum Gardens, By Miklós Vay, 1861.

Kazinczy Fountain
I. Bécsikapu tér. By János Pásztor, 1936.

Kisfaludy, Károly, poet and dramatist (1788-1830)
VIII. Museum Gardens. By István Ferenczy, 1875. Destroyed in the Second World War, it was remade in 1952.

Kisfaludy, Sándor, poet (1772-1844)
VII. Museum Gardens. By Döme Petrovics. Damaged in the Second World War, it has since been restored.

Kossuth, Lajos, statesman, leader of the War of Independence (1802-1894),
V. Kossuth Lajos tér. The statue of Kossuth is the work of Zsigmond Kisfaludi Strobl; the auxiliary figures were designed by András Kocsis and Lajos Ungvári, 1952.

Kossuth, Lajos
II. Mátyás király út. By István Tóth, 1913. The statue stands where Lajos Kossuth was arrested on May 4, 1837.

Kölcsey, Ferenc, poet (1790-1838)
II. Batthyány tér. By Ede Kallós, 1939.

Lechner, Ödön, architect (1845-1914)
IX. Üllői út 33-37, in front of the main façade of the Museum of Industrial Arts. By Béla Pankotai Farkas.

Lendvay, Márton, actor (1807-1858)
VIII. Blaha Lujza tér. By László Dunaiszky, 1860.

Liberation Monument
XI. Gellért Hill. By Zsigmond Kisfaludi Strobl. Figures of bronze, pedestal of limestone. The central figure is 14 metres tall. The Soviet engineers B. Joffan and A. Gerassimov rendered help in carrying out the architectonic work of the monument. The monument was unveiled on the second anniversary of Hungary's liberation, April 4, 1947.

Liszt, Ferenc, composer (1811-1886)
XIV. City park, Artists' Promenade. By Dezső Erdei, 1952.

Madonna Column
V. Martinelli tér. By Dezső Erdei, 1941.

Matthias Fountain
I. Buda Castle. By Alajos Stróbl. Architectonic work by Alajos Hauszmann. Bronze fountain.

Mikszáth, Kálmán, novelist (1847-1910)
XIV. City Park, Artists' Promenade. By János Sóváry, 1953.

Mikszáth, Kálmán
VIII. Mikszáth tér. By András Kocsis.

Millenary Monument
XIV. Hősök tere. The architectonic work is by Albert Schickedanz. Sculptures: St. Stephen by Károly Senyei; St. Ladislas by Ede Telcs; Könyves Kálmán by Richárd Füredi; Andrew II by Károly Senyei; Béla IV by Miklós Köllő; Charles Robert by György Kiss; Louis the Great by György Zala; János Hunyadi by Ede Margó; Matthias Corvinus by György Zala; Gábor Bethlen by György Vastagh; István Bocskai by Barnabás Holló; Ferenc Rákóczi II by Zsigmond Kisfaludi Strobl; Imre Thököly by Jenő Graubner; Lajos Kossuth by Zsigmond Kisfaludi

Strobl. The other statues of the monument: "Genius", "War", "Peace", "Árpád and the Chieftains", all by György Zala.

Monument to the recapture of the Fortress of Buda
I. Bécsikapu tér. By Béla Ohmann. Erected in 1936, on the 250th anniversary of the retaking of Buda.

Móricz, Zsigmond, novelist (1879-1942)
XIV. City Park, Artists' Promenade. It is the work of the Greek sculptor Agamemnon Makris who is living in Budapest, 1952.

Munkácsy, Mihály, painter (1884-1900)
XIV. City Park, Artists' Promenade. By Walter Madarassy, 1952.

Pallas Athena
I. Szentháromság tér. By Adami Carlo, 1927. The pedestal is the work of Rezső Hikisch.

Petőfi, Sándor, poet (1823-1849)
V. Petőfi tér. Bronze statue by Adolf Huszár, the grey granite pedestal is the work of Miklós Ybl, 1882.

Petőfi, Sándor
XIII. Szent István körút, in front of the Comedy Theatre, By György Baksa-Soós.

Pósa, Lajos, poet (1850-1914)
XIV. City Park, Népstadion út. By Ede Margó, 1930.

Rákóczi, Ferenc II (1676-1735)
V. Kossuth Lajos tér. By János Pásztor. Equestrian statue of bronze, pedestal of Swedish granite. Unveiled in 1937, on the 200th anniversary of the death of Ferenc Rákóczi.

Salamon, Ferenc, historian (1825-1892)
V. Roosevelt tér, in front of the Hungarian Academy of Sciences. By Gyula Jankovich, 1902.

Eugene of Savoy (1663-1736)
I. Garden of the Buda Castle. By József Róna. Equestrian statue. Eugene of Savoy was a leading figure in the wars against the Turks.

Ságvári, Endre (1913-1944)
V. Városház utca 9-11. By György Baksa-Soós. The bust of the communist leader who died a martyr was erected in 1949.

Sebők, Zsigmond, fabulist (1861-1916)
II. At the Buda abutment of the Margaret Bridge. By Gyula Maugsch, 1934.

Semmelweis, Ignác, physician (1818-1865)
VIII. Rákóczi út, in front of the Semmelweis Hospital. By Alajos Stróbl, 1906. Carrara marble, pedestal of limestone.

Sitting Girl
XIII. Margaret Island, in the pond of the rock garden. By Imre Csikász, 1955.

Sport Rider
V. Danube Promenade, at the corner of Szende Pál utca. By Pál Pátzay.

St. Christopher
XIV. Népstadion út, at the Art Gallery. By László Hűvös, 1913.

St. Imre, son of King Stephen I (1007-1031)
XI. Móricz Zsigmond körtér. By Zsigmond Kisfaludi Strobl, 1930.

St. Gellért (Gerard), bishop, educator of St. Imre
XI. Gellért Hill. By Gyula Jankovich, 1904. Badly damaged in the Second World War, the statue was later restored.

St. Ladislas, king of Hungary (1077-1095)
X. Pataki István tér. By Károly Antal, 1940. The head is modelled after the well-known herma of St. Ladislas.

St. Stephen (King Stephen I), first king of Hungary (1001-1038)
I. Fishermen's Bastion. Equestrian statue by Alajos Stróbl, pedestal by Frigyes Schulek.

Soviet War Memorials
V. Szabadság tér,
V. Vigadó tér,
XI. Gellért tér.

Soviet Parliamentary, Memorial of the
XI. at the fork of the Balaton highway and Budaörsi út.
By Jenő Kerényi, 1951. This is the Ostapenko Memorial,
raised at the spot where Captain Ilya Afanaseyevitch Ostapenko and two of his comrades were shot in cold blood
by the German fascists on December 29, 1944, when they
approached the German positions as parliamentaries bearing a flag of truce.

Soviet Parliamentary, Memorial of the
XVIII. Vöröshadsereg útja. By Sándor Mikus, 1958. This
statue stands at the spot where the German fascists mas-
sacred Captain Steinmetz and his two comrades, truce-
bearers of the Red Army, in 1944.

Szarvas, Gábor, editor of the periodical journal "Magyar
Nyelvőr" (Hungarian Purist) (1832-1895)
V. Roosevelt tér, in front of the Hungarian Academy of
Sciences. By Gyula Jankovich.

Széchényi, Ferenc, founder of the National Museum (1754-
1820)
VIII. Museum Gardens. By János Istók. 1902.

Széchenyi, István, statesman, leading figure of the Reform
period (1791-1860)
V. Roosevelt tér. By József Engel, pedestal by Antal Weber,
1880. The principal figure and the four auxiliary figures are
of bronze, the pedestal of limestone. The auxiliary figures
represent Minerva, Vulcanus, Neptunus and Ceres.

Széchenyi, István
XII. Széchenyi Hill, at the lookout tower. By Alajos
Stróbl, 1891.

Széchenyi Fountain
V. Szabadság tér. By Ede Telcs, 1930.

Szondy, György, fortress commander during the Turkish wars (d. 1552)
VI. Körönd. By László Marton, 1958.

Táncsics, Mihály, writer and publicist (1799-1884)
XIV. City Park. Artists' Promenade. By Mihály Pál. 1953.

Tinódi Lantos, Sebestyén, poet (b. between 1505 and 1510, d. 1556)
X. Könyves Kálmán körút. By Gyula Bezerédi.

Tompa, Mihály, poet (1817-1868)
XIII. Margaret Island. By János Pásztor, 1940.

Trefort, Ágoston, reformer of the Hungarian educational system (1817-1888)
VIII. Múzeum körút. In the garden of the University. By György Kiss, 1904.

Vak Bottyán (Bottyán the Blind), army general in the war of independence under Rákóczi (1635-1709)
VI. Körönd. By Gyula Kiss Kovács, 1958.

Veres, Pálné, educationalist, pioneer of the education of young girls (1815-1895)
V. Engels tér. Carrara marble, on pedestal of limestone. By György Kiss, 1906.

Vörösmarty, Mihály, poet (1800-1855)
V. Vörösmarty tér. Statue of Carrara marble by Ede Kallós, Géza Márkus and Ede Telcs, pedestal of limestone, 1908.

Washington, George
XIV. City Park, George Washington Promenade. By Gyula Bezerédi, 1906.

Wesselényi, Miklós (1796-1850), memorial tablet
V. Kossuth Lajos utca. On the wall of the Franciscan church. Relief by Barnabás Holló, 1905.

Zrínyi, Miklós, poet (1620-1664)
XIII. Szent István körút, in front of the Comedy Theatre. By István Tar, 1952.

Zrínyi, Miklós, military leader (1508-1566)
VI. Népköztársaság útja, at the Körönd. By József Róna, 1902.

Zsigmondy, Vilmos (1821-1886)
XIV. City Park, in front of the Széchenyi Baths. The statue of the initiator of the drilling of artesian wells in Pest was modelled by Antal Szécsi, 1929.

CEMETERIES

There are eleven cemeteries in Budapest. The largest and most important of them are:
Farkasréti temető, XII. Németvölgyi út 99.
Kerepesi temető, VIII. Mező Imre út 16.
Új Köztemető, X. Kozma utca 8-10.

RECOMMENDED SCHEDULE FOR SIGHTSEEING

FOR A HALF-DAY

Visitors who spend only a few hours in Budapest should not miss a stroll along the Pest Danube embankment. It offers a superb panorama at every point. An especially lovely view can be obtained from the Promenade before Vigadó tér, from the Pest abutments of the Margaret Bridge and the Liberty Bridge. If there is still some time left a little walk through the following streets is recommended:
Vörösmarty tér—Váci utca—Kígyó utca—Felszabadulás tér—Petőfi Sándor utca—Martinelli tér—Kristóf tér—Váci utca—Vörösmarty tér. (Thirty minutes.)

FOR ONE DAY

In the morning: Felszabadulás tér (Franciscan church)—Szabadsajtó útja—Március 15. tér (Inner City Parish Church)—Petőfi tér (statue of Petőfi, Greek Orthodox church)—Promenade Danube—Vigadó tér (Soviet War Memorial, Vigadó)—Deák Ferenc utca—Vörösmarty tér (statue of Vörösmarty)—Vigadó utca—Vigadó tér—Danube Promenade—Eötvös tér (statue of Eötvös)—Roosevelt tér (Suspension Bridge, statues of Deák and Széchenyi, building of the Hungarian Academy of Sciences)—Széchenyi rakpart—Kossuth Lajos tér (Parliament, statues of Rákóczi and Kossuth, National Gallery, Ministry of Agriculture)—Ságvári Endre tér—Vécsey utca—Szabadság tér (Soviet War Memorial, House of Technology, Studios of the Hungarian Television, Hungarian National Bank, Hungarian Foreign Trade Bank)—Október 6. utca—Zrínyi utca—Szent István tér (Basilica)—Bajcsy-Zsilinszky út—Népköztársaság útja (Opera House, statues of Jókai and Ady)—November 7. tér—Népköztársaság útja—Körönd—Népköztársaság útja—Hősök tere (Art Gal-

lery, Museum of Fine Arts, Millenary Monument, Vajda-
hunyad Castle, City Park)—Népstadion út—Thököly út
(People's Stadium, National Sport Hall)—Baross tér (East-
ern Railway Terminal)—Rákóczi út—Kenyérmező utca—
Köztársaság tér (Erkel Theatre)—Luther utca—Rákóczi
út (Great Boulevard intersection, National Theatre, St.
Roch's Chapel, statue of Semmelweis)—Múzeum körút
(National Museum, Museum Gardens, statue of János
Arany)—Calvin tér (Calvinist Church)—Tolbuhin körút
(Market Hall)—Dimitrov tér (bust of Dimitrov, Karl Marx
University of Economic Sciences)—Belgrád rakpart—Már-
cius 15. tér—Szabadsajtó út—Felszabadulás tér. (Three
and a half hours.)

In the afternoon: Gellért tér (Technical University, Soviet
War Memorial, Gellért Medicinal Baths)—Gellért rakpart (Rudas Baths)—Döbrentei tér (Imre Baths, Roman
watch tower)—Apród utca—Ybl Miklós tér (statue of
Miklós Ybl, Castle Bazaar, Várkert Kioszk)—Clark Ádám
tér ("0-kilometre" stone, Tunnel)—Hunyadi János út
(statue of János Hunyadi, Jesuit Stairs, approach to the
Fishermen's Bastion)—Dísz tér (Honvéd Monument)—
Tárnok utca (at No. 14, a glance into Balta köz)—Szent-
háromság tér (Castle Museum, Holy Trinity Statue, Mat-
thias Church, equestrian statue of St. Stephen, Fishermen's
Bastion, ruins of the Dominican church)—Hess András
tér (statue of Pope Innocent XI, "Red Hedgehog" house)
—Táncsics Mihály utca (No. 9)—Bécsikapu tér (Vienna
Gate, Kazinczy Memorial Fountain, Lutheran church)—
Fortuna utca—Szentháromság tér—Országház utca (Nos.
2, 18 and 22)—Kapisztrán tér (Capistrano Memorial, Mary
Magdalene Church)—Tóth Árpád sétány (War History
Museum, Esztergom Round Bastion)—Kapisztrán tér—Petermann bíró utca—Bécsikapu tér—Várfok utca—Moszkva
tér—Széna tér—Mártírok útja (ruins of the old Buda ramparts, Franciscan church, Buda abutment of the Margaret
Bridge)—Bem József tér (statue of József Bem)—Fő utca
(Florian Chapel, Király Baths)—Batthyány tér (Nos. 3
and 4, St. Anne Church)—Fő utca (No. 20)—Clark Ádám
tér. (Three and a half hours.)

For the tour above take the following transportation:
In the morning: From the beginning of Népköztársaság
útja to Hősök tere: bus No. 1. After visiting the People's
Stadium, from the corner of Thököly út and Dózsa György
út to Rákóczi út, and after a visit to Erkel Theatre, from
Luther utca to Felszabadulás tér: bus No. 7.

In the afternoon: From Gellért tér to Clark Ádám tér: bus No. 1, from Clark Ádám tér to Dísz tér: bus No. 16. From Moszkva tér to the Buda abutment of the Margaret Bridge: bus No. 12.

FOR TWO DAYS

If the visitor has two days at his disposal, we would recommend for the first morning the itinerary of the one-day programme above, putting off the proposed afternoon tour to the morning of the second day.

First day. *Afternoon:* An excursion to Gellért Hill: Felszabadulás tér—Károlyi utca (No. 16)—Egyetem tér (University Church)—Eötvös Loránd utca—Nyáry Pál utca—Váci utca (Church of the order of Mary Ward Nuns)—Dimitrov tér—Liberty Bridge—Gellért tér. Walk up the southern slope of Gellért Hill to the hilltop—descent on the northern slope (statue of St. Gellért)—Döbrentei tér—Attila út—Krisztina tér (Krisztinaváros Parish Church)—Alagút utca—Tunnel—Clark Ádám tér.

Evening programme: In winter the Opera House, in summer a performance at one of the many open-air theatres.

Second day. *Afternoon:* Excursion to Margaret Island by water bus, or by bus No. 26 from the corner of Szent István körút and Pannonia utca.

FOR THREE DAYS

First day. *Morning:* Felszabadulás tér (Franciscan church) —Szabadsajtó út—Március 15. tér (Inner City Parish Church, Péterffy House, relics of a Roman Castrum)—Petőfi tér (statue of Petőfi, Greek Orthodox church)—Danube Promenade—Vigadó tér (Soviet War Memorial, Vigadó)—Deák Ferenc utca—Vörösmarty tér (statue of Vörösmarty)—Vigadó utca—Vigadó tér—Danube Promenade—Eötvös tér (statue of Eötvös)—Roosevelt tér (Suspension Bridge, statues of Deák and Széchenyi, Hungarian Academy of Sciences)—Széchenyi rakpart—Kossuth Lajos tér (statue of Rákóczi, Parliament Building, statue of Kossuth, National Gallery, Ministry of Agriculture)—Ságvári tér—Vécsey utca—Szabadság tér (Soviet War Memorial, House of Technology, Studios of the Hungarian Television, Hungarian National Bank, Hungarian Foreign Trade Bank)—

303

Aulich utca (Perpetual Light to the memory of Batthyány)—
Báthori utca—Kossuth Lajos tér—Széchenyi rakpart—
Jászai Mari tér (Pest abutment of the Margaret Bridge)—
Szent István körút (Comedy Theatre)—Marx tér (Western Railway Terminal)—Lenin körút—November 7. tér
—intersection of the Great Boulevard and Rákóczi út
(National Theatre)—József körút—Rákóczi tér—Baross
utca intersection—Üllői út intersection (Museum of
Industrial Arts)—Ferenc körút—Boráros tér—Pest abutment of the Petőfi Bridge—Ráday utca—Calvin tér (Calvinist church)—Múzeum körút (Hungarian National Museum, Museum Gardens, statue of János Arany)—Kecskeméti utca—Egyetem tér (Eötvös Loránd University, University Church)—Károlyi utca (Károlyi Palace, University
Library)—Felszabadulás tér.

Afternoon: Excursion to Gellért Hill: Felszabadulás tér—
Szabadsajtó út—Váci utca (Church of the order of Mary
Ward Nuns)—Dimitrov tér (Market Hall, Karl Marx University of Economic Sciences, bust of Dimitrov)—Liberty
Bridge—Gellért tér (Soviet War Memorial, Technical University, Gellért Hotel and Medicinal Baths)—Walk up to
Gellért Hill on its southern slope—top of Gellért Hill (Liberation Monument, view of the town, Citadel)—descent
on the northern slope (statue of St. Gellért)—Döbrentei
tér—Attila út—Krisztina körút—Krisztina tér (Krisztinaváros Parish Church)—Alagút utca—Tunnel—Clark Ádám
tér.

Second day. *Morning:* Felszabadulás tér—Petőfi Sándor
utca—Pilvax köz—Városház utca (buildings of the County
Council of Pest, and the Budapest City Council)—Martinelli tér (Servite church)—Kristóf tér—Váci utca—Vörösmarty tér—Harmincad utca—Engels tér (Central Bus Terminal)—Deák Ferenc tér (Lutheran church)—Bajcsy-Zsilinszky út—Szent István tér (Basilica)—Bajcsy-Zsilinszky
út—Népköztársaság útja (Opera House, visit through
Nagymező utca, Terézváros Parish Church, Liszt Ferenc
tér: Academy of Music)—November 7. tér—Népköztársaság útja—Hősök tere (Art Gallery, Museum of Fine Arts,
Millenary Monument)—by the underground railway to
Vörösmarty tér, walk through Vigadó utca to Vigadó tér,
and from there along the Danube Promenade to Március
15. tér, and back through Szabadsajtó út to Felszabadulás
tér.

Afternoon: Gellért tér—Gellért rakpart (Rudas Baths)—
Döbrentei tér (Imre Baths, Roman watch tower)—Attila
út (Tabán Parish Church)—Apród utca—Ybl Miklós tér
(statue of Miklós Ybl, Castle Bazaar)—Clark Ádám tér
("0-kilometre" stone, Tunnel)—Hunyadi János út (statue
of Hunyadi, Jesuit Stairs)—Dísz tér (Honvéd Memorial)—
Tárnok utca (at No. 14, a glance into Balta köz)—Szentháromság tér (Castle Museum, Holy Trinity Statue, Matthias Church, equestrian statue of St. Stephen, Fishermen's
Bastion, view of the town from the Fishermen's Bastion,
statue of Julianus, ruins of the Dominican church)—Hess
András tér (statue of Pope Innocent XI, "Red Hedgehog"
house, doorway of the house at No. 4)—Táncsics Mihály
utca (No. 9)—Bécsikapu tér (Vienna Gate, Kazinczy Memorial Fountain, Lutheran church)—Fortuna utca—Szentháromság tér—Országház utca (Nos. 2, 14, 20 and 28)—
Kapisztrán tér (Tower of the Mary Magdalene Church,
statue of Capistrano)—Tóth Árpád sétány (War History
Museum, view from the Esztergom Round Bastion)—Kapisztrán tér—Petermann bíró utca—Bécsikapu tér (ruins
of the old Buda ramparts, Buda Franciscan church, Buda
abutment of the Margaret Bridge)—Bem József rakpart—
Bem József tér (statue of József Bem)—Fő utca (Florian
Chapel, Király Baths)—Batthyány tér (Nos. 3 and 4, St.
Anne's Church)—Fő utca (No. 20)—Clark Ádám tér.

For the evening: Theatre performance. In the State Opera
House in winter, or at an open-air stage in summer.

Third day. *Morning:* From Vörösmarty tér by under-
ground railway to the Zoological Gardens, a walk in the
Zoo, Széchenyi open-air and medicinal baths, a walk in the
City Park—Népstadion út (Geological Institute, People's
Stadium, National Sport Hall)—Thököly út—Baross tér
(Eastern Railway Terminal)—Rákóczi út—Kenyérmező
utca—Köztársaság tér (Erkel Theatre)—Luther utca—
Rákóczi út (Great Boulevard intersection, National The-
atre, St. Roch's Chapel and Semmelweis Hospital, statue
of Semmelweis)—Kossuth Lajos utca—Felszabadulás tér.

Afternoon: An excursion by water bus or by bus No. 26.
from the Comedy Theatre (Szent István körút, corner of
Pannonia utca) to Margaret Island, or an excursion from
Buda to Aquincum.

FOR SIX DAYS

If the stay in Budapest can be extended to six days the above mentioned itinerary may be taken as a basis:

First day. *Morning:* As the first morning of the three-day programme.

Afternoon: As the first afternoon of the three-day programme.

Second day. *Morning:* As the second morning of the three-day programme.

Afternoon: Excursion to Margaret Island.

Third day. *Morning:* As the second afternoon of the three-day programme.

Afternoon: A trip by the Pioneers' Railway from Széchenyi Hill to Hűvösvölgy, or a visit to the Castle Museum, and a walk on Castle Hill and its surroundings.

Fourth day. *Morning:* As the third morning of the three-day programme.

Afternoon: Excursion on board of the pleasure steamer on the Danube, or a cinema or concert performance, or an exhibition.

Fifth day. *Morning:* Visit to an open-air bath, or medicinal bath, or to a museum.

Afternoon: An excursion to Óbuda and Aquincum.

Sixth day: An all-day excursion to Visegrád, Esztergom, Dobogókő, to Lake Balaton or to the Mátra Mountains. Theatre programmes: Opera House, Operetta Theatre. For programmes other than those given above, one should turn to the Budapest Municipal Tourist Agency (V. Roosevelt tér 5. Tel.: 380-581 or 180-609), which also supplies guides if desired. The Tourist Agency organises regular sightseeing bus tours.

THE HUNGARIAN LANGUAGE

The Hungarian language is a member of the Finno-Ugric family of languages, together with Finnish and Estonian. It bears no relationship to other European languages classified as Indo-European. Grammatical gender is unknown in Hungarian. Prepositions are non-existent, but suffixes are added to the words to express time, place or other relations. The original word stock has been enriched by borrowing from the Turkic and Slavic languages, German, Latin and even French. Towards the end of the eighteenth and in the early nineteenth century an extensive language reform made the Hungarian language more suitable for modern usage, adding to it a great many newly coined words.

A few notes on the pronunciation of Hungarian may be useful to visitors making their way about the country by helping them in the pronunciation of place names. Other readers of this book may also wish to know the correct pronunciation of proper names appearing in the text.

Vowels:

Among the vowels in Hungarian we should notice the following differences from the English pronunciation:

á is pronounced like the *a* in English *father.*
a has a short, open sound, similar to the *o* in English *not.*
é like the *a* in state.
e like a the e in *men.*
í like the e in *she.*
ó has a long close sound similar to the *o* in English *sole.*
ö denotes an open sound somewhat similar to the er in *bigger.*
ő the same as *ö* but longer.
ü denotes a sound which does not exist in English, but is like the French *u,* in *vu,* or the German ü in *müde.*

The length of the vowels should be strictly observed. Nonobservance may lead to misunderstandings, e.g. őrült (mad), örült (he was glad); kor (age), kór (disease).

The *stress* in Hungarian is *always* on the *first syllable*.

Consonants:

The consonants that are pronounced unlike their English counterparts are the following:

c has a special sound, as if *ts* were pronounced as one sound.

cs is treated as a single consonant, pronounced like the *ch* in English *church*.

g is always pronounced like the *g* in English *good*.

gy is treated as a single consonant, having a sound similar to that of the *d* in English *due*.

j is pronounced like the *y* in English *year*.

ly is treated as a single consonant, having the same sound as *j*.

ny is treated as a single consonant, pronounced like the *ny* in English *canyon*.

s is pronounced like the *sh* in English *short*.

sz is treated as a single consonant, pronounced like the *s* in English *son*.

ty is treated as a single consonant, having a sound similar to that of the *t* in English *tune*.

zs is treated as a single consonant, pronounced like the *s* in English *pleasure*.

A FEW ESSENTIAL WORDS

HUNGARIAN-ENGLISH

ajándékbolt	gift shop
állomás	station, stop
áruház	department store
Ápisz	stationery shop
asszony	woman
asszonyom	Madame
autóbusz	bus
balra	to the left
balra hajts	keep to the left
bejárat	entrance
bélyeg	postage stamp
bocsánat	I'm sorry; excuse me; I beg your pardon
bolt	shop, store
bor	wine
borkóstoló	wine tasting
borbély	barber('s shop)
cigaretta	cigarette
cipész	shoemaker
cipőbolt	shoe store
csemege	delicatessen; dessert
csengő	bell
cukrászda	pastry shop
divatüzlet	ladies' and gentlemen's outfitters
dohány	tobacco
dohánybolt	tobacconist's
ebéd	lunch
édességbolt	sweet-shop, candy-shop
egyenesen	straight on

309

előre	forward, onward
elvtárs	comrade
emelet	floor, storey
érkezés	arrival
eszpresszó	coffee shop
étlap	bill of fare
étterem	restaurant
fasor	avenue
felvilágosítás	information
férfiak(nak)	for men, men's room
férfifodrász	gentlemen's hairdresser
fiú	boy
fizetni	to pay, "bill please"
fodrász	hairdresser
foglalt	occupied, busy
földalatti	underground, subway
főváros	capital
fűszer és csemege	delicatessen shop
gőzfürdő	steam bath, Turkish bath
gyógyfürdő	medicinal bath
gyógyszertár	chemist's pharmacy
gyufa	matches
gyümölcs	fruit
hajó	ship, boat
határ	frontier, border
ház	house
háztartási bolt	household store
hegy	mountain, hill
híd	bridge
hideg	cold
honvéd	soldier of the Hungarian Army
hordár	porter
hölgyek(nek)	for ladies, ladies' rest room
hús	meat
húsbolt	butcher's shop
igen	yes
illatszerbolt	perfumery
indulás	departure
iszap	mud
itt	here

jegy	ticket
jobbra	to the right
jó éjszakát	good night
jó estét	good evening
jó napot	good day, good morning, hello
jó reggelt	good morning
kalauz	conductor
kávé	coffee
kávéház	café
kenyér	bread
kérem	please
kérem?	I beg your pardon?
kijárat	way out, exit
kórház	hospital
könyv	book
könyvesbolt	bookshop
körút	boulevard
köszönöm	thank you
Közért	provision store, grocery shop
köztársaság	republic
kultúrház	cultural centre (building)
lány (leány)	girl
lassan hajts	drive slowly
leves	soup
levél	letter
levélpapír	note paper
levelezőlap	post card
magyar	Hungarian
Magyarország	Hungary
magyarul	in Hungarian
MSZMP	HSWP (Hungarian Socialist Workers' Party)
megállóhely	stop, bus stop, tram stop
meleg	hot, warm
menetjegy	(bus, etc.) ticket
mosni	to wash, to launder
mosás	laundering, washing
mozi	cinema, movie
munkás	worker

311

nem	no, not
népi demokrácia	people's democracy
népművészeti bolt	shop of folk-art products
női fehérnemű	lingerie, ladies' underwear
női fodrász	ladies' hairdresser
női szabó	dressmaker, ladies' tailor
nők(nek)	ladies' rest room, for ladies
nyitva	open
Ofotért	cameras and optical instruments
olcsó	cheap
óra- és ékszerbolt	watchmaker and jeweller's shop
ország	country
országgyűlés	parliament
orvos	doctor, physician
ott	there
pályaudvar	railway terminal or station
paraszt	peasant
párt	party
pénz	money
pénztár	box office, booking office, cash register
peron	platform
pincér	waiter
poggyász	luggage, baggage
portás	porter, reception clerk
posta	post office
reggeli	breakfast
rendőr	policeman
repülőgép	aircraft, aeroplane
repülőtér	airport
Röltex	haberdashery
ruhatár	cloakroom
segítség	help
sofőr	driver, cabman
sör	beer
strand	beach, open-air bath
sütemény	cake, pastry
szabad	free, unoccupied
szabad?	excuse me please; may I?

szabadság	liberty, freedom
szálló, szálloda	hotel
szépségápolás	cosmetics
színház	theatre
szivar	cigar
szoba	room
szobalány	chambermaid
tánc	dance
taxi	taxi(cab)
tea	tea
tej	milk
templom	church
tér	square
tessék	please
tészta	pastry, noodles
tilos	forbidden, not allowed
tilos a dohányzás	no smoking
trafik	tobacconist's
úr	gentleman
urak	gentlemen
uszoda	swimming pool
úszóknak	for swimmers
uzsonna	afternoon snack
út, utca	road, street
útlevél	passport
üdít	refreshes
vacsora	dinner, supper
vám	customs duty
város	town, city
Városliget	City Park
vasalni	to iron (linen)
végállomás	terminus
vendéglő	inn, restaurant
veszélyes	dangerous
vigyázz	look out, careful, watch your step
villany	electricity
villamos	tram(car)
virág	flower
Virágért	florist's shop
viszontlátásra	good-bye
víz	water

vonat	train
völgy	valley
zárva	closed
zöldség- és gyümölcsbolt	fruit and vegetable shop

ENGLISH-HUNGARIAN

abroad	külföldön
address	cím
airplane	repülőgép
all right	rendben
America	Amerika
American	amerikai
armchair	karosszék, fotel
arrival	(meg)érkezés
baggage	poggyász
barber	borbély
bath	fürdő
beautiful	szép
bed	ágy
beer	sör
bell	csengő
big	nagy
bill	számla
bill please	fizetni!
boat	hajó
book	könyv
booking office	jegypénztár
border	határ
bottle	üveg
boy	fiú
bread	kenyér
breakfast	reggeli
bridge	híd
bus	autóbusz
butcher's shop	húsbolt
cab	taxi
cable	távirat, sürgöny
to cable	táviratozni, sürgönyözni
café	kávéház

railway	vasút
reception clerk	portás
refreshing	üdítő
refreshment	üdítő ital
republic	köztársaság
restaurant	étterem
revolution	forradalom
right (direction)	jobb
river	folyó
road	út
room	szoba
ship	hajó
shop	bolt, üzlet
soap	szappan
sorry	bocsánat
south	dél
square	tér
stamp	bélyeg
station	állomás
stationery	írópapír, írószerek
statue	szobor
steam bath	gőzfürdő
stop	megálló(hely), állomás
store	üzlet, bolt
storey	emelet
straight (on)	egyenesen
street	út, utca
streetcar	villamos
subway	földalatti
suitcase	koffer, bőrönd
supper	vacsora
swimming pool	uszoda
table	asztal
to take care	vigyázni
tea	tea
telegramme	távirat, sürgöny
terminus	végállomás
thank you	köszönöm
theatre	színház
there	ott
ticket	jegy
time	idő
tobacco	dohány

tobacconist's	trafik
today	ma
tomorrow	holnap
to the left	balra
to the right	jobbra
town	város
train	vonat
tramcar	villamos
trip	utazás, kirándulás
trunk	bőrönd
Turkish bath	gőzfürdő
underground	földalatti
underground railway	földalatti villamos
valley	völgy
village	falu
waken	felébreszteni, felkelteni
warm	meleg
to wash	mosni
watch	óra
watch your step	vigyázz
water	víz
week	hét
west	nyugat
what	mi, mit
what's the time?	hány óra van?
weather	időjárás
when	mikor
where	hol, hova
who	ki
why	miért
wine	bor
wine shop	italbolt
to wire	táviratozni, sürgönyözni
woman	asszony
word	szó
work	munka, dolog
worker	munkás
yes	igen

INDEX

THE AUTHORS:

NÓRA ARADI
IMRE DEMETER
ZOLTÁN HALÁSZ
ZSIGMOND HAVAS
LÁSZLÓ HOPPE
LÁSZLÓ HUBA
SÁNDOR LÁNG
EMIL NIEDERHAUSER
FERENC PAPP

ANTAL PÉNZES
LAJOS PESTI
TIBOR PETHŐ
ÖDÖN SCHULHOF
PÉTER SELLEI
DEZSŐ SZABÓ
LÁSZLÓ SZÉKELY
LÁSZLÓ TARR
JÓZSEF VENESZ

ANDRÁS VITÉZ

DRAWINGS BY
ENDRE MORVAY

MAPS BY
ERZSI RUSZNYÁK

PRINTED IN HUNGARY 1964
KOSSUTH PRINTING HOUSE, BUDAPEST

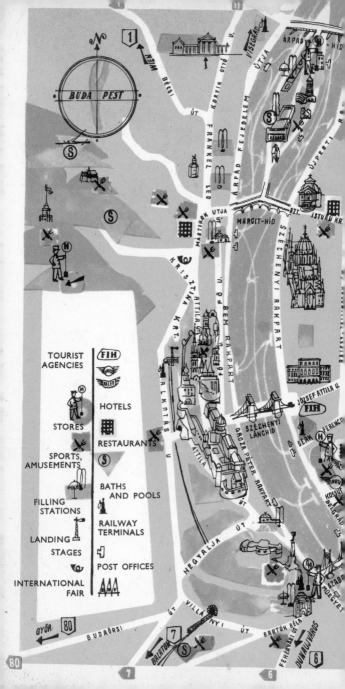